THE YAO VILLAGE

PLATE I

CHIEF KAWINGA THE SIXTH

He wears the traditional necklace of lions' claws which are medicated to
protect him from the bullets of his enemies.

THE
YAO VILLAGE

A STUDY IN THE SOCIAL STRUCTURE OF A
MALAWIAN PEOPLE

by

J. CLYDE MITCHELL

Professor of Urban Sociology, University of Manchester
Sometime Professor of Sociology, University College of
Rhodesia and Nyasaland
Sometime Director, Rhodes-Livingstone Institute, Lusaka

Published on behalf of

THE INSTITUTE FOR AFRICAN STUDIES
UNIVERSITY OF ZAMBIA

by

MANCHESTER UNIVERSITY PRESS

© 1956, Institute for African Studies, Lusaka
Published by the University of Manchester
at THE UNIVERSITY PRESS
316–324 Oxford Road, Manchester M13 9NR

First published, 1956
Reprinted, with minor corrections, 1966
Reprinted, 1971

Distributed in the U.S.A. by
The Humanities Press, Inc.
303 Park Avenue South, New York, N.Y. 10010

ISBN 0 7190 1020 9

PRINTED IN GREAT BRITAIN

This book is dedicated

to my

FATHER

and

the memory of

my

MOTHER

PREFACE

THIS book is the fruits of field work from September 1946 to September 1947, and from September 1948 to June 1949, as a Research Officer of the Rhodes-Livingstone Institute, among the Yao of Southern Nyasaland. Between June and September 1949 I was employed by the Nyasaland Government on a survey of the Domasi District where a Development Scheme was to be inaugurated. The detailed results of the Domasi survey have already been published separately,[1] and the general results have been incorporated here by permission of the Nyasaland Government.

By the very nature of his work a sociologist must depend heavily on others for help. As with all sociologists my greatest indebtedness is to the people amongst whom I worked. Here I must mention in particular Chiefs Kawinga and Chiwalo, and Village Headmen Cigwaja and Kapaloma, whose hospitality in one way and another helped me appreciably. I also thank Rajabu Kumpulula, who was my clerk and main informant during the second field trip.

I am grateful to the Nyasaland Government for assistance in many ways, and to several officers of the Administration for their kindness and hospitality to me. In particular, Mr. E. C. Barnes, then Provincial Commissioner in Blantyre, encouraged me by his interest in my research. Mr. Martin Lewis and Mr. R. P. Errington, successive District Commissioners at Zomba, by their sympathetic understanding of the rôle of an anthropologist, and their hospitality in Zomba and Blantyre, did much to make field work less of a burden than it might have been. The hospitality of Mr. Richard Leach and Mr. H. Gardner, then of the Agricultural Department, and of Mr. E. Hemmings of the Native Tobacco Board, also eased the discomforts of field life.

To my teachers and colleagues I owe a special word of thanks. I would like to acknowledge here my debt to two of my teachers at the Natal University College who, during my undergraduate

---

[1] 'An Outline of the Social Structure of Malemia Area', *The Nyasaland Journal*, iv, 2 (July 1951), 15–48.

days, imbued me with enthusiasm for scientific research. Dr. P. de Vos's lectures on social theory, particularly on the teachings of Simmel and von Wiese, stood me in good stead when I came into contact with Professor Radcliffe-Brown's ideas in the study of non-literate societies. Dr. H. Coblans gave me my first introduction to statistical methods : his influence on my interests is immediately apparent.

Early in 1946, when I first took up my appointment with the Rhodes-Livingstone Institute, I went with Dr. Max Gluckman, then Director of the Institute, Mr. J. A. Barnes, also newly appointed to the staff of the Rhodes-Livingstone Institute, and Mr. Max Marwick, a Colonial Social Science Research Fellow, on a field-training trip to the Lamba people in Northern Rhodesia. I owe much to that short trip, and to the period of training that followed it at the University of Cape Town. Dr. Elizabeth Colson, who joined us at Cape Town, Barnes and myself, under the direction of Gluckman, formed the first research team of the Rhodes-Livingstone Institute. It was in Lambaland and Cape Town that we worked out our common approach to field problems. While we were at Cape Town we were under the tutelage of Professor I. Schapera. I acknowledge gratefully his tuition, and also his insistence on a high standard of scientific scholarship, both in commenting on work done at Cape Town and later in meticulous reading of the manuscript of this book.

Max Marwick went to make a study of the Cewa people in eastern Northern Rhodesia, who are culturally and sociologically similar to the Yao. In many discussions with him, particularly on the subject of sorcery and witchcraft beliefs, I have been greatly stimulated.

After my first field trip the Trustees of the Institute decided to send Colson, Barnes and myself for our initial period of writing-up to Oxford where Dr. Gluckman had become a lecturer. There I came under the influence of Professor E. E. Evans-Pritchard and Dr. M. Fortes, who contributed considerably to my training.

Throughout my study of the Yao, in the field and in analysis, I have been supported in every way by the Rhodes-Livingstone Institute and its staff. Not only did the Institute provide the finances for academic and disinterested research, but it also created the framework in which a group of sociologists, of divergent interests and background, could work on common problems. Each was able to present his own particular viewpoint, but all were stimulated to adopt a common frame of reference. In this sense the book is as much my colleagues' as it is my own. Barnes, Colson (who later became Director of the Institute), and later Dr. Ian Cunnison, have consistently worked on the material I have submitted to them, individually and in conference, in Central Africa, at Cape Town, at Oxford, and finally at Manchester. I would like to record my special gratitude to Max Gluckman, who was not only my Director in the Institute but also my supervisor at Oxford. To him I owe more than to any other of my colleagues. I would like to say in appreciation that both Max Gluckman and Elizabeth Colson, as successive Directors of the Rhodes-Livingstone Institute, have always given me complete freedom in the conduct of my research and have only given me ' direction ' when I asked for it.

I am glad also to record my appreciation to the Trustees of the Rhodes-Livingstone Institute, and particularly to His Excellency Sir John Waddington who was their President when I was in Nyasaland, for the freedom they allowed me in my work, and for their beneficence in allowing me to come to the United Kingdom in 1947 and again in 1949 where most of my writing has been done.

I am grateful to Mrs. U. K. Stevenson who has read the draft and to Mr. T. Baxter for help with the bibliography.

Lastly, I thank my wife, who not only shared with me the difficulties and frustrations of life in the field, but who has always encouraged me at times when I thought that this book would never be finished. She has in fact had the major share in its preparation.

J. C. M.

NOTE TO SECOND REPRINTING

In this reprint slight alterations have been made to the tables in Chapter IV following a re-analysis of the data. The estimation of the ranks of Administrative Village headmen on pages 104–6 has been made on a different basis and an Appendix E dealing with the interrelationship of factors affecting the prestige of village headmen has been added. Otherwise, apart from these additions and the correction of a few typographical errors, the text is the same as in the first printing.

J. C. M.

NOTE TO THIRD PRINTING

In this reprinting the phrase 'Malawian people' in the sub-title has been substituted for 'Nyasaland tribe'. The Protectorate of Nyasaland became the independent state of Malawi in 1964, so that Nyasaland is now superseded. The word 'tribe' and its adjectival form 'tribal' have subsequently taken on social and political connotations I did not imply when the book was first published. I used the word 'tribe' then to denote a set of people who saw themselves as sharing an indigenous way of life. Accordingly the word 'people' might be more appropriate to-day. The words 'Nyasaland', 'tribe' and 'tribal', however, have not been systematically changed through the book since this would have entailed considerable expense. Where 'Nyasaland' appears in the text, therefore, it should be taken to refer to the country before independence and where 'tribe' or 'tribal' appear they should be taken to refer to a people who see themselves as sharing, or to the quality of, a common indigenous way of life.

1 May, 1971.

J. C. Mitchell.

CONTENTS

xi

Contents

LIST OF PLATES

LIST OF TABLES, DIAGRAMS AND MAPS

B   xv

LIST OF CASE HISTORIES AND TEXTS

NOTE

Where I have used abbreviations for kinship terms I have followed the Rhodes-Livingstone Institute convention :

M = mother	B = brother	H = husband
F = father	Z = sister	W = wife
D = daughter	S = son	G = sibling

Other symbols are built up on these, so that 'father's sister' is FZ and 'mother's father's sister's son's daughter's husband's brother' is MFZSDHB. Seniority is indicated by a plus or minus, so that 'older brother' is + B and 'younger brother' is — B. I have used the combination XC to stand for 'cross cousin'.

CHAPTER I

THE PROBLEM IN ITS ECOLOGICAL SETTING

THE PROBLEM

AT a joint meeting of the Royal Anthropological Institute
and the International African Institute in 1948, Gluckman
said : ' Many District Officers have described the village headman
as the invaluable Non-Commissioned Officer of native administration. Yet despite various references in earlier literature to his
important political, legal and ritual responsibility for his dependants, there has not yet been an adequate appreciation of his key
position in the social structure.' [1]

In this essay, I have tried to examine this problem in relation to
one of the tribal groups in British Central Africa. Gluckman
pointed out that one fact among the diverse characteristics of
Central African peoples is constant—people live in villages.
This was observed by the earliest travellers in the region, who
gave the English word ' village ' to the groupings of huts they
saw, and so this important point passed imperceptibly into the
descriptions of the social organization of the peoples. Yet,
perhaps because of its very obviousness, it is an interesting fact
that no studies have been made of the position of the village as
such in the social structure. It is clear that Lozi villages [2] and
villages along the Luapula River, where the environment sets a
stamp on the village composition,[3] are different from Nyakyusa
villages where boys of one age-grade strike out to found a new
village,[4] or from Ngoni villages where a diversified set of kinsmen

[1] Gluckman, M., Mitchell, J. C., and Barnes, J. A., ' The Village Headman in
British Central Africa ', *Africa*, xix, 2 (April 1949), 89–106.

[2] Gluckman, M., *The Economy of the Central Barotse Plain*, Rhodes-Livingstone Paper, No. 7 (1941), and his contribution to the symposium, *Seven Tribes
of British Central Africa*, eds. Colson, E., and Gluckman, M., Oxford University
Press for the Rhodes-Livingstone Institute (London, 1951).

[3] Cunnison, I., *Kinship and Local Organization on the Luapula*. Communication from the Rhodes-Livingstone Institute, No. V (Livingstone, 1950).

[4] Wilson, G., ' An Introduction to Nyakyusa Society ', *Bantu Studies*, x, 3
(1936), and Wilson, M., *Good Company*, Oxford University Press for the International African Institute (London, 1951).

adhere to a headman whose position is fixed in an historically determined hierarchy.[1] Yet it stands the test of observation that there are in all tribes of this region small concentrated settlements of people who look upon themselves as groups, and who play an important part in the political activities of the community.

In my analysis of the social structure of the Yao, I have taken the village and tried to see it as a unit in a larger field of political relations. I have also tried to see it as a unit in itself, internally differentiated. I have taken the district under the jurisdiction of a Native Authority as the whole, the universe, which is to be resolved into parts. Before the British forces subjugated the tribes of Nyasaland, there had been a period of intensive tribal movement and intertribal warfare. Some groups had gathered around successful warriors and maintained their identity ; others had been broken and dissolved by stronger forces. The British conquest ended the period of military adjustment, and for administrative purposes the country was divided into districts. Within these districts some adherents gathered around their former leaders while others preferred to remain where they were. Tribes such as the Nyanja, who were the original inhabitants, remained in residence ; newcomers such as the Lomwe immigrated from Portuguese East Africa. But when the Administration later officially recognized chiefs in these districts it was the successful Yao invaders who were recognized and not the indigenous Nyanja or immigrant Lomwe.

While the war-making units of the Yao—the tribal groups under numerous chieftains—were broken up by the British forces, the smaller component units, the villages, survived. From early records and from the tales told by old men who can still remember something of the pre-White days, we know that the people have always lived in villages, though their structure has probably changed since those days. The villages were far and away the most important social units within any of the chiefdoms. The 'village' was and still is a key concept in Yao thought. I shall demonstrate later that it was the smallest group acting in the political field. At the same time it was, and still is, the field in which kinship was most significant. This is why I have taken

[1] Barnes, J. A., in his essay 'The Fort Jameson Ngoni', *Seven Tribes, and Politics in a Changing Society*, Oxford University Press for the Rhodes-Livingstone Institute (Cape Town, 1954).

the village as the fundamental unit in my description of Yao social structure. I have tried to describe other social groups in a village context : for example, how lineages and families make up the village ; how the religious congregations, particularly the Moslems, still organize their relationships on a village basis ; and so on.

The position of the village in the social structure therefore has to be analysed from two aspects. Firstly, it is a unit within an organized whole—the chiefdom. Secondly, the village itself is a whole, with its own structure and morphology. Dividing the total structure into two sections and considering the village both as a part of a whole and as itself an organized whole, simplifies description. In fact, there is one continuum of social relationships, and the internal organization of a village reflects its position in the total structure. For example the fission of a matrilineage is significant in both the fields of kinship and politics, since through it kinsmen separate and found new villages.

Throughout this essay I use the word ' village ' to mean both a concentration of huts and a social group. The two ideas are inseparable in Yao thought and it will be clear from the context of the sentence which meaning I intend. A word of warning is necessary here for those who are familiar with Administrative terminology in Nyasaland. The Administrative use of the word ' village ' is different from mine. To me a village is a discrete cluster of huts occupied by a group of kinsmen who recognize their own identity against similar groups. The Administration has for its own purposes classified the population of each district into ' villages ' under remunerated ' village headmen '. Very frequently these do not fall directly within the scope of this study. Wherever I refer to the villages in the Administrative sense I shall use the phrase ' Administrative village ' ; otherwise the word ' village ' refers to the indigenous social group which I have defined.

In order to burden the reader with as few strange-sounding names as possible, and to spare him the task of learning many general village backgrounds, I have tried as far as possible to draw my illustrations from two villages, Ali Kasunka and Cikoja.[1]

---

[1] These names and the names of most of the characters in this book, except those of the well-known chiefs, are fictitious, so that their anonymity might be preserved.

But I have used illustrative material from other villages where it was more complete or less confusing. In Appendices, I set out genealogies, hut censuses, and plans, of the two villages. In the text I use reference numbers in these genealogies, by generation and position in generations, to identify people.

It is necessary to select illustrations because the structural uniformities I wish to describe are often hidden by the idiosyncrasies of particular examples. The general principles of social structure, as I present them here, have been abstracted from my observations over a period of two years, not only in Cikoja and Ali Kasunka villages, but in many others in the Machinga area. I present my illustrations not with any belief that they prove my analysis, but only to help the reader set the principles I describe in the reality of Yao life.

THE FIELD WORK

I spent the first two weeks of my stay in Nyasaland talking over my proposed field work with the Administrative officers of the Nyasaland Government. The Provincial Commissioner suggested that I should do a round trip of the Yao area with the District Commissioner at Zomba. After this tour, in consultation with Chief Kawinga and the District Commissioner, I decided that the best place for me to start would be in Chief Chiwalo's area. The District Commissioner then took me to Chiwalo who indicated a site in his court-village where I could pitch my tent.

For the first week I held meetings with the chief and some of the older men of the vicinity and spent most of my time making notes on material culture, 'customs' and history. On the first page of my notes I find that there is a good description of Yao beliefs in sorcery, all described as if it were in the past : a full year was to pass before my informants were prepared to admit that these beliefs were still held. After a week or two of this general activity I decided to try my first village census. The results were hardly encouraging. Often when villagers knew I was coming they slipped away into the bush. Those who were left frequently refused steadfastly to answer my questions. Many rumours arose to explain my presence. I heard, for example, that I had been sent by the Government to record the names of those to be taken away as soldiers for the next war. I heard that I was an American spy, and also that I was a spy for the Portuguese, because Nyasaland, or at least the Yao area of it, was going to become part of Mozambique. I spent much of my enforced idleness during these early months copying down texts in Yao from my clerk and translating them into English.

Towards the end of 1946, when the rains had set in, I decided to move into a vacant house on a tobacco market about five miles from where I had first pitched my tent. I then started to make a census of the nearest village. Here the attitude of the people was markedly different and I established friendly and happy relationships with them. For some weeks I systematically made censuses of the surrounding villages, and got my first insight into the structural principles of Yao villages. I left this area to attend a conference of research officers of the Institute, and when I returned I pitched my tent in the village into which my personal servant had married. By this time I was speaking some of the language and had started to talk to people directly. I now began to establish a set of informants who would come to my tent in the afternoons and dictate texts to me in Yao on various topics of interest, which I immediately translated into English. The mornings I spent out in neighbouring villages. It was during this period that I gradually heard about the various ceremonies that were being performed and was able to attend them. My wife too was able to attend some of the women's ceremonies. Some months later I moved down to Kawinga's area and pitched my tent in one of the largest and most complex villages I could find and made a complete census of it. I chose this village so that it would be sufficiently close for me to attend Kawinga's court, which was the largest in the area. I left the field in September 1947, and in September 1948 returned to Chiwalo's village. I now engaged a new clerk who could speak no English and who came from the village in Chiwalo's area where I had originally settled. During my second trip I visited Jalasi, Katuli and Kalembo chiefdoms, all in different parts of the Yao country, and made village censuses in each.

The procedure I adopted in making village censuses was as follows. Usually I visited the headman a day or so in advance to explain my intention to him. Most of the villages I studied were fairly close to that in which I was camped so that the people knew as a rule what information I wanted. On an appointed day I went to the village in the early morning. My first task was to make a rough sketch of the position of the huts and to number them. Then with the aid of some of the men of the village (who were usually the wardens of sorority-groups) I went from hut to hut completing a Rhodes-Livingstone Institute standard census form for each adult person who lived in the hut. Later I found that if I completed the census forms for certain key personalities who were dead, I could sometimes construct most of the genealogy of the village without having to question the headman any further. More commonly, however, especially in the larger and more complex villages, I found that it was necessary for me to meet the headman and some of the older men afterwards to complete the genealogy of the village. When I did this it was customary for the men of the village to gather in the common shelter or around me under the verandah of the hut where I was working. The women were not invited near, at least at the beginning of the interview. Soon, however, the men became more and more confused. At some stage or other they would begin shouting questions over to the women, who were sitting discreetly under the verandah of an adjoining hut or in the shade of a conveniently close tree, from where they could hear the proceedings. Eventually, almost without fail, the older women were brought closer and the difficulties straightened out. In time I became accustomed to this procedure and accepted the fact that the first genealogy would have to be discarded and a second made later with the help of the women.

It was during the house-to-house census that many valuable leads emerged. During the census-taking, for example, unusual types of marriage with kinsmen appeared which I was able to follow up immediately in terms of an actual case history ; or, if it were likely to be embarrassing at that moment, I noted it down and made specific enquiries later, for the census-taking was usually done in public.

The quantitative material presented in Chapter IV on Prestige and Rank among Village Headmen was collected at the chief's courts. I worked with the chief's tax-clerk and one or two of the chief's councillors. We worked through the tax-register, and the councillors answered a set of questions about each village headman. In two areas the chiefs called the village headmen into a public meeting and each answered the questions personally. Where the information was not known, I made special enquiries to obtain it. Later I transferred this information on to small cards which I subsequently used in the statistical analysis. During my survey of Malemia chiefdom I was able to employ six African clerks whom I trained to record genealogies. They surveyed a 20 per cent random sample of villages in the chiefdom. The material from these genealogies has been transferred to Hollerith cards for statistical analysis at some future date. During this period, Mr. Carrall Wilcocks, who was then Agricultural Instructor at the Jeanes' School, and I were able to make a map with chain and compass of every garden cultivated by members of a large village. While the general results of this study have been included here, a detailed analysis is still to be made.

The material used in the chapters which deal with the pre-White times has been derived mainly from the published works quoted in the Bibliography. I was also able to consult records in the Central African Archives. By permission of the Nyasaland Government I was allowed to read through the District Books at Fort Johnston and Zomba, and through some of the files which contained information collected by early District Officers. I was also able to consult the detailed returns of the 1945 Census at the District Commissioner's office in Zomba. The Agricultural Officer at Fort Johnston, under whose jurisdiction the area where I was working fell, was kind enough to let me read some reports and to give me statistics of sales of tobacco and other agricultural produce at the Government-controlled markets, as well as details of rainfall and temperature.

The ideas in this book have been developed in a number of Rhodes-Livingstone Institute staff conferences and at seminars at Oxford. During a preliminary period of writing at Oxford between September 1947 and August 1948 I prepared the manuscript of what was later to become my contribution to the symposium *Seven Tribes of British Central Africa*. I cannot over-emphasize the importance of this essay in setting the problems examined in this book and in clarifying my approach to them. It brought home to me more than anything else the truth in the aphorism : the hardest part of field work is writing it up.

Topography and Surface Water

The Protectorate of Nyasaland lies between latitudes 09° 45′ S. and 17° 16′ S. and longitudes 33° E. and 36° E. It includes most of the surface of Lake Nyasa, the most southerly of the African Great Lakes. This dominant topographical feature, from which Nyasaland has taken its name, is part of the Great Rift Valley which runs from north to south through the territory. On the western, northern and eastern shores of the lake the coastline is fringed by great mountain masses, some of which drop sheer to the lake without a coastal shelf. In the south, the broad base of the valley forms a plain through which runs the Shire River which issues from Lake Nyasa. The western edge of the Rift Valley is fringed by the Kirk Range which sweeps north-westwards to form the Dedza Highlands. On the eastern fringe the valley forks to the east to form a plain between the Mangoche Highlands, the highest point of which is 5400 feet above mean sea level, and the great mass of the Shire Highlands, the highest point of which is 11,000 feet above mean sea level. This plain rises sharply about 800 feet in a mile or two to 2000 feet above mean sea level, eastwards from the Shire River. This forms the scarp of the Great Rift Valley. From the scarp it slopes gently to the west to the smaller lakes Chiuta-Amaramba and Shirwa which lie on the Portuguese East Africa border. Between the Mangoche Highlands and the Shire Highlands the plain is broken by the Chikala-Chaoni Range which protrudes almost to the shores of the Lake Shirwa, just to the north of its centre. This range, which forms an outstanding natural fortress, has played an important rôle in the history of Kawinga's followers.

The Mangoche Highlands, the ridge along the scarp of the Great Rift Valley and the Shire Highlands, here form the watershed between the rivers which flow into the Shire and thence the Zambezi, and the rivers which flow into the Chiuta-Amaramba, thence into the Lujenda and to the Rovuma River, or into Lake Shirwa which has no outlet. All the main rivers flow to the Indian Ocean. While the Great Rift Valley is well drained by the Shire River, the plain is inefficiently drained by the rivers which flow to the two smaller lakes. The shores around Chiuta and especially Shirwa are liable to inundation during the rainy season : hence the area depicted on the map is not all suitable for

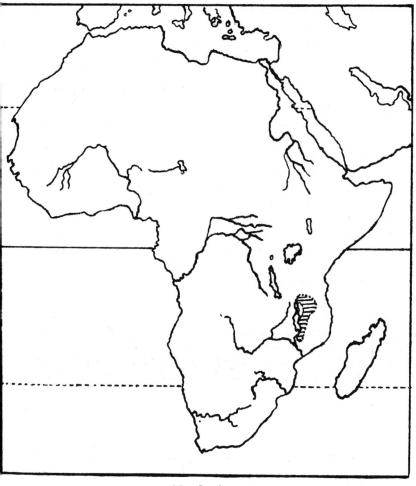

MAP I. AFRICA.
The shaded portion shows roughly where the Yao live.

human habitation. Large areas around Lake Shirwa are in fact marshlands in the wet season, and stretches of poor sandy and slightly saline soil during the dry season.

Generally speaking the distribution of surface water throughout this area is variable. The highlands are on the whole well supplied with streams which rise in the mountains and flow

swiftly throughout the year. In the plains many small rivers
flow quite strongly during the rainy season but dry up shortly
afterwards and by July or August the water shortage becomes
acute for many villages. In the rainy season plenty of shallow
pools supply the wants of the people ; as these dry up the women
must go farther and farther afield to find water. To the east of
the watershed of the plain the distance they may have to go is
still within the bounds of possibility, but on the valley lip this is
no longer so,[1] and large areas of the escarpment, especially to the
south towards the Shire Highlands, are unpopulated. The
Administration has been sinking wells in an attempt to increase
the amount of land available for human habitation. It reports
that soon after wells had been sunk villages moved there and
started gardens :[2] this indicates the pressure of the population on
the land. Within the area where most of my study was made,
i.e. from the northern fringe of the Shire Highlands, agricultural-
ists describe the soil as ' variable '. The Agricultural Officer at
Zomba, writing of this area, said :

In the valley of the Shire the soils may be described as rich sandy
alluvium. Around the hills the soil is chiefly red with a high percentage of clay and a small percentage of sand. Much of the soil
in the ridge of highland stretching from the Chikala hills in the south
to the hills near Mount Mangoche in the north is sandy and poor,
with pockets of good rich soil here and there. The soil improves
as the land slopes down each side of the ridge to the west to the Shire
Valley, and to the east to the shores of Lake Shirwa and Lake Chiuta.[3]

CLIMATE

The climate is the tropical monsoon type. The average annual
rainfall over the years 1944–6 at the three stations, Jalasi, Nyambi
and Mlomba, i.e. placed at even intervals throughout the area
of study, was 41·89 inches.[4] The rainfall is slightly heavier in
the higher areas. This rain falls almost entirely during the

[1] The relation of water supply to population distribution in Nyasaland is discussed by Dixey, F., ' The Distribution of the Population of Nyasaland ',
Geographical Review, xviii (April 1928), 274 ff.
[2] *Nyasaland Protectorate Report on Native Affairs* (Zomba, 1931), 47.
[3] *Report of the Agricultural Officer, Zomba, to the Director of Agriculture* (1944),
(unpublished).
[4] I am indebted to the Agricultural Officer, Fort Johnston, for this information.

months November to March inclusive. Diagram 1 shows the distribution of the rainfall during the year. Very little rain falls during other months. The initial rains of the year are ushered in by convectional storms and very heavy downpours. This causes a heavy run-off, flooding of the rivers and lake shores, and much erosion of the parched land which by this time has become

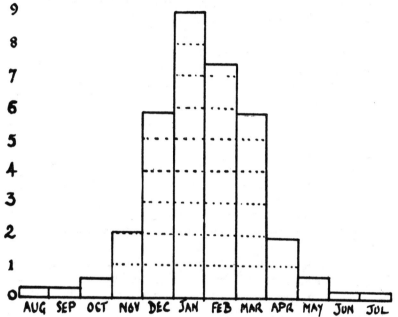

DIAGRAM 1. RAINFALL IN LIWONDE AND FORT JOHNSTON DISTRICTS.
This diagram shows that almost the whole of the rainfall occurs between November and April.

very dusty. During December there is usually little rain for a short period of a week or two. After that the rains change their character and become more steady and drenching. They decrease in March and April, and thereafter, little rain falls.

The Yao concept of the seasons follows this feature of the climate. The year is divided into two seasons, called *cuku*, the wet season, and *cau*, the dry season. The wet season is the one in which most agricultural activity is carried out. The gardens are hoed up and planted, weeded and tended, and the crops harvested, between the months of October and May. During the dry season, in contrast to the busy wet season, there is much visiting and social activities are resumed. Dances and initiation ceremonies also are mostly held during the dry season. The only agricultural work done during this time is the clearing of the bush and the stacking of the brushwood ready for burning.

The temperatures are high. I have no records for the three stations in the area because recording has started only recently. It is hottest during the months just preceding the rains, i.e. September to December, and coldest during May to August. I have never heard of frosts in the area so it is unlikely that the temperature falls below freezing point. Hornby records the mean maximum temperature for Liwonde as 82·3° F. and the mean minimum temperature as 59·3° F. These are for Liwonde station which is in the Shire Valley. The temperature for the plains and the highlands is probably a few degrees less.

VEGETATION

The natural vegetation in this area varies from thick rain forest along the permanent watercourses to open grassland in the marshy patches. In forestry reserves and other places where the vegetation has not been cut out, trees 20 to 30 feet high predominate with thin undergrowth. Along the Shire Valley much of the vegetation is untouched, but in the highlands and on the plain most of the unprotected forest has been cut out for garden lands. In the open spaces between trees the land is covered by elephant grass six to eight feet high.

POPULATION

The density of the population in Nyasaland as a whole is high in comparison with that in the surrounding territories.[1] Within the Territory itself the densities in some districts are as high as anywhere in Africa.[2] The population as a whole is concentrated in the highland districts of Dedza and the Shire Highlands. The districts in which I worked are less densely populated than most of the districts in the Southern Province, but of average density

[1] Expressing densities as total population per square mile. Nyasaland, 55·5 (1945); Tanganyika, 17·0 (1946); Portuguese East Africa, 14·5 (1938); Southern Rhodesia, 11·5 (1946); Northern Rhodesia, 5·0 (1946).

[2] Chiradzulu district, 309·8; Cholo, 191·9; Zomba, 152·4. *Nyasaland Census,* 1945, Table 8.

(*a*)   Patchwork cultivation in Chiwalo area.   Note how the natural vegetation has been cleared for staple gardens.   Patches of ash from burnt garden refuse can be seen to the left.   There are also two small villages in the foreground and a large village distinguishable by the dark patch of mango trees at the foot of the hill in the top left-hand corner.

(*October 1948*)

(*b*)   A small village in typical surroundings in Chiwalo area.

(*August 1948*)

PLATE II

for the Territory as a whole. Within these districts [1] there is a population of 117,035. This estimate is based on an actual count and is probably more accurate than the usual questionable estimates of African population. The population as shown by the censuses over the last 35 years has been increasing rapidly. Between 1931 and 1945 in Kawinga, Liwonde and Nyambi areas it increased from 39,154 to 64,840 which represents an annual rate of increase of 3·5 per cent. This is due partly to immigration and partly to natural increase, but it is difficult to estimate which is the more important since immigration figures for Africans are unobtainable.[2] The density of the population in these areas, in 1945, is set out in Table I.

TABLE I

DENSITIES OF POPULATION IN TRIBAL AREAS : 1945

Chiefdom	Area in sq. miles	Total Population	Density per sq. mile
Jalasi.	800	40,287	50·4
Nyambi. . . .	131	7335	56·0
Kawinga . . .	682	44,789	65·7
Liwonde. . . .	396	12,176	30·7
Malemia . . .	50	12,448	248·9
All areas . . .	2059	117,035	56·8

Sources : Areas from the Provincial Commissioner, Southern Province. Population from the detailed returns of the 1945 Census.

Of these areas Malemia has the highest density, 248·9 per square mile. This is on the fringe of the highlands which are the

[1] From the 1945 Census. These areas are Kawinga, Liwonde, Nyambi, Jalasi and Malemia. Other Machinga chiefdoms are Mponda (18,701), Kalembo (11,260), Nsamala (11,582), and Ntumanje (17,467), but in these I have spent only a few days and I do not include them in the main analysis. I also spent some time in Katuli area (12,245) in Fort Johnston district, and Ntaja area (17,195) in Blantyre district, but these are not Machinga Yao, and I only refer to them to illustrate points. My generalizations do not apply to them.

[2] There is some evidence that the natural rate of increase would double the population in 25 years. See Mitchell, J. C., 'An Estimate of Fertility in some Yao Hamlets of Liwonde District of Southern Nyasaland ', *Africa*, xix, 3 (Oct. 1949), 293–308.

economic centre of Southern Nyasaland and much land has been alienated to Whites there. Liwonde area, which has only 30·7 to the square mile, has large parts that are unpopulated because of the lack of surface water on the escarpment of the Rift Valley.

This population is by no means homogeneous, tribally or linguistically, but culturally the tribes are all very similar. The Yao, Nguru and Nyanja, who comprise most of the population, live in villages under village headmen ; marry uxorilocally ; have similar practices and beliefs in sorcery and disease. Table II

TABLE II

TRIBAL COMPOSITION OF THE CHIEFDOMS : 1945

Chiefdom	Total Population	Percentages of Tribes			
		Yao	Nguru	Nyanja	Ngoni
Jalasi	40,287	81·3	12·4	5·9	0·2
Nyambi	7335	73·2	26·8	0·0	0·0
Kawinga	44,789	48·7	35·7	14·4	1·2
Liwonde	12,176	75·2	19·6	5·2	0·1
Malemia	12,448	75·1	9·6	13·7	1·6

Sources : Nyasaland Census, 1945. Abstracted from the detailed returns at the District Commissioner's Offices at Zomba and Fort Johnston.

shows the tribal make-up of the five areas with which I am concerned. Three-quarters of the population in all these areas are Yao. In Kawinga area, in which non-Yao tribes are most numerous, only one-half of the people are Yao, but included in this area are the two Mpotola subordinate chieftains Ngokwe and Chikweo, whose followers are predominantly Nguru (42·7 and 55·7 per cent).[1] If we exclude these two chiefdoms, the proportion of Yao in the rest of Kawinga area is 55·6 per cent. Nyambi and Kawinga areas, lying as they do against the Portuguese East African boundary, have the greater proportion of Nguru. Within Kawinga area the concentration of the Nguru along the boundary is also shown. Chiwalo chiefdom, which lies to the west of Kawinga area, has only 15 per cent Nguru,

[1] It seems here that the Mpotola may have been enumerated as Nguru and Nyanja.

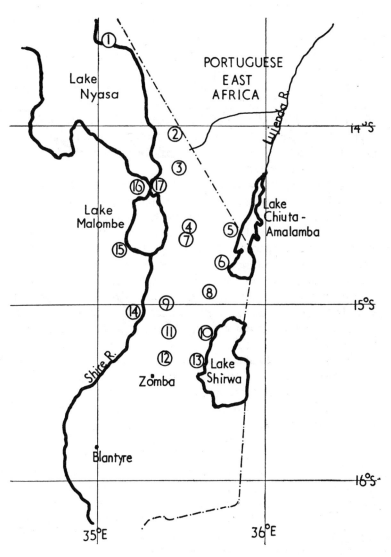

MAP II. SOUTHERN NYASALAND.

Showing the positions of Machinga and other Chiefs.

1. Makanjila (Masaninga)
2. Katuli (Chisi)
3. Jalasi (Machinga)
4. Nyambi (Machinga)
5. Ngokwe (Mpotola)
6. Chikweo (Mpotola)
7. Chiwalo (Machinga)
8. Kawinga (Machinga)
9. Liwonde (Machinga)
10. Mposa (Machinga)
11. Chamba (Machinga)
12. Malemia (Machinga)
13. Ntumanje (Machinga)
14. Msamala (Machinga)
15. Kalembo (Machinga)
16. Mponda (Machinga)
17. Nankhumba (Nyanja)

slightly more than the extreme southerly chiefdoms, Mposa and Chamba. As we have seen, half the population of the two most easterly chiefdoms is Nguru.

The Nyanja are concentrated mostly along the Shire River banks and around the Lake Shirwa shores. Most in Kawinga are at the north end of the Lake Shirwa or in Mposa at Lake Shirwa [1] and, according to the census, in Ngokwe in the extreme north-east. It is possible that in Ngokwe some of the Mpotola have been enumerated as Nyanja.

Although my study was of the Yao, I cannot exclude these other ethnic groups from it. The specific percentages must not be considered as exact reflections of the tribal make-up in the area. Though the villages of the three main tribal groups tend to be distinct, and intermarriage is not as great as might be expected, there are increasing numbers of children of mixed tribal parentage. There is some value in the figures, but we must take into consideration the general political situation in these chiefdoms. I enlarge upon this theme later. Generally speaking, however, the Yao have come in as invaders, while most Nguru have come in as immigrants. The Yao have greater prestige both in the eyes of the Whites and in the general structure of the chiefdoms. Many Nguru therefore, who have been in this area for some time, have come to call themselves Yao if they are asked, especially by a White man. This is especially true of the Mpotola people where they are living under Yao chiefs. The Mpotola are technically Nguru but most have lost their own language and speak only Yao. The Administration did not classify the Mpotola as a separate tribe in the Census and it is difficult to decide whether they were included as Yao or Nguru. Most of the Mpotola headmen I have met in Yao chiefdoms have called themselves Yao until they were prevailed upon to qualify their claim. Allowing for some discrepancies in the figures, the table shows nevertheless that numerically the Yao outnumber any other tribe in the area. In general, the other tribes are members of the chiefdoms and take part in most of the social activities which occur within them. I outline later the position of their headmen in the general political structure, but I wish to set out here some general notes on the tribal background of the non-Yao groups.

The term Nguru is applied to a large group of people who call

[1] 32 per cent of the population in Mposa's area is Nyanja.

themselves Alomwe. These people came from that part of Portuguese East Africa immediately to the east of Nyasaland. They speak a group of dialects mutually intelligible and widely different from either Yao or Nyanja. Culturally and structurally they are similar to the Yao and Nyanja, practising matrilineal descent and uxorilocal marriage, and living in small groups of matrilineal kin. Their religious and mystical beliefs are also the same. Some of the linguistic groups that form this congeries are the Shirima, Kokhola, Metho, Thokwani, Ratha, Kuwa, Nahara, Marenje, Nyamwelo, Mihavani and Nikhukhu. These people have been migrating into Nyasaland over the last fifty years, and now predominate in the Cholo and Chiradzulu districts.

The Nyanja were the original inhabitants in these areas, but have been almost completely displaced by the Yao, except in Liwonde along the Shire River and in Kawinga along the Lake Shirwa shores. Linguistically they are more akin to the Yao than to the Lomwe, but their language is still unintelligible to the Yao. Culturally they appear to be similar to the Yao, and they have accepted certain Yao institutions such as the boys' initiation ceremonies (*lupanda*), and have been fitted into the social and political structure.

The Ngoni, of whom there are very few here, are concentrated on the south side of the Chikala Range, in the areas of Chamba and Mposa, who are subordinate chiefs to Kawinga. They are the remnants of various Ngoni armies that raided into Nyasaland during the last two or three decades of the nineteenth century. As far as I could ascertain they have adopted Nyanja ways and language.

HISTORICAL BACKGROUND TO THE MODERN ECONOMIC SITUATION

Nyasaland to-day, as part of the British Empire, is in the general world economic system, and the Africans in the tribal areas participate in this system, though not to the same degree as the White planters in the Shire and Dedza Highlands. If the Yao were ever a people who supported themselves by their agriculture alone, they had adopted a more complex economy long before the Whites came to Nyasaland. Later, when I discuss their historical background, I outline briefly the position that the Yao occupied in Central Africa as middlemen and traders. As far back as 1798 Laçerda described the Yao rôle as active traders. They bartered ivory, slaves, beeswax and tobacco with the Arabs along the East Coast of Africa for guns, gun-powder, cloth and beads. We cannot easily estimate what proportion of the population was engaged in whole-time slaving and trading. The larger proportion must have found it necessary to cultivate their gardens of finger-millet and sorghum in the rainy season to supply them with the major food crops. It seems likely that slave-raiding and trading were occupations mostly followed during the dry season.

The Yao therefore had become accustomed to a variation of activities and division of labour, at least a century before the Whites came to Nyasaland. Their wants at this time had already become sufficiently diversified to include cloth, beads, gun-powder and guns. All these trade goods are more durable than the foodstuffs which are the measure of wealth among a people who support themselves entirely by their own produce. But the individual want for these trade goods was limited, and the Yao used their surplus rather as capital for trading farther inland with other tribes.

There is considerable evidence, both from my informants and the writings of early travellers, that these trade goods—ivory, cloth and slaves—came to be used as currency, and most people recognized a fixed relationship between the three commodities. A female slave could be exchanged for an amount of calico or ivory that was constant over fairly large parts of Central Africa ; the value of a tusk of ivory could be expressed in calico in the same way. By enterprise, therefore, in trading and raiding, an individual could accumulate wealth in the form of calico, guns, beads, ivory or slaves. But the personal consumption of trade goods is of necessity limited, so that the Yao preferred to accumulate their wealth in the form of slaves. The reason for this lies in the general political structure of the early chiefdoms, which I describe later. Slaves were not only labourers and serfs ; they also increased the military and political power of their masters. At the same time slaves could be sent to the coast in a caravan and bartered for cloth, or, since they were always prized, they could be used to settle claims for compensation from aggrieved neigh-bours. The slave trade therefore, although related to domestic slavery in that a trader could at any moment send some of his own slaves to the coast, was actually quite a separate institution.

Although the advent of the White Administration stopped both domestic slavery and the slave-trade to the coast, both of which were vitally important elements in Yao economy, it did nothing to decrease or reduce the variety of the wants of the Africans. On the contrary, it obviously increased those wants. The missionaries, who were the first Whites to settle in Nyasaland, were forced to import large quantities of cloth and beads so that they could buy foodstuffs and pay their labourers. They quite unintentionally, therefore, became competitors with the Yao in this trade. By some accounts their goods were both superior and cheaper. As early as 1878 the African Lakes Company was sponsored by the Church of Scotland Mission, so that it could take over the trading part of their dealings with the Africans. The planters and traders who began to settle in the highlands after 1890 brought more and more cloth, beads and other trade goods into Nyasaland to pay wages and buy foodstuffs.

When the Protectorate was proclaimed in 1891 and the Administration started to put down domestic slavery and the trade in slaves to the coast, the monopoly of trade in goods fell directly into the hands of the Whites. After 1893, when coinage was introduced, the economy of the country rapidly changed from one based on barter with slaves and ivory as the main outgoing commodities, and slaves, calico, beads and brass rings as the incoming commodities, to an economy in which the wants had become even more diversified. In 1895, the *British Central African Gazette* could record :

The wants of the people of this part of the world not long ago were limited to sufficient calico to clothe the family, but in one short year their wants now include boots, size and quality a minor point, turbans, coats, and in fact at a distance the half-naked native of yesterday has the appearance of Sikh soldiery.[1]

That the Yao took to the use of money is illustrated by the Acting Commissioner's statement in 1897 : ' The Yao thoroughly appreciate having a currency. It has proved, in fact, a great step towards civilizing the native of this part of Africa. He is now able to accumulate his earnings, which formerly in the days of a

[1] Vol. i, 2 (Sept. 26th, 1894).

calico currency was an impossibility.'[1] The Africans could hardly have resisted the change over to a money economy. The taxation system introduced in 1893 was based on the Governor of Zululand's Proclamation III of 1887, and ruled that a tax defaulter was liable to be conscripted for labour until he had earned the amount of his tax. Coffee estates owned by Whites in the Highlands were at the same time in need of labour.[2] Tax was then taken in kind but it was soon changed to cash as a further inducement to Africans to come on to the labour market. The Africans were forced into the cash economy of the Protectorate even if they were unwilling. The measures were so successful that in 1899 the *Gazette* announced that the labour market in Blantyre was flooded.[3]

MODERN ECONOMIC STRUCTURE

In modern Nyasaland, the wants of the Africans have become even more varied than they were in the earlier days. Most younger men wear European-type clothing and shoes. Many own bicycles and sewing machines. Many houses have glass windows and panelled doors and most of them are furnished with some rough furniture which has been bought from local craftsmen. Many have beds and mosquito nets. Few women cannot boast of enamel dishes to replace their clay pottery or china cups to replace drinking gourds. The food habits of the peoples too have broadened. Most households use sugar these days, and many people drink tea. I should say that all households occasionally buy soap. Certainly all need salt, which formerly was burnt from the saline grass around Lake Shirwa or dissolved out of special soils in Portuguese East Africa. The stock-lists of an Indian-owned village shop in Chiwalo's area and of an African-owned canteen in the same area, which I have set out in Appendix A, indicate the range of the wants of the modern African.

It is clear that these wants are over and above food requirements. The people in these tribal areas live primarily on the

[1] *Report of the Consul and Acting Commissioner Sharpe on the Trade and General Condition of the British Central African Protectorate for April 1896 to March 1897.* C. 8438.

[2] See the *B.C.A. Gazette*, iii, 5 (March 1895), and iii, 17 (Sept. 15th, 1896), which print advertisements offering 'native labour arranged for and supplied to plantations at a commission of 7s. 6d. a head'.

[3] *B.C.A. Gazette*, vi, 6 (June 24th, 1899).

crops grown in their gardens. For their other wants they need cash, and they obtain it either by the sale of their agricultural produce, by trading with their fellows, or by seeking work either within or outside the area. The sale of agricultural produce is probably the most important. A few Africans earn a small living as blacksmiths, bicycle repairers, diviners and leeches, fish pedlars and tailors. There are some African canteen or small shop owners, but this field is dominated by the Indians, who between them have a few dozen village and roadside stores.

A certain amount of money is sent or brought home by labour migrants. I could not estimate how much this is for each household. It cannot be very high on the average, because not a great proportion is working at labour centres outside the area of study.[1] Within the Territory there are few opportunities of earning wages. In Jalasi's area there are one or two White tobacco estates, which employ at the most a few hundred labourers, and a number of Indian storekeepers who may between them employ a hundred men. Otherwise the Government itself, through the Agriculture Department in particular, may employ a hundred or more labourers. There are more opportunities south of Chikala and in the densely populated Malemia area where a considerable number are employed in the neighbouring township, Zomba, and on the surrounding estates. The cash income per adult, male and female, in the area where this study was made probably does not exceed £40 to £50 per annum, and the Yao rely mainly on the sale of their own produce to earn this amount.

[1] I estimate from genealogies that about 22 per cent of the men over the age of 18 were at labour centres in 1947–8. Table 3 of the 1945 Census shows that, excluding those in the Army, 28 per cent of the men over the age of 18 were away from Liwonde and Fort Johnston districts when the census was taken.

CHAPTER II

THE HISTORICAL BACKGROUND TO THE MODERN SITUATION

Before the Whites came

TO understand the Yao we must start with the Arab coloniza-tion of the east coast of Africa. We know that the Arabs had colonized it as early as A.D. 700. They were a mercantile people, and their trading was so well advanced that by the end of the twelfth century they had founded Kilwa, due east of the north end of Lake Nyasa, as an entrepôt.[1] When Vasco da Gama sailed up the east coast in 1498, he found that the Arabs had well-established posts all along the coast. The Portuguese and the Arabs became rivals for the trade of the African interior, and this rivalry was to continue for many centuries. In 1698 the Imam of Oman drove the Portuguese out as far south as Cape Delgado, and the Arabs had sole control of the east coast[2] up to that point.

The Yao say that their traditional home is between the Lujenda and Rovuma Rivers, east of Lake Nyasa. There can be no doubt, therefore, that Arab trading expeditions passed through the Yao territory, especially since the Rovuma Valley is the most convenient route into Central Africa from Kilwa. We can be fairly certain that Yao contact with the Arabs began at least 200 years before the Europeans came.

Although it is fairly certain that the Jesuits from the Zambezi had explored the Shire Valley and the Lake regions, they left no easily available records of the inhabitants of those areas.[3] One of the earliest references to the Yao is recorded by Dr. Franscisco Jose de Laçerda in a letter dated March 22nd, 1798, addressed to the Minister of State of Portugal. In it he outlines his pro-

[1] Hichens, W., 'Islam in Africa', in Arberry, A. J., and Landau, R., *Islam To-day* (London, 1943).

[2] Pim, A., *Economic History of Tropical Africa* (London, 1940), 19.

[3] Burton mentions in a footnote to *Laçerda's Journey to the Cazembe in 1798*, John Murray (London, 1852), 37, that a missionary Joaõ dos Santos resided in this area from 1586 to 1597.

posed visit to the Kazembe of Luapula regions, known then as the Wisa country. It is quite obvious that the Yao were serious competitors with the Portuguese for the land trade. Laçerda writes :

The dry goods hitherto imported into this country [i.e. Wisa country], have been bought by the Mujao, indirectly or directly, from the Arabs of Zanzibar and its vicinity. Hence these people received all the ivory exported from the possessions of the Casembe ; whereas formerly it passed in great quantities through our port of Mozambique.[1]

It is reasonable to assume that because of their geographical position the Yao had conducted a considerable trade between the interior and the coast, mainly cloth and guns for slaves and ivory—the two were inseparable since the cheapest means of transporting ivory to the coast was by slaves. The Yao trade in slaves led to their major conflict with the British.

When Livingstone made his expedition up the Rovuma in 1866, he found abundant evidence of the influence of the Arabs. Speaking of the Yao chief Mataka, he says : ' He gave me a square house to live in, and indeed most of the houses here are square, for the Arabs are imitated in everything.'[2] Livingstone mentions in particular the trade in slaves that the Yao were conducting in Kilwa. He records that :

The Waiyau generally are still the most active agents the slave-traders have. The caravan leaders from Kilwa arrive at a Waiyau village, show the goods they have brought, are treated liberally by the elders and told to wait and enjoy themselves, slaves enough to purchase all will be procured : then a foray is made against the Manganja who have few or no guns. The Waiyau who come against them are abundantly supplied with both by their coast guests. Several of the low coast Arabs, who differ in nothing from the Waiyau, usually accompany the foray, and do business on their own account.[3]

Even before Livingstone had made his expedition up the Rovuma Valley, there had been a large-scale movement in all directions of the Yao from their traditional home. The tradition is that the name Yao is taken from a hill, grass-covered but

[1] Burton, *Laçerda's Journey*.
[2] Waller, H., *The Last Journals of David Livingstone in Central Africa from 1865 until his Death*, John Murray (London, 1874), 73.
[3] Waller, *Last Journals*, 78.

treeless, which is situated somewhere between Mwembe (in Portuguese East Africa) and the Luchilingo Range.[1]

It is convenient to divide the history of the Yao into two major episodes : firstly the movement from the Yao Hill to other hills, and secondly the movement into and within the Nyasaland Protectorate.

EPISODE I : THE SCATTERING OF THE TRIBES FROM THE YAO HILL

The exact cause of the scattering of the tribes from their traditional home is not clear. Yohannah B. Abdallah suggests that it must have been some internal dissension.[2] Whatever the cause, the tribe broke up into a number of sections, each of which settled at yet another hill from which it took its name. Abdallah lists ten divisions [3] but we need consider only the four that penetrated into British Nyasaland.

These were :

1. The *Achisi Yao*, who settled at Mchisi hill.
2. The *Amasaninga Yao*, who settled near the Lisaninga hill (near the Lutwisi River in Portuguese East Africa).
3. The *Amangoche Yao*, who settled at Mount Mangoche near Fort Johnston, south of Lake Nyasa.
4. The *Amachinga Yao*, who settled near the Mandimba hill. They are called Amachinga because of the serrated edge of the range in which the Mandimba hill is situated. [*Licinga*—a fence.]

EPISODE II : THE DISPLACEMENT OF THE DIVISIONS FROM THEIR HOMES [4]

In time, each of the four sections mentioned found its way into Nyasaland. Briefly the details are :

1. The *Achisi Yao* are represented in Nyasaland by the people under Native Authority Katuli in Fort Johnston district. The 1945 Census showed that there were 12,187 Yao under this chief, i.e. 4·3 per cent of the total Yao population of British Nyasaland. However, not all Yao under Katuli are Achisi Yao, and there are no doubt Achisi Yao elsewhere in small numbers ; but even

[1] Abdallah, *Chiikala cha Wayao*, 7, edited and translated by Meredith Sanderson as *The History of the Yao*, Government Printer (Zomba, 1919).
[2] Abdallah, *Chiikala*, 8.   [3] Abdallah, *Chiikala*, 9.
[4] For information on areas which I did not visit I have drawn heavily from the Administrative file 'Historical Notes on Districts'.

if we estimate the total proportion as 5 per cent, it is still a small and relatively unimportant group.

2. The *Amasaninga Yao* are represented in British Nyasaland by the people under Native Authority Makanjira, and they are roughly 5 per cent of the total population of the Yao of the Territory. Makanjira himself is said to have been of Nyanja origin. He moved first to the Lisaninga Hills, where he acquired a mixed following of Amasaninga Yao and Nyanja ; and then by conquest he moved on to the area round Fort Maguire, where he is now established. There are offshoots of the group in Dowa district across Lake Nyasa.

3. The *Amangoche Yao* are of much greater importance, and at present constitute about half of the Yao population of the Territory. During the early part of the nineteenth century, while this group was at Mangoche mountain, it was successfully attacked by the Amachinga Yao under Nkata and Kawinga, and scattered in all directions. Most of the people migrated southwards and settled in the Shire Highlands, where Mlumbe, Chikowi, Kapeni, Matipwiri and other representatives are found to-day.

4. The *Amachinga Yao* [1] were probably displaced from their traditional home, at Mandimba on the Lujenda River in Portuguese East Africa, by attacks from the Lomwe inhabitants in the east. They say that wide-spread famines followed the war and forced most people to migrate. Present-day representatives of this group are Nkata, Jalasi, Mponda, Kalembo, Nsamala, Nyambi, Kawinga, Liwonde, Malemia and Ntumanje in the Fort Johnston and Zomba districts.

The Yao invasion into Nyasaland was not a military incursion of the Ngoni type. Definite evidence on the exact form of the invasion is not available, but informants maintain that many of the first immigrants came into the country peacefully and in family groups (*mbumba*). Often the immigrants found succour with Nyanja groups. Sometimes this hospitality was claimed because the Yao had the same clan names as the Nyanja. The Yao soon took the opportunity presented by internecine struggles among the Nyanja to consolidate their position in the country.

[1] For a more detailed history of this group, especially of the Malemia group, see Stannus, H. S., ' The Wayao of Nyasaland ', *Harvard African Studies*, iii (1922), 233 ff.

When Livingstone passed the Lake in 1866 he found Mponda living in approximately the same place as his successor does to-day, and he mentioned that Kawinga was living on the west of Lake Malombe.[1] He also mentioned that the Machinga dominated the whole of this area, showing that by this time there had been considerable movement into it. When the Church of Scotland Mission was established at Blantyre in 1876, Duff MacDonald recorded that the disposition of the chiefs was as follows : Mlumbe to the north-west of Zomba ; Kapeni near Blantyre at Sochi ; Mpama at Chiradzulu ; Kawinga at Chikala ; Malemia on the south-west side of Mount Zomba, and the Matipwiri at Mount Mlanje.[2] These groups, except for Kawinga, still occupy the same positions to-day. At this time most of the movement into Nyasaland had ceased, and the Yao invaders had already set themselves up as rulers over the indigenous Nyanja. At the same time the Ngoni were making frequent forays into the Shire Highlands and the rest of Southern Nyasaland, so that the position was far from stable.

The distribution of the Yao to-day reflects the history of their movement into Nyasaland. The districts nearest and fanning out from the point of entry into Nyasaland, viz. the area due east of Fort Johnston, contain the largest proportion of Yao. The more distant the districts are, the smaller the proportion of Yao in them.

The Entry of the Missionaries

The Missionaries were the first Whites to settle in Nyasaland. When he was in Britain in 1858, Livingstone had recommended the Shire Highlands as a suitable place for the establishment of a Mission. Inspired by his reports, the Universities Mission to Central Africa was founded, and in 1861 Dr. Mackenzie was sent out to establish the Mission. It was an ill-starred venture.[3] From the sociological point of view its significance is that it

[1] Waller, *Last Journals*, 109.

[2] MacDonald, D., *Africana or The Heart of Heathen Africa*, Simpkin Marshall (London, 1882), i, 31.

[3] Rowley, H., *The Story of the Universities Mission to Central Africa, from its commencement under Bishop Mackenzie, to its Withdrawal from the Zambesi*, Saunders, Otley & Co. (London, 1886), and *Twenty Years in Central Africa*, Wells Gardner, Darton & Co. (London, 1889), 3rd Edition.

initiated the relationships of Black and White in Nyasaland ; and its failure was partly a result of the ambivalent attitude to colonial peoples at that time. The people of Britain were horrified at the cruelties of slavery, but the Mission drew upon itself severe public censure because it took up arms against the Yao slavers in its vicinity. The Mission had to face a very difficult problem. It was ostensibly a teacher of the Gospel. Yet about it the Yao were performing deeds of violence, robbery and murder, and were taking slaves from the Nyanja inhabitants in the area. At the same time hundreds of fugitives and runaway slaves were seeking protection at the Mission. To take in fugitives and runaway slaves was, in African eyes, as political an action as to take physical action against the slavers. Should the Mission close its eyes to these un-Christian barbarities, since they were a part of the secular life of the people, or should it take action against them ? Livingstone had had no compunction in releasing slaves, and the U.M.C.A. followed his lead, and not only took in fugitives but actually carried out assaults on parties of slave-raiders. This was the time when the first of the Yao groups under Mpama and Kapeni were penetrating into the highlands. The indigenous Nyanja, whose political and military organization was very weak, ranged themselves around the Missionaries, and tried to use them against the Yao invaders. The situation soon developed into a struggle between the Missionaries and the Yao slavers, in which the Nyanja headmen played very little part. Disaster followed upon disaster, and eventually the Missionaries decided that it would be politic to withdraw from the highlands and allow the situation there to stabilize before they returned. In Britain, however, public opinion had been roused by their militant treatment of the slavers, and the Mission, after losing three of its members, including Bishop Mackenzie, through illness, was moved to Zanzibar in 1862.

After 1862 there were a few expeditions to Nyasaland, but none of great political importance. In 1876, a second and this time successful settlement was made in the Shire Highlands. The Church of Scotland founded a Mission in Blantyre, which comprised a lay section of artisans and a clerical section of preachers. It was particularly careful that any political action should be taken by the lay, and not by the clerical, members, because it was anxious to avoid the censure which its earlier colleagues had suffered. This Mission also felt it could not stand by and see cold murder done in front of its eyes. Yet fugitives came to it as they had to the U.M.C.A., so that the Mission, despite its unwillingness, was inexorably drawn into political relationships with the Yao in the area. The lay members severely punished certain wrongdoers. Eventually an African was murdered at the Mission. They tried the murderer, found him guilty, and allowed a local headman to execute him. The Home Authorities looked upon this action as a trespass from the Mission's proper function. The Mission suffered severe public censure, and several of the lay members were dismissed. It was clear that a Mission in the Territory could not be a mission alone ; it could not escape the political implications of the situation, and for the success of its venture some civil authority had to be established.

THE ESTABLISHMENT OF BRITISH RULE

In the meantime Livingstone's publications were bringing the horrors of the slave-trade home to the people of Britain, and more and more pressure was exerted to bring it to an end. As a result, in 1878, Captain Elton, the Consul at Mozambique, obtained permission to conduct an expedition to Lake Nyasa to enquire into the slave-trade. The British population in the Shire Highlands was now increasing so much that in 1883 a British Consul was appointed. From then on, until the close of the century, Britain followed a militant policy against all slave-traders, amongst whom were the Yao. No active steps were taken to institute a formal government over the territory, until in 1889 the Portuguese appeared at the confluence of the Ruo and Shire Rivers with a large military expedition which they maintained was scientific. Accordingly, on November 21st, 1889, the Acting-Consul declared the territory north of the Ruo to be a British Protectorate. The next year, Mr. A. Sharpe made treaties with most of the Native chiefs in the area. These treaties were later ratified by the Anglo-Portuguese convention of June 1891. It is clear that the British Government was protecting the treaty chiefs against the slave-raiders, and ensuring that no other European power assumed responsibility for this service.

The pacification of Nyasaland after this was largely the suppression of the slave-trade. The Commissioner of the Protectorate (H. H. Johnston) wrote in 1891 :

I felt bound to make our Protectorate of Nyasaland a reality to the unfortunate mass of people who are robbed, raided and carried into captivity to satisfy the greed and lust of the Yao race, these again being incessantly incited to engage in internecine war and slave-raiding forays by the Arab and Swahili slave-traders who travel between Nyasaland and the German and Portuguese littoral. The big men in this part of the Protectorate with whom it behoved me to deal and whom I must either persuade or coerce into acceptance of an anti-slave policy and sufficient subservience to the new administration as would put an end to further civil wars and inhumane practices, were the following :

Makanjila and Kazembe, ruling on opposite coasts of the south end of Lake Nyasa.

The Makandanje clan of chiefs (Tshindamba, Zarafi, Nkata) which dominates the country between the east bank of the upper Shire, Lake Pamalombe and the Portuguese boundary.

Mponda, the powerful chief holding the Shire where it leaves Lake Nyasa, and possessing a large tract of country along its western bank.

The Angoni chief Tshifusi, who dwells behind Mponda.

Tshingwalu-ngwalu and Msamara, Yao chiefs along the western bank of the upper Shire, half-brothers and bitter haters of Mponda.

Liwonde, chief ruling an exceedingly rich tract of land along the east bank of the upper Shire.

Tshikusi, the great Angoni chieftain dominating all the hill country between the west bank of the Shire and the Portuguese frontier.

Kawinga, one of the most powerful of the Yao chiefs who dwells near the north-west corner of Lake Shirwa and who commands a great slave-route to the coast, and lastly

Tshikumba, who after being for ten years a roving bandit living on the plunder of the missionary caravans between Blantyre and the upper Shire, has at last settled down on Mount Mlanje to a steady career of slave-trading.[1]

Except for the two Angoni, all the chiefs mentioned are Yao, and three of them, Jalasi, Kawinga and Liwonde, were forbears of the chiefs in whose areas I made my study. The history of the Administration's activities of the next five years is almost

---

[1] *Papers relative to the Suppression of Slave Raiding in Nyasaland.* C. 6699 (1892). Commissioner Johnston to the Marquis of Salisbury, Nov. 24th, 1891.

entirely a story of the subjugation of this list of chiefs. Acting-Commissioner Sharp wrote in his annual report in 1897 : ' The Yaos . . . were the chief slave-raiders for the Arabs, and in consequence nearly all our expeditions for 1891 to 1895 were undertaken against various sections of this tribe.' [1] The British South Africa Co. had made available a sum of £10,000 a year for providing a police force. As early as 1891, a raid was made on Cikumbu, a Yao slave-trader who had attacked a European coffee plantation in the Mlanje area. After this, there was a continual series of punitive expeditions against various native groups, usually after some slaving incident which precipitated British action. Captain Maguire was killed in 1891 by Makanjila's men, and shortly afterwards the British forces suffered a reverse at the hands of Jalasi. Unsuccessful attacks had been made on Kawinga's stronghold at Chikala. In 1893, two contingents, each of 100 Sikhs, arrived, and with this force more active measures were taken to control the slave-route to Quilamane through Mlanje district. In 1894, the Yao chief Makanjila was attacked and thoroughly defeated. In 1895, there was a concerted effort by the chiefs Kawinga, Jalasi and Matipwiri to oust the British from the Highlands. This commenced with an attack by Kawinga on the friendly chief Malemia, in Zomba area. A force was sent to protect the Missionaries at Domasi, and it stopped the main onslaught. After that, the stronghold of Chikala was scaled and Kawinga completely dislodged. He retreated to the east, and Matipwiri and his relative Mtirimanje were captured. The power of these chiefs was completely broken and no more expeditions were necessary. In 1896, Katuli, a neighbour of Jalasi's, was captured and in the same year Liwonde, who had so far eluded capture, was apprehended and sent as a political prisoner to Chiromo in the extreme south of the Protectorate.

In the meantime the Portuguese were making similar punitive expeditions into the region due east of the Protectorate, and many refugees came into the Territory from Portuguese East Africa. Notable amongst these were the Mpotola groups under Chikweo and Ngokwe, who are to-day settled near Lake Chiuta.

In those parts of the Territory where military action was no longer necessary the framework of the Administrative system was

[1] *Annual Report, 1896.* C. 8438, p. 12.

soon erected. As early as 1893 the Protectorate was divided into Administrative divisions and Collectors were appointed in each. Coinage was issued ; a hut tax of 3s. was introduced ; European claims to land and mineral rights were settled with the chiefs—all large estates were issued with certificates of claim ; and a postal system was initiated. The old order of independent chiefdoms had gone for good and the Africans had to adjust their way of living to a new order.

THE VILLAGE AS A UNIT IN PRE-WHITE TIMES

Though there are earlier records of villages among related tribes, the earliest we have of the Yao are those of Livingstone.[1] In the records of his journeys up the Shire and the Rovuma Rivers, he states that the people lived in villages. Rowley's reports [2] of the Shire Highlands in 1861 show that the Nyanja were organized in villages similar to those of to-day, but the best reports on the Yao village are by Duff MacDonald, who worked as a missionary in the Shire Highlands and the Zomba area from 1878 to 1881. Duff MacDonald published both a general ethnographic account of the Yao around Blantyre and a journal of day-to-day events on the mission. From these descriptions we are able to reconstruct much of the political organization of Yao groups before the Whites came to Nyasaland. Though the information from these early accounts about the internal structure of villages is scant, the reports of the importance of domestic slavery are good, and this is valuable in assessing its effect on the internal structure of modern Yao villages.

From MacDonald's description it appears that each Yao chiefdom was a congeries of almost autonomous villages. The headman of these villages recognized the superiority of one of their number whom we may call ' chief '. The unity of each village and its corporateness were expressed in many ways. One of these was in connection with the worship of ancestor spirits. MacDonald writes :

[The village headman] is the recognized high priest who presents prayers and offerings on behalf of all that live in his village. . . . It

---

[1] Livingstone, D. and C., *Narrative of an Expedition to the Zambesi and its Tributaries, and of the Discovery of Lakes Shirwa and Nyassa. 1858–64*, John Murray (London, 1865). Waller, *Last Journals*.

[2] Rowley, *The Story of the Universities Mission*.

is his relatives that are the village gods. Everyone that lives in the village recognizes these gods but if anyone removes to another village he changes his gods. He now recognizes the gods of his new chief. One wishing to pray to the god (or gods) of any village naturally desires to have his prayers presented through the village chief, because the latter is nearly related to the village god, and may be expected to be better listened to than a stranger.[1]

In this quotation the word 'chief' is used for village headman. In Yao the same term is used for both the chief of the country and the chief of the village (*mwenye*).

It is clear from MacDonald's description that foreign villages were looked upon as undifferentiated wholes. When discussing punishment in general he writes :

We find that almost every offence may be punished by death, but when an offender is not redeemed, the particular punishment is left to the headman of the injured party. For instance, if a headman of Kumpama's go and say, 'Chenyono has killed a subject of mine ; I have caught a subject of his and want to kill him,' the chief's answer will be, 'He has done you wrong, do according to your heart (*poli mtima wenu*).' The punishment is thus inflicted not by the criminal's own chief, but by the injured party, and it may fall, not on the guilty person, but on one connected with him.[2]

For example, he describes how some children had been carried off from Che Lomoni's village one night in 1880.

Towards the end of 1880 [he recounts], Che Lomoni, a Blantyre headman, captured two men from Mpingwi, and put them in slave-sticks. They belonged to the village that had kidnapped the children a few months before, and native law did not require proof that the men were personally guilty. They were undoubtedly innocent. Still they were kept in close confinement till their friends returned the captives in February.[3]

The village headman—called the 'owner of the village' (*asyene musi*)—was the representative of the village in all public transactions, and also the representative of such higher authority as existed, to the village members. Duff MacDonald writes : 'A chief represents and is responsible for all his people. If anyone wish to treat with a native village it is with the village

---

[1] MacDonald, *Africana*, i, 65.
[2] MacDonald, *Africana*, i, 186.   [3] MacDonald, *Africana*, ii, 234.

chief that he must deal. If we give a present to a village it is to the village chief that we must give it'; and, 'It is when a man transgresses against his own village chief that *personal responsibility* is brought home to him. When he transgresses against another village, his own chief pays for him.' [1] The village headman accepted liability for offences committed by his villagers against members of other villages, but could punish his own villagers by fines and by putting them into slave-sticks. Within the village, according to MacDonald,

The headman cannot make his villagers hoe his farm for him, or do such private work. Neither does he exact tribute from them. . . . Still he expects them not only to stand by him in war, but to support his government on all occasions, and to render special assistance in the trial of judicial cases. . . . He may pronounce a capital sentence, or order as large a penalty as the fine of four slaves—especially if he be a higher headman. But his judgements may be complained of by any of his free subjects (only such appeals are rare, unless by parties that want to leave his village altogether). His decision may be revised by some other headman, as the ruler of the village from which his own settlement broke off; but the ultimate appeal is to the chief of the country. While the village headman settles all smaller disputes without troubling the chief, he usually reports graver cases. [2]

THE CHIEF AND THE VILLAGE HEADMEN : THE POLITICAL PROCESS

The village headmen in any particular area recognized the superiority of one of their number, the chief of the land (*asyene cilambo*). MacDonald classifies the headmen under one chief as follows :

1. Chief's blood relatives, usually called ' younger brother '.
2a. Settlers or refugees (*alambi*) who have come over with a large following from a hostile chief.
2b. Men who have gained the chief's favour by their services and been sent to occupy new spots in the kingdom.

'Other village headmen arise when a large village increases and sends forth smaller hamlets.' [3] All in the territory of a chief were integrated by a chain of authority. As he explains,

1. Headmen are under higher headmen and under the chief.

---

[1] MacDonald, *Africana*, i, 186. Original italics.
[2] MacDonald, *Africana*, i, 153.   [3] MacDonald, *Africana*, i, 156.

2. Free men are under their elder brother in the first instance, but they may carry their cases to the headman of their village or even to the chief of the country.
3. Slaves were entirely under their own master.[1]

The headmen's subservience to the chief is described in the following passage :

In all public transactions the headman represents his village. He receives the chief's orders and sees them carried out. When he kills an elephant he sends one of the tusks to the chief. Should he kill twenty elephants he is not expected to give up twenty tusks—two or three would be sufficient. If he shoots a large buck he gives one haunch of venison. For all such tributes he expects to receive in return a present (generally a little powder). . . . He is expected to attend the chief's parliament unless he is under an elder brother in which case he is not allowed to speak, except when especially commissioned. Headmen are expected to report all cases of war, but they often attack enemies without telling their chief beforehand, saying, ' Let him hear of the enterprise when it succeeds.' Yet this is dangerous unless they are sure of success, and well acquainted with the chief's private sentiments. On reporting an attack they present the chief with part of the booty. In times of war each headman when summoned, must follow his chief's flag, otherwise his village is burned down, and all that fail to escape are killed or enslaved.[2]

Yet within the framework of this organization villages were markedly autonomous. MacDonald's description, which I have just quoted, brings this out very well. Elsewhere he writes : 'The chief may often have less influence than powerful headmen, and we have known cases where he simply contented himself with grumbling when his headmen acted contrary to his desire.' [3] The chief did not differ greatly from his more powerful headmen. A certain amount of ritual in terms of ancestor worship embellished his position, and he had some ascendancy over village headmen to whom he had given land. Yet, in the last analysis, the chief had to rely on his personal following and military power to subjugate headmen who were becoming too powerful. The chief was therefore in direct competition with his subject village headmen, and involved in a constant struggle with them for followers. MacDonald describes how the chief himself was a

[1] MacDonald, *Africana*, i, 155.
[2] MacDonald, *Africana*, i, 157.   [3] MacDonald, *Africana*, i, 155.

village headman and had to administer his slaves and relatives in his village in the same way as a village headman.[1]   MacDonald shrewdly observes :

> Where the chief sees occasion to interfere with his subordinates he generally consults his own interest.   He will say to a headman, ' I see that you have been behaving badly to that subject of yours. You cannot get on with him : he must leave you and come and dwell in my own village.'   The chief thus secures another servant.[2]

Another writer observed, ' As a chief's power consists of the number of his subjects the loss of a man is a serious matter.' [3]

A village headman also tried to strengthen his position against the chief and against other village headmen by attracting to himself as many followers and dependants as he could.   The process whereby a man might increase his status is described as follows :

> However large the settlement may become, the man that is first in the field is the chief or headman.   In course of time he adorns his position by acquiring wealth.   He may shoot some buck and get possession of their skins.   With these he goes to the Mangoni country and buys slaves.   An old person he obtains for a single skin, but a young slave costs two, and women cost much more than men.   The female slaves thus bought are his junior wives and he keeps them busy in hoeing the farm, and all such female duties.   The male slaves he employs in farming, building, making baskets, sewing garments and such masculine pursuits.   He keeps all these persons strictly at their duties, and at the same time welcomes an opportunity of selling them at a profit.   If his daughters were unmarried, he would give them slave-husbands.   The natives aim at ' replenishing the earth and subduing it '.   As it is no expense for them to rear families, they are all desirous to have many children.
>
> Besides this increase of the village from the chief's own resources, there may be an accession of freemen.   After the settlement is begun, a man may come to its founder and say, ' I wish to live with you.' The village chief gives him permission and calls him ' younger brother '.   The newcomer brings his family, builds a house, and cultivates a farm in the same way as his chief.   A freeman may leave his present chief and take up his abode with another, whose subject he becomes.   His former chief has no longer any authority over him

---

[1] MacDonald, *Africana*, i, 154.   [2] MacDonald, *Africana*, i, 155–6.
[3] Hynde, R. S., ' Among the Machinga People ', *The Scottish Geographical Magazine*, viii (1891), 656–63.

whatsoever. But a man often decamps by night taking with him many slaves belonging to his fellow-citizens ; he then goes to some influential chief who may be only too glad to give the fugitive ground and to establish him as a sub-chief. Freemen who thus leave are detested by their former chief, who welcomes every opportunity of shooting or capturing them.[1]

In this way village headmen, by increasing their following, increased their power against the chief. MacDonald records :

When a person has acquired several villages, he becomes a higher headman, intermediate between the chief and the owner of a single village. Each headman lives in the village he likes best, and leaves his 'brothers' to manage his other villages. But a headman of great ambition often places his 'brothers' all around him, decides their cases, and practically governs a small kingdom of his own. If he lives far from his chief, one might suppose that he was quite independent. When a quarrel arises between the chief of the country and an important headman, the latter may rebel, and found a new kingdom, thus depriving the old chief perhaps of one-third of the villages in his dominion.[2]

MacDonald cites the case of Mkanda of Chiradzulu, who was at first a headman of KuMpama's but rebelled, and went to live on the southern side of the mountain.[3] He also observes that on the other hand, ' a headman may keep up his chief's authority in a district that the latter could not otherwise hold '.[4] Elsewhere he says :

In and around his own village the chief of the country is a terrible power, and his government is supported by the most prompt and severe punishments. But in distant parts of his dominions, where influential headmen live, he may be little known, although as a matter of theory he is supposed to settle all graver disputes even in remote villages.[5]

The history of the Yao chieftaincies in MacDonald's time, and as told to me by my informants, is that of constant division into independent chiefdoms. In the Zulu and Bemba polities a strong state structure included a pattern of civil war and the main-

[1] MacDonald, *Africana*, i, 147–8.   [2] MacDonald, *Africana*, i, 156–7.
[3] MacDonald, *Africana*, i, 32.
[4] MacDonald, *Africana*, i, 157.   [5] MacDonald, *Africana*, i, 154–5.

tenance of the whole state under a new king,[1] but the Yao political units seem to have split into two factions when divisions appeared within them. The dissident faction left the parent chiefdom and established itself somewhere else as an independent entity.

The picture my informants have given me substantiates Mac-Donald's account, though his contact was mainly with Mangoche and not with Machinga Yao. My informants, however, placed greater emphasis than he did upon the importance of trade with the coast. A slave-trading trip was not a venture which the ordinary village headman could undertake with equanimity. The journey to the coast, to Quilimane or to Kilwa, was long and arduous, and strong military protection against bandits was needed. A caravan could only be sent by a chief or someone of like status, so that the coastal trade became the monopoly of the chiefs. Headmen who had ivory and slaves to send to the coast included them in the chief's caravan. When it returned, the headmen were able to collect calico and beads to the value of their contribution. Gun-powder also seems to have been a chief's monopoly. Thus, in fact, he did have some physical control over the military activities of his subject village headmen, since he could withhold supplies of gun-powder if he wished. But in a society where minor chieftains were inimically poised against each other, the maxim ' a chief without people is nothing ' had much more significance than it has to-day : a village headman's ultimate sanction was that he could withdraw his support from one chief and give it to another.

THE EFFECTS OF WHITE CONQUEST

It was into a society thus organized that the first Missionaries came. I have already described how the Missionaries, by taking in runaway slaves, and by occasional armed combat, entered into political relationships with the chiefs. With the establishment of the Protectorate, the policy, clearly expressed in Sir Harry Johnston's letter,[2] was to stamp out slavery. This was done in numerous campaigns against the Yao chiefs [3] so that by

---

[1] See Gluckman, M., ' Succession and Civil War among the Bemba : An Exercise in Anthropological Theory ', *Human Problems*, xvi (1954), 6–25.
[2] See f.n., p. 29.   [3] See Chap. II, pp. 29–30.

1896 the superior British militia had completely subjugated all the Yao chiefs who had resisted them.

British power initially became merely an element in the political relationships of chiefs : they used it against their rivals, as Kalembo used it against Cingwalungwalu,[1] or Malemia against Kawinga. Yao chiefs did not unite in the face of their common enemy.[2] As the campaign against the slave-traders progressed, however, Yao chief after chief fell to superior British arms. They, who only a few years earlier were accepting the submission of refugees, themselves had now to ' grasp the leg of the White people '.

It is clear that they looked upon their submission to the Whites in much the same way as they looked upon the submission of refugees to themselves. To submit to a man was to accept slave or near-slave status. According to informants, Kawinga sent a large tusk of ivory [3] to the British as a placatory gift. His ceremonial knife, and the knives of his important headmen, were taken from them by Robert Codrington, Assistant Collector of the northern part of Zomba.[4] A chief with whom I was once discussing slavery expressed neatly the attitude of the Yao chiefs to their subjugation. He said : ' There is no slavery to-day— we are the slaves of the Government '. The chiefs who returned to the Protectorate, therefore, returned as subjects, and were fully aware of this. In the new regime, the former chiefs had to recognize a superior authority and the British Administration provided the framework within which the old rivalries had to be rephrased.

The chief's position in relation to his subjects as a result of this catastrophic change was, of necessity, weakened. When the slave caravans stopped, the chief's source of wealth disappeared, and with it much of his power. He was no longer much wealthier than his subjects. The wants of the people could now be more easily satisfied by the numerous trading stores which

[1] Mitchell, J. C., 'The Political Organization of the Yao of Southern Nyasaland', *African Studies*, viii, 3 (Sept. 1949), 141–59.

[2] Johnston maintains that Matipwiri, Jalasi and Kawinga had planned a joint attack against the British in 1895. If this is so, the attempt was completely unsuccessful. See Johnston, H. H., *British Central Africa*, Methuen & Co. (London, 1897), 130. See p. 30.

[3] *The British Central African Gazette*, ii, 18 (Nov. 15th, 1895), reports that Kawinga sent in some ivory as ' indemnity ' but was told to pay more and to send in 60 more guns.

[4] They are to-day in the Southern Rhodesia National Museum, Bulawayo.

began to appear in the Territory. The chief in this situation had the same wants as his subjects but was in no way able to satisfy them. He was precluded by his position from becoming a labourer and thus securing a cash income, while his subjects, until recently dependent on his monopoly for their wealth, had been drawn into the new economy of the Protectorate and were comparatively affluent.

The cessation of warfare and slavery thus affected the prestige of the chiefs seriously. The Administration's policy was at first to impose a fine of guns on those who broke rules. In July 1894, for example, Chapola village on the south-west corner of Lake Malombe was fined 30 guns for being in possession of slaves.[1] Later the Administration introduced an ordinance requiring the registration and licensing of guns, and many guns were confiscated on account of breaches of this regulation. Not only were the Yao disarmed, but the Administration also punished those who broke the peace. At the same time the Government was pursuing an active policy against domestic slavery. For example, in the village of Chapola mentioned above, 26 slaves were released. The slaves, formerly bound to their masters by the physical sanction of being liable to death at his hands in cases of desertion, were now liberated. It is not surprising to find the Collector at Mlanje reporting, in 1895, that the power of Kuntirimanja and Matipwiri was failing, and that they were losing people.[2]

Statements of informants confirm that slaves were then starting to leave their erstwhile masters to set up villages of their own. In 1904, the Administration reported: ' The tendency is for the old large communities to be broken up ; for the small man to collect a surrounding of friends and go off and build new hamlets in other localities '.[3]

From my own investigations, there appear to have been two possible reasons for this. First, communities may formerly have lived in consolidated groups in order to protect themselves from slave-raiders and other assailants. With the disappearance of the slaver and of war, the bond of the need for security would,

[1] *B.C.A. Gazette*, i, 10 (July 28th, 1894).
[2] *B.C.A. Gazette*, ii, 8 (June 15th, 1895).
[3] *The Annual Report of the Territory, 1903–4*, quoted by S. S. Murray (ed.), *Handbook of Nyasaland*, Crown Agents for the Colonies (London, 1932), 188.

therefore, be weakened, and the component parts of the village scattered. This is what the Administration argued when it wrote about the split-up of communities : ' This tendency is to some extent gratifying, in that it originates in the native's sense of his complete security under the existing Government.'[1] I have not much evidence that this is true, and in fact do not think it is.   Second, there is little doubt from my village histories that the slave-groups attached to various village headmen were deserting their former masters and setting up independent villages.

It is significant that the report speaks of the ' old large communities '.   Duff MacDonald, writing of the Blantyre area in the period 1877–81, says : ' Usually the natives live in small villages containing 10 or 11 huts, occasionally in large villages containing three times as many.   They do not like to pack themselves closely.   In time of peace few villages contain more than 100 people.'[2]   Hynde, writing of the Domasi area, says : ' Sometimes a village consists only of five or six huts ; more commonly twelve or twenty and rarely above thirty.   The chief's village at Domasi consists of more than 100 houses but that is an exceptional case.   The villages occur at intervals of quarter to one mile.'[3]   In July 1895, the Collector at South Nyasa made a census of all the villages on the west bank of the Shire (64 villages).   These were mainly Yao, but also included some Nyanja.   The modal size of villages, calculated from his published figures, is 26 huts.[4]   The reports of MacDonald and Hynde agree well, although they describe different areas.   The Collector's average was slightly larger, but one is not sure that he has not included two or three settlements under one headman. A village, Changali, was marked as having 217 huts, but a note indicated that they were scattered.   Also the numerical accuracy is not above question because a large proportion of hut totals end in 0 or 5, indicating estimation rather than enumeration.   From my own observation, the arithmetic mean of a sample of 37 villages in two separate areas was 11 huts (mode was 8 huts).

It seems, therefore, that the optimum size for Yao villages has always been about 10 to 15 huts, and that the disintegration

[1] *Annual Report of the Territory, 1911–12*, Murray, *Handbook*, 128.
[2] MacDonald, *Africana*, i, 145.
[3] Hynde, R. S., ' Among the Machinga People '.
[4] *B.C.A. Gazette*, ii, 3 (Sept. 1895).

noted by the Administration in 1904 was in fact the break-up of larger communities under important village headmen. These communities were, as is evident from MacDonald's writings, largely made up of slaves and their descendants. In the light of the internal structure of modern villages, I believe that the fragmentation going on at that time was due to the breaking of the bond between captor and slave—a bond formerly rein-forced by physical sanctions that included the killing of a slave by his captor. Therefore, while the groups thus linked to the headman may have moved out of his village, his matrilineal kinsmen, who were bound to him by bonds of deep sentiment and religious beliefs, remained. The irreducible 10 to 15 huts were therefore likely to have been those of the headman's own matrilineal kinsmen. When the Administration ascribed the continuing tendency all over the Protectorate to the splitting up of villages into small family groups [1] it was probably describing the splitting off of descendants of slave-wives to found villages of their own. While this process of readjustment was going on, the Administration stepped in with legislation designed to control what it considered to be unchecked social disorganization. The Administration spoke of the necessity to

build up an organization to control the rising generation of natives who, finding themselves without the restraining influences to which their parents were accustomed, have of recent years evinced an inclina-tion to emancipate themselves from the disciplinary responsibilities of village life and obedience to authority, and to adopt habits prejudicial to native family life.[2]

To accomplish this task the Government introduced the District Administration (Natives) Ordinance of 1912. This was the Ordinance about which the Administration wrote in 1913 :

Framed, as it has been, in accord with native ideas and practice, it is a measure which none the less avoids the defects of the archaic system of tribal rule and which has as its aims the gradual formation of a subsidiary local government by means of Sectional Councils of Headmen chosen as far as possible by natives themselves and presided over by the District Resident.[3]

---

[1] *Annual Report, 1911–12*, Murray, *Handbook*, 128.
[2] *Annual Report on the Protectorate for 1912–13*, Murray, *Handbook*, 129.
[3] Murray, *Handbook*, 129.

Under this Ordinance, the Administration provided first of all for the formation of ' villages '. A Rule made under Section 3 of the Ordinance and published in Gazette Notice No. 113 of 1913, gave the Resident the power to concentrate the native population, where necessary, into organized villages of not less than 20 huts and to disallow the erection of isolated huts. ' In order to give effect to this policy the erection of new huts was to be confined to existing villages, and the occupants of isolated huts were to be instructed to remove, as opportunity offered, to an approved village.' [1]

The Ordinance then proceeded to create a line of authority from the District Resident to the villagers through Village Headmen and Principal Headmen. Districts in the charge of Residents were divided into Administrative Sections. A Principal Headman was put in charge of each. The Sections in turn were sub-divided into Village areas (groups of villages), each in the charge of a Village Headman.

Under the Ordinance, Principal Headmen and Village Headmen were given specific duties and responsibilities in their respective areas. The Principal Headman, for example, was:

to be responsible for the good order of his Administrative Section, the maintenance of discipline, the reporting of crime and the apprehension of criminals, sanitation, the control of the movement of cattle, reporting outbreaks of epidemic disease, and for any other matters in the interest of law and order and the general welfare of the native community. [2]

The Principal Headman was also to ' secure the attendance at the Magistrate's court of natives whose presence was required in connection with deceased estates, remittances, government labour and so on, and to exert his influence to accelerate the payment of hut and poll taxes '. These duties in turn devolved upon Village Headmen—they were responsible for their smaller areas as the Principal Headmen were responsible for the larger.

Unfortunately we have no information about the way in which Principal and Village Headmen were chosen. Murray records that

Residents were not necessarily to recommend those natives who had hitherto been recognized as Chiefs or Headmen. It was considered

---

[1] Murray, *Handbook*, 132.　　　　　　[2] Murray, *Handbook*, 130.

that in some cases the previous records or age of such persons would be found to be such as to preclude their selection to transact the responsible duties of Headmen under the Ordinance, and in such circumstances Residents were to consider the claims of other natives of good standing, intelligence and reputation residing in the section, who, having assisted the Resident in native administrative matters in the past, might be expected to carry out the duties efficiently, and who, at the same time, were known to enjoy the confidence of the natives with whose supervision they were entrusted.[1]

Elsewhere Murray writes, ' The system introduced by the Ordinance was in no way intended to revivify or perpetuate government by native chiefs. The position of Principal Headmen under the Ordinance was in no sense to be similar to the archaic one of the chief.' [2]   Yet in the area in which I worked it was precisely the traditional chiefs who were made Principal Headmen—Jalasi, Nyambi, Kawinga, Liwonde and Malemia. In retrospect it is difficult to see how it could have been otherwise. Considering the sentiment attached to the chief in Yao society, it seems scarcely possible to conceive of leaders who ' enjoyed the confidence of the natives with whose supervision they were entrusted ' who were not chiefs in the traditional sense.

In spite of its avowed intentions not to ' revivify or perpetuate government by native chiefs ', the Administration proceeded to invest the traditional chiefs with its own power. ' Residents ', Murray writes, ' were to indicate carefully by their attitude towards and dealings with Principal Headmen the fact that they were officially recognized as chiefs of their respective sections and that, as such, they were entitled to the respect and obedience of their people.' [3]

It would be wrong to imagine that the military actions at the end of the last century had completely destroyed chieftainship. Those who had resisted the Whites were driven out of British Territory but were allowed to return very soon afterwards. These chiefs then took up the threads of their life as best they could under the changed conditions. The degree to which the new Administration had become a force in Yao politics is illustrated by an entry in the District Book in Zomba. Kawinga III had died in August 1905, and the record reads : ' There were two

[1] Murray, *Handbook*, 131.
[2] Murray, *Handbook*, 130.   [3] Murray, *Handbook*, 130.

claimants to the succession, Kumlomba and Chiwalo. Their claims were really very equal and His Majesty's Commissioner (April 1906) called in Kumlomba and the most important headmen and decided the succession by their vote.' District Books have many entries dating before 1912 showing that the Administration did not consider chiefs and village headmen insignificant.

The appointment of village headmen needed the approval of the Provincial Commissioner, but presumably the recommendation came from the District Resident. It is reasonable to suppose that the District Resident in turn had discussed appointments with the principal headmen. Whatever the mechanics of the appointment, however, the outcome was that most village headmen who held positions of prestige in the indigenous system of ranking became village headmen under the Ordinance.

The District Administration (Natives) Ordinance thus made official the unofficial relationship which had previously existed between the Administration and the chiefs and the village headmen. The traditional relationship of chief to village headman and village headman to villager, however, became suffused with a new significance. These relationships had become part and parcel of the extensive administrative organization of the British Empire.

THE MODERN ADMINISTRATIVE STRUCTURE [1]

The Native Authority Ordinance of 1933 and the Native Court's Ordinance provide the legislative framework for the modern administrative system. Under Section 23(a) of the Native Authority Ordinance, the rules, orders, proclamations, notices and appointments made under the District Administration (Natives) Ordinance were not repealed. The duties which had so long been incumbent upon chiefs and village headmen, therefore, continued unaffected.

The chief, however, was set up at the centre of a bureaucracy and given autonomy in a number of directions. The Native Court's Ordinance gave him legal powers to inflict punishment on his subjects; the treasury under his authority could raise

---

[1] I have dealt in some detail with the position of the chief in the modern situation in my article ' Political Organization of the Yao of Southern Nyasaland '.

funds and could spend them. The chief could make rules and regulations in specific matters.

Burnt-brick court houses, burnt-brick offices and clinics have appeared at the traditional headquarters of the chiefs. A court clerk collects court fees and fines, issues receipts and records the cases in a register. A tax clerk issues licences and collects taxes, receives correspondence addressed to the chief and writes the chief's replies. In addition, there are other functionaries—community workers, forest guards, agricultural demonstrators, sanitary inspectors, market clerks, well inspectors and so on.

In other words, the position of the chief is becoming more and more that of an administrative head-of-department.[1] His position *vis-à-vis* his subjects is coloured by this. The chief is at once the people's representative to the Administration and the Administration's representative to them.

[1] Compare Barnes's statement about the Ngoni: ' the great warrior chief has become in effect the only member of the Administration who never goes home to Britain on leave '. Barnes, J. A., *Politics in a Changing Society*, 172.

E

CHAPTER III

THE COMPOSITION OF MODERN CHIEFDOMS

Chiefdoms in the Administrative Mould

NO less than in MacDonald's time, modern chiefdoms are in the first place organizations of villages. Physically, the villages consist of solid pole and daub huts of varying sizes. Some huts are rectangular, twenty feet long and fifteen feet wide, with glass windows, panelled doors, and thatched roofs. Others are small and round, about eight feet in diameter. There is also a considerable variation in the compactness of villages : often the huts are only a few yards apart, but sometimes at least a hundred yards or more. Most villages, however, could be circumscribed by a circle of a quarter-mile diameter, though, of course, there are many exceptions. There is a slight tendency for the village to spread itself along a path, in a way faintly suggesting ribbon development, but on the whole there is no particular physical pattern to the Yao village. In fact, though most villages have fairly distinct physical boundaries, and are definitely discrete clusters of huts, some are difficult to identify in this way. To the minds of the local people, however, the village is quite clear and distinct. This is because they see the village primarily as a social unit, and tend to impute into physical boundaries more definition than actually exists. It is in the social sense that I use the word here : the ' village ' is a spatial group which recognizes its identity against similar groups.

The importance of the village in Yao structure can hardly be over-emphasized. Membership of a village provides the first index whereby people determine a stranger's background. If, after village membership is fixed, no other links can be found with a stranger, such as distant kinship, the relationship will remain at that level. A gossip identifies the person about whom he is speaking by giving his or her name and the name of his or her village. He says, ' Bt.[1] Mwana of Cigwaja village '.

---

[1] I use this abbreviation for the Arabic ' binti ', ' daughter of '. Binti, pronounced ' biti ' by the Yao, with Ali and Wadi, ' son of ', appear commonly in Yao names.

(*a*)   Villages on the floor of the Rift Valley near Fort Johnston.
(*December 1949*)

(*b*)   A village in the Domasi Valley near Zomba.
(*September 1949*)

PLATE III

The chief identifies a man who comes to see him in exactly the same way, and the Administration has adopted a similar system, except that it has its own definition of the village. During the initiation ceremonies, the initiands [1] are housed in long grass sheds which are subdivided into sections. Each section or room of the long shed houses the boys or girls from one village. If villages share a burial ground, they have allotted portions where they bury their dead separately. In these and many other ways the village is looked upon by the Yao as a distinct unit in the chiefdom.

The chiefdom in the old days was distinctly a territorial unit and all the villages within that area recognized the superiority of the chief. The boundaries of the old chiefdoms were marked by rivers and hills and fixed after conquest and agreement. They are still well remembered. Modern chiefdoms are defined in their limits partly by Government decree and partly by custom. When Principal Headmen were appointed, the districts under them were demarcated with ' due regard being given to the composition of the Native population '. The traditional areas under the various chiefs, therefore, were recognized by the Administration as districts, so that the districts or their sections almost coincided with the chiefdoms. Some disputes between chiefs over boundaries have occurred from time to time and the Administration has had to arbitrate. For example, the Provincial Commissioner of the Southern Province reported a difference between Liwonde and Kawinga in 1936,[2] but through time these differences have been eliminated.

Traditional and Administrative boundaries do not coincide in a few places, for two reasons. Firstly, the Administration has accepted an obvious and physical boundary in preference to an indistinct and social boundary. It has taken the Domasi River as the boundary between Ntumanje and Mposa, though in fact a few villages under Mbela, Kawinga III's son, live on the south side of the river, and fall for Administrative purposes in Ntumanje's area. Mbela is still very strongly associated with Kawinga in ritual and kinship matters. His dealings with the

---

[1] I am grateful to Prof. Schapera for suggesting this word for those who are undergoing initiation ceremonies. The parallel is with graduands, i.e. those who are undergoing graduation ceremonies.

[2] *Report of the Provincial Commissioner, Southern Province* (1936), 20.

Administration, however, must be through the chief Ntumanje.

Secondly, some discrepancy has arisen because the Administration has not recognized all the indigenous chiefs. This has occurred mainly in Jalasi's area where there are at least two headmen who as far as I can judge were chiefs in their own right before the British conquest. These are Mkumba and Namwera.

Mkumba was the father of Nkata, the original Invader of this area whose chieftaincy later took the name of Jalasi. Mkumba moved into the southern part of Nkata's chiefdom where he settled. Nkata occupied the north. As far as I can gather, Mkumba held rights to the ivory in his area and made sacrifices for rain—the main attributes of chieftainship. He still holds both types of initiation ceremonies and tries cases not involving large compensation. Nowadays, the office still commands some respect, though the present incumbent himself is not highly respected. The village under him has broken up since his accession.

Namwera came into the area before the White invasion with a small following from Mataka's area in Portuguese East Africa. He obtained chieftaincy rights over a large tract of land. Though I have not been able to check this in Government records, informants tell me that he was originally a Principal Headman, but that he was deposed largely because of the intrigues of Jalasi III with a Government clerk. Nowadays, Namwera claims to be independent of Jalasi and is markedly hostile towards him. The village headmen who came into the area still recognize Namwera's authority and take their cases surreptitiously to him, if they do not involve compensation. But as far as the Government is concerned he is merely one of Jalasi's headmen, and if it comes to a trial of strength, Namwera will have to recognize the authority of Jalasi.

In general, however, the Administrative system, in incorporating the main indigenous chieftains, incorporated the indigenous organization in its framework. Kawinga as a Native Authority is the superior of Chiwalo, his ' sister's son ' ; of Chamba, his ' son ' ; of Mposa, his ' brother's son ' ; and of Ngokwe and Chikweo who came to seek his protection. Kawinga holds his position both by virtue of his indigenous rank as a descendant of the original Invader Kawinga, and also as a Government representative. Liwonde, also a Native Authority, resists Kawinga's claims to primacy, and by the ideology of the kinship system is equivalent in status. In Jalasi's area, once again, the indigenous status of the chieftaincy is shown by the Administrative recognition of Jalasi against Mkumba, who was a minor chief, and Namwera, who had come to 'ask land from Jalasi', and who had to give some slaves and some ivory for his chieftaincy rights in the area.

The relationships of Native Authorities to each other to-day are thus fixed partly by the Administrative structure, and partly by their historical backgrounds, and I have indicated that the structure the Administration imposed in the Yao areas was very largely determined by the indigenous structure which existed at that time.[1] The Administrative system to-day, therefore, supports the traditional structure.

The five chiefdoms with which this study is concerned stretch from Zomba in the south, almost to Fort Johnston to the north-east of the Shire River. These chiefdoms are Malemia in the north of Zomba district, whose area lies along the Malosa range of mountains north of Zomba as far as Mount Chaoni. Liwonde district stretches from Mount Chikala and Mount Chaoni in the south to Mount Msili in the north. This district contains the chiefdoms of Liwonde and Kawinga and the minor chieftains under them. In Fort Johnston district which stretches from the north of Mount Msili to Lake Nyasa are the chiefdoms of Jalasi, Nyambi, Katuli, Makanjila and an Nyanja chief Nankhumba. The chiefdoms of Jalasi and Nyambi abut those of Kawinga and Liwonde, and it is with these that we are mainly concerned.

Malemia, whose clan-name is *amwale*, was apparently the first of the Machinga chiefs to move into present-day Nyasaland from present-day Mozambique.[2] His group moved south-west past the north end of Lake Chiuta and settled for a while on Mount Msili. Malemia was closely followed by Nkata, from whom the Jalasi chieftaincy developed and whose clan-name was *ambewe*, and his 'father' Mkumba, who moved in westwards past the north end of Lake Chiuta into the Mangoche Highlands. Here, together with the help of Kawinga and Liwonde, they attacked the so-called Mangoche chiefs (Mlumbe, Chikowi, Kapeni,

[1] Chap. II.
[2] The history of this chieftaincy is set out more completely in 'An Outline of the Social Structure of Malemia Area'.

Matipwiri, etc.), displaced them southwards and so established chiefdoms of their own. Mkumba moved to the south and Nkata set up a fortress on Mount Mangoche, from which vantage-point he resisted British conquest for many years. Kawinga and Liwonde, whose clan-name was also *ambewe*, had moved in with Nkata but continued across the Shire River to settle in the Kongwe Hills to the west of Lake Malombe. Later, Kawinga and Liwonde re-crossed the Shire and moved south-eastwards until they reached Mount Chikala. This in the meantime had been occupied by Malemia. Kawinga and Liwonde succeeded in dislodging Malemia who retired to the Malosa Range, where he is situated to-day. Liwonde then left the mountain to settle on the east shore of the Shire River.

The arrangement of these particular chiefdoms in Administrative districts therefore reflects the social relationships among the chiefs. Between Malemia and the two *ambewe* chiefs, Kawinga and Liwonde, there is an uninhabited forest reserve and a mountain range. Liwonde and Kawinga who can trace their descent matrilineally from a common ancestress and who are to-day perpetual [1] brothers, together with their minor chiefs, share the Liwonde district. In spite of the opposition of these two chiefs which arises from their position as chiefs of independent chiefdoms, they sometimes meet and visit each other. Chiwalo, who from the Administrative point of view is under Kawinga, is in fact more closely related to Liwonde and has much more to do with him. But Chiwalo's headmen usually appeal to Kawinga, not Liwonde, in their difficulties. Within Kawinga's area at a funeral or an installation ceremony of an important headman in the northern areas, representatives of the nearby chieftaincies Ngokwe, Chikweo, Chiwalo and Kawinga will be present. In the south, the representatives of only Chamba, Mposa and Kawinga are likely to be present. Headmen, if they come from Liwonde's area, do so because of kinship connection and not because they are representatives of Liwonde.

The relationships of Jalasi and to some extent Nyambi, with Kawinga and Liwonde, are much more distant. Kawinga and Liwonde stand opposed to Jalasi in spite of the fact that Jalasi shares their clan-name. I have never known of Jalasi coming to visit Kawinga or Liwonde. Jalasi's area extends well down

[1] i.e. the offices are fixed perpetually in this relationship. See p. 122.

the Shire River to within about 15 miles from Liwonde's head-quarters, and though he frequently tours his chiefdom in this area I have never known him to cross his boundary. The position of Nyambi here is interesting in that originally Nyambi's chiefdom was part of the Liwonde district. It was made part of this district in the early days of the Administration when Nyambi II, Nkata's sister's son who founded the chiefdom, opposed the reigning Jalasi and moved into the area where the chiefdom is now situated. The implication of Nyambi's being in Liwonde district was that he had to sit on District Councils in Zomba with Kawinga and Liwonde instead of with Jalasi in Fort Johnston. I understand that since the original Nyambi died his several successors have made requests to the Administration to be included in the Fort Johnston district. Finally in 1948 the request was granted and Nyambi's chiefdom was once more linked with his perpetual son's in Fort Johnston district.

The opposition of the chiefdoms as wholes appears in other situations as well, often when it is not expected. For example, there are two tobacco markets in the area studied. One is in Nyambi's area and the other is about 25 miles away at Mlomba's village in the extreme south of Kawinga's area. Mlomba is a uterine brother of the present Kawinga. Chiwalo's chiefdom abuts Nyambi's and tobacco growers need to transport their produce only six or seven miles to the market in Nyambi's area. Yet several growers told me that they were taking their produce the 25 miles to Mlomba market because they felt in some vague way that the Chiwalo people got lower prices for their tobacco in the Nyambi market than the Nyambi people.

The cleavage between the chiefdoms is also expressed in their religion. Kawinga, Liwonde, Jalasi and Nyambi are all Moslems and very few of their followers are Christian. Malemia is a Christian and very few of his followers are Moslems. But between Kawinga and Liwonde on one hand, and Jalasi and Nyambi on the other hand, there is a cleavage in terms of a schism among the Moslems. One group, the *twaliki*, became centred at Jalasi's court village Majuni. The *twaliki* believe that Islamic devotions should be accompanied by loud singing and chanting of Arabic tracts and by particularly vigorous dancing. Even at funerals this type of prayer is required. The other sect, the *sukutu*, centred at Kawinga's and Liwonde's court villages, advocates the more orthodox type of Islamic devotion in which a quiet restrained manner is emphasized. As far as I know the *twaliki* sect are confined entirely to Jalasi's chiefdom and the *sukutu* to Kawinga and Liwonde. In this matter, Nyambi's people side with Kawinga's and Liwonde's.

On the other hand, local informal organization is well developed so that Chiwalo who is at the point of juxtaposition of Kawinga, Liwonde, Nyambi and Jalasi chiefdoms, may try cases involving headmen from any of these areas, and they usually accept his arbitration. His is the nearest court house. The actual boundaries of the four areas, however, are very clearly recognized and Chiwalo realizes the limits of his jurisdiction. Though he may arbitrate in a difference between headmen, he would not dare to apportion land outside his area. Headmen living on the boundaries of two chiefdoms arbitrate in each other's cases ; the villagers under them intermarry. A village in Chiwalo's may procure garden lands in Jalasi's area, and children may be initiated at ceremonies held by headmen in other chiefdoms. There is no clear break in the normal social relationships of people across the boundaries of chiefdoms, and their members interact as freely with each other as members of two villages of the same chiefdom. The cleavage between the villages on different sides of the boundary of a ·chiefdom becomes apparent only in special situations.

The formal relationships of the chiefs, set by the history of their conquests and their kinship, and incorporated in and slightly modified by the Administrative framework, are overlaid by an informal local organization where the interaction of village headmen only conforms to the formal pattern when no agreement can be reached.

The Position of the Modern Chief

In ritual situations a chiefdom is clearly differentiated from its neighbours, and many of these situations arise in the cult of tendence on the ancestor spirits. The ancestor cult has fallen away almost completely among village headmen, but among the chiefs it is still strong, and appears particularly in the rain-prayers and the initiation ceremonies. Later, I shall discuss at length the importance of the chief's sanction before headmen may conduct initiation ceremonies. This is because the spirits of the ancestors of the chief are supposed to affect the welfare of the initiands. Though some village headmen may conduct initiation ceremonies they are unable to offer rain-prayers. These are offered by a chief on two occasions. The first is in November, before the rains have started. The chief's wife and some women from the bigger villages in the near vicinity of the chief's village gather at his hut. They brew beer—*ukana wacisoka*, the beer of the spirits—to be used as a libation. At sunset on the appointed day the chief goes to the shrine tree where some headmen have gathered, and pours some of the beer into a pot, partly buried at the root of the tree, while he invokes all the spirits of his departed ancestors—mainly matrilineal but occasionally some patrilateral. He then entreats the spirits to send some rain and to look after their ' children ' in the land. Sometimes a length of calico is hung on the tree as an extra offering. Should no rain fall the chief will have to repeat the offering until it does fall. When the rains have ended in March he makes a second offering ' of thanks '.

In the context of the present discussion, the important point is that it is only the chief who can make this libation and offer this prayer. If his plea fails the whole area starves, and no headman may supplicate his ancestors on his own behalf or approach the chief's ancestors through his own ancestors. The grain for the beer comes from the various villages, but not on a fixed rate of levy. Some villages never contribute. The chief buys the offered cloth on behalf of his people. When in 1948 the cloth on the shrine tree was stolen, Chiwalo imposed a levy on the village headmen in the area so that a new cloth could be bought. Here the boundaries of the chiefdoms are important, and no headman outside Chiwalo's area was approached. A village headman from Jalasi's area, though geographically much closer to Chiwalo, relies on Jalasi's rain-offerings and may not approach Chiwalo or plead with him to offer a rain-prayer to his ancestors.

Another ritual situation in which the limits of the chiefdom appear is during the institutionalized pillage on the death of a chief. I have not been in any area when the chief has died, so that I rely here on the tales of informants. During the mourning rites certain feasts are held. The food for the mourning feast of a commoner or village headman is provided from his estate by his relatives. For the feasts during the mourning at a chief's death the food is acquired by institutionalized pillage (*cipinimbe*). The villagers in a chiefdom are often first informed of the death of a chief by the appearance of men from his village. These men are by custom allowed to take from a village any article of food they can find—flour, a goat, some chickens, prepared relish, or whatever is lying around in the village. The owners of the food may not charge them with theft. This food is used in the funeral feast. The excesses to which the chief's men may go became circumscribed after the White conquest. Previously, almost any crime short of murder could be committed under the guise of *cipinimbe*. More recently, owing to Government opposition, it has been restricted to the taking of smaller articles of food, such as flour and chickens. Some people are beginning to object even to this. The chief's funeral is a public affair and all his subjects may attend it. The effect of the *cipinimbe* is to bring together enough food for the chief's funeral feast. Here, as before, the chief's men may not cross the boundary for fear of reprisals, and the effect is to impose a levy in an informal way over most of the villages in the chief's area.

The Chief as a Symbol of Unity

The chief is a representative of his people and it is his particular duty to ensure their welfare and that of the chiefdom as a whole. His symbolic representation of the unity of his people is brought out clearly by his right to fines in cases involving bloodshed and arson. Strife and division in a chiefdom in the old days were likely to end in spilt blood and burnt huts so that the Yao associate bloodshed and hut-burning with dissension within the chiefdom.

Most other offences are against the individual and not the chiefdom as a whole : the case is brought to the chief so that compensation may be awarded. Adultery and theft thus are definitely civil offences. Nowadays, a fine is imposed, but this is seen to be a White innovation, and the money from it is looked upon as ' Boma ' money.[1] In disputes where blood has been shed, however, the chief is entitled to fine the guilty party on his own account. The chief is said to be ' blinded ' by the blood and a payment must be made to him before he may ' see '

[1] i.e. Government money.

again.   In the past, disputes hinging on murder had this aspect, though they were usually settled by a feud.   Nowadays, of course, all murder cases are lifted altogether out of the hands of the chief, but the special fine for bloodshed is still levied in cases of assault.   When a man is convicted of assault in the chief's court he will have to pay three separate amounts : one to the victim as compensation, one as a fine to the Native Treasury, and one to the chief ' so that he may see again '.

A similar provision applies to cases of arson.   When a case is brought to the chief because a man has burnt another's hut, the chief will say that the guilty man has ' brought a torch into his country '.   The man convicted of arson will have to pay a special fine to the chief in the same way as the man who caused blood-shed.   The association of the unity of the chiefdom with fire probably has some place in the attitude of the chief here.   People who have come to a chiefdom as strangers are said to have come to ' seek the chief's fire ',[1] and all the fires in the chiefdom are supposed to have been kindled from one flame.   This expresses the unity of the chiefdom : the burning of the hut, therefore, symbolizes the introduction of discordant elements, as well as being a serious crime in itself.

The Chief's Judicial Functions

It is clear from MacDonald's writings that in pre-White days the chief settled most of the serious disputes in his chiefdom. Nowadays, this function of the chief has been given legal sanction under the Native Courts' Ordinance of 1933.   ' A ' grade courts have the power of imposing fines not exceeding £5, or 6 months' imprisonment and 12 strokes whipping ; and ' B ' grade courts may impose fines not exceeding £1 and imprisonment including hard labour not exceeding one month, but not corporal punishment.   The Native Authorities, Jalasi, Nyambi, Kawinga and Liwonde, all have ' A ' courts ; the Subordinate Native Author-ities, Chikweo, Ngokwe, Chiwalo, Chamba, Mposa, Mlomba, Stora, have ' B ' courts.   Only a certain proportion of disputes is brought for trial in these Native Authority courts.   This is because, firstly, the Administration does not admit the legality of some disputes.   Most of these centre on charges of witchcraft,

---

[1] A similar view of fire in the village context is discussed in Chap. V, p. 112.

but some also on having killed children by *ndaka* [1] (a disease caused by the mystical influence of sexual intercourse). Secondly, other cases not brought to the court are petty squabbles which do not involve heavy compensation. Examples of these disputes are personal quarrels, disputes over land ownership, petty theft and so on. The Native Authority's court handles mainly cases arising from adultery, which involve compensation varying from £1 10s. to £5 ; and theft and assault for which similar compensation may be payable. If the case is brought up to the chief's court there is a mechanism whereby the compensation may be enforced. Ordinarily, in those cases which are not tried in the court house, there is no legal sanction behind the payment of the compensation, so that if a man defaults in payment no legal pressure can be brought to bear on him. It is for this reason that such cases are tried in the court house.

The cases are heard by the court assessors who call the witnesses and cross-examine them. Sometimes a chief or his representative is in the court, as at Kawinga's court, but sometimes as in Chiwalo's court, the chief never comes to the court house at all. After the evidence is sifted, one court assessor takes the case to the chief and tells him about it. On the basis of the court assessor's analysis he awards compensation and imposes fines. The court assessor then takes this information back to the court house, reassembles the protagonists, and announces the chief's decision. The losing party has then the opportunity to appeal, first to the court of the Native Authority, if the case was tried in a Subordinate Native Authority's court, and then to the District Commissioner.

Cases tried by the chief in his extra-Administrative capacity are usually tried outside the court house. The same personalities take part in the trial but they act now with reference to a different set of values. The procedure is exactly the same, except that in Chiwalo's area the chief is present at the hearing. He sits somewhat aside from the main body of people but within hearing distance, weaving a mat or making nets while the case is being tried.

In minor cases, if either of the parties is dissatisfied with the decision, he may take the case up to the chief for arbitration and, theoretically, may then take it from him if he is a Subordinate

[1] See Chap. V, p. 112.

PLATE IV

A dispute in settlement at Chiwalo's hut. The assessor is sitting under the veranda behind the pole. A village headman can just be discerned in the shade under the veranda. The commoners sit in the sun.

(*October 1948*)

Native Authority, to the Native Authority, and eventually to the District Commissioner if the case is one which he will countenance. In practice, most cases reach the chief and go no further. Most people accept his decision. Thus the chief has important judicial functions.

THE CHIEF AS HIS PEOPLE'S REPRESENTATIVE

In special situations where the welfare of the chiefdom as a whole has been endangered by an infringement of the mores, the chief may take action. For example, a chief prosecutes a village headman who allows a woman in his village to bear her first child before she has been through the *litiwo* ceremony. Every woman who becomes pregnant for the first time must undergo this ceremony, during which she is instructed in child welfare and child care. If she bears a child without undergoing the ceremony, she is said to have 'spoilt the country' (*ajalwice cilambo*), in the sense that she has besmirched its reputation.[1]

Chiefs usually call in magicians 'to smell out' those responsible for keeping back the rain.[2] When the rains fail as they did in 1948–9, their failure is held to be due to the magic of some evilly disposed person. It then becomes the chief's duty to call in a magician to indicate who this person is. The fees for this duty are paid by the chief himself on behalf of his people.

The chief also acts as a representative of his people when they are affected as a whole. For example, Nyambi called in a magician after man-eating lions had taken some of his subjects. This magician called for the hearth-stones and domestic utensils from all the villages in the area, and built them up into a pyramid over which he made some anti-lion medicine. This was to clear the whole chiefdom of man-eating lions.

Nowadays, the chief's representation of his people is seen most clearly in his position in the Administrative framework.[3] The chief represents the Administration to his people since they approach it through him. At the same time the Administration clearly treats him as the representative of his people and consults

---

[1] I was told in Mponda's area that the women undergo this ceremony *after* the birth of the child, but that it is still obligatory.

[2] *Kutawa ula*—lit. 'to tie or bind the rain', in the sense of to make it a prisoner.

[3] I have dealt with this aspect more fully in 'The Political Organization of the Yao of Southern Nyasaland'.

him about the laws it intends to introduce which affect his people. The Administration transmits new Ordinances and Regulations to the chief and he must then relay them to the village headmen. When it advises the chief of a new law it thereby advises the people of his chiefdom.

THE ORIGIN OF VILLAGES IN MODERN CHIEFDOMS

We have thus far been looking at the chiefdom as an organization of villages united by their common interests in and association with one chief. But the villages that compose the chiefdom are not all equally closely integrated into the political structure. This is most clearly seen against the background of how the modern chiefdoms came into being.

By the time that the 1912 Ordinance was introduced the social composition of the chiefdoms had undergone some change from what it was before the White conquest. Before the White conquest the Yao chiefs had overcome the indigenous inhabitants of Southern Nyasaland. Some of these had been allowed to remain in the area as subjects. Others were enslaved. There were some Nguru, Nyanja and Mpotola village headmen who had come to seek the protection of the Yao chiefs.

During the conquest, the territory was thrown into confusion, and villages fled in abandon from their own into neighbouring chiefdoms both in Southern Nyasaland and Mozambique. When the Administration allowed the chiefs to return, most of the important village headmen and their followers returned with them. Kawinga, for example, was allowed to return, not to Mount Chikala but to the area immediately to the north of it. He brought back with him most of his important headmen who had fled with him to the country of the Mpotola chief Nkanyela, in Mozambique. Jalasi was allowed to return from Portuguese Territory in 1906,[1] not to his mountain fortress Mangoche, but to a smaller hill Sakalwe some miles to the east. He gathered round him a few of his important headmen.

When hostilities ceased, there was a certain amount of internal readjustment. Some villages which had fled to other chiefdoms in the Protectorate started to come back while others stayed behind. To-day there are villages here and there which had left their chiefdoms in the confusion and had then joined their present

[1] District Book, Fort Johnston.

chiefs. Mpumbe's village, which in 1947 was about $2\frac{1}{2}$ miles from Kawinga's court village Nanyumbu, was originally one of Jalasi's adherents. Mpumbe fled with many others when the British attacked Mangoche in 1896. He went to the place where Lake Amaramba spills into the Lujenda River in Portuguese East Africa. When things seemed more peaceful, Mpumbe did not return to Jalasi's area, but preferred to seek his son Ngongondo, who had fled with a section of the village to Kawinga's area. He found Ngongondo at approximately the present site of the village, and settled with him. Ngongondo later moved eastwards to his present home in the Liwonde area. Both village headmen have achieved a certain amount of prestige in their new chiefdoms. Mpumbe was once a court assessor of Kawinga, and now holds girls' initiation rights. They have lost all touch with their former chief and are most unlikely to return to him.

A considerable number of Kawinga's villages moved into Mposa's and Chamba's areas, when they returned to the Protectorate. Their descendants to-day say that they did so because the soil was better in those areas than in Kawinga's.

Shortly after the British expedition, i.e. between 1896 and 1900, the Portuguese Government launched a punitive campaign against the Africans along the Portuguese–Nyasaland boundary. Many thousands of refugees came pouring into the Protectorate. Most of these were Mpotola and Nguru. The great majority settled where they crossed the boundary, i.e. round Chiuta, and Ngokwe chiefdom arose from some of them. After the Portuguese campaigns ended many other migrants came into the area. All those I questioned gave Portuguese ill-treatment as the reason for their coming across.

During the first decade of the century the movement, as in the initial invasion, was predominantly south-westwards—from Lake Chiuta towards the Shire River and Highlands. Now, however, the movement is gradual. The first movement of a group may bring it just within the boundary. Then the next movement may take it to the south and west deeper into Nyasaland. Some of my village case histories show this. Table III sets out some movements within Kawinga–Liwonde area (except Chiwalo).[1] I asked about the place of origin of all the villages

[1] I use Kawinga–Liwonde area to include the chiefdoms Kawinga, Liwonde, Mposa, Chamba, Ngokwe, Chikweo and Chiwalo.

TABLE III

Movement of Villages within Kawinga-Liwonde Area

Losers:	\multicolumn{6}{c}{Gainers:}	Totals
	Ngokwe	Chikweo	Kawinga	Liwonde	Mposa	Chamba	
Ngokwe .	—	—	7	2	—	—	9
Chikweo .	—	—	2	—	1	—	3
Kawinga .	—	—	—	27	1	20	48
Liwonde .	—	—	—	—	—	4	4
Mposa	—	—	—	2	—	9	9
Chamba .	—	—	—	—	—	—	—
Totals .	—	—	—	2	—	2	73

Totals above the diagonal represent movements south-westwards. Totals below the diagonal represent movements north-eastwards.

extant in Kawinga's section, which had arrived since the White conquest. My enquiries about the headmen who are recognized by Government were easy, but for those who are not recognized I had to rely on the memories of my informants and I know that many were left out. I am not aware of any bias, but realize that wide generalization from the figures is not safe. A glance at Map II shows that Ngokwe area is the most north-easterly area and Chamba the most south-westerly. The others are intermediate. Of the 75 villages only two had moved counter to this direction, i.e. from Mposa to Liwonde in a north-westerly direction.

I have no measure of the number of villages which have moved entirely out of the Kawinga–Liwonde area, either to other parts of Nyasaland or back to Portuguese East Africa. I have never heard of a village's moving back to Portuguese East Africa, though I have heard of their moving westwards and southwards, and of a few moving northwards.

In Table IV, I set out the origin of villages which have arrived in Kawinga–Liwonde area since the White conquest, and which are still there. This table shows quite clearly, that by far the biggest influx into these areas has been from Portuguese East

TABLE IV

ORIGIN OF VILLAGES WHICH HAVE ARRIVED IN THE KAWINGA-LIWONDE AREA
SINCE THE WHITE CONQUEST AND ARE STILL THERE

Origin	Ngokwe	Chikweo	Kawinga	Liwonde	Mposa	Chamba	Total
Northern Areas :							
Fort Johnston . . .	—	—	—	6	—	1	7
Nyambi	—	3	—	1	1	2	7
Jalasi	1	—	10	6	1	3	21
Southern Areas :							
Malemia and Ntumanje	—	—	—	8	7	28	43
Zomba	—	—	—	4	7	4	15
South of Zomba . .	—	—	—	2	1	3	6
Other Nyasaland Areas :	—	—	—	3	—	2	5
Port. E. Africa . . .	13	76	111	37	6	30	273
Unrecorded	—	—	—	2	1	31	34
Total	14	79	121	69	24	104	411

Africa. We have no record of how many villages have been lost to the Southern or Northern area from Kawinga–Liwonde area, so that we cannot evaluate the significance of the gain of 64 villages from Southern areas, and of only 35 from the Northern areas. The density of population in Malemia's area is 268 per square mile, and the average density of the Shire Highlands is about 156·6. It may well be that there is now a movement out of the Shire Highlands into the less densely populated I iwonde–Kawinga area.

THE PRINCIPLE OF PRIMACY

Migration and invasion have been the keynote of Machinga histories : village headmen recount with pride how their ancestors moved into Nyasaland with their bands of slaves and followers. 'The East' is the traditional home of the Yao and even young men who have never been there proudly say, 'We come from the East'. This sentiment is reflected in the belief that the rains from the east are beneficial and give rise to good crops, while the rains from the west are detrimental and cause

F

crop failures. Also I was told that important village headmen
are buried with their heads pointing to the east.

The Yao concept of the past is reflected in the principles of
political organization of these Machinga chiefdoms. The invasion is the datum point from which rank mainly stems. We
may classify modern headmen into : those who were in the
area before the Yao invasion, i.e. the Aborigines ; the Invaders ;
and those who have come in since the invasion and have had to
submit themselves to the Machinga chief, i.e. the Newcomers.
The principle behind this classification of headmen is fundamental
to Yao political structure. Stated most simply it is the rule that
MacDonald quoted in describing the development of local organization : ' However large the settlement may become the man
that is first in is the chief or headman.' [1] This is, of course,
somewhat of a simplification, but the rule contains the essence
of the principle. It was reversed for the Aboriginal Nyanja
because the Yao subjugated them. But the claims of the Nyanja
chiefs to rank because they had occupied the land first were
recognized by the Yao who absorbed them into the social
structure in positions of high rank.

But the principle holds among the Yao themselves, and for
the Nguru in their movements after the White conquest. The
operation of the principle is clearest in the structure of small local
areas such as Chiwalo's. When Chiwalo's area was first settled,
just after World War I, there were large tracts of unoccupied
land. The first headmen to move into this region were Cigwaja,
Kapaloma, Nyanje, Makata and Mumbwa. The local chief
Chiwalo followed Cigwaja, but as Cigwaja was one of the
Invader headmen under Chiwalo during the period of invasion,
he now recognized Chiwalo as the chief. The area that is now
Chiwalo's chiefdom was divided out among these five headmen.
As other headmen came into the area they had to approach one
of these five for land rights. These, when granted, were granted
irrevocably in a block to the new village headman who then
had sole rights to distribute the land afterwards. If he had the
land to spare, he may have granted a portion of it to yet another
village headman, and this action was also irrevocable. The land
occupation pattern in any particular area is therefore extremely
complex, because in addition to the village garden areas, indivi-

[1] MacDonald, *Africana*, i, 147. See p. 35 above.

duals may hold garden plots in other village areas which they have temporarily borrowed in a private arrangement with the individual owner. But when the system is seen in relation to the pattern of occupation of the area, it is greatly simplified. Each garden may be traced back to the original owner through three or four village headmen. The pattern of the reversion of rights follows the same system. The garden land of a village which has recently moved in and is moving out again reverts directly to the village headman who granted it. If he has moved out it reverts back to the village headman from whom it was in turn acquired.[1] These original landholders form the central points of locally organized areas to-day. For example, in Chiwalo's area there is Chiwalo at the top of the scale, then there are Kapaloma, Cigwaja, Mumbwa, Makata and Nyanje as the most important village headmen, and they take precedence over any of the other village headmen. All the others who have come into the area since then, of whom many are Nguru, rank very much lower.

From the smallest village to the chiefdom as a whole, therefore, there is a series of overlapping areas of organization. In any particular area chosen at random in a chiefdom as large as, say, Kawinga's, there will probably be two or three small villages which recognize the primacy of one of their number. The headman of this village may be called in to arbitrate in disputes over land or personal quarrels or even in the private consultations held after the death of a village member (*mapeto*). But the superior headman in turn recognizes *his* superior who was in the area before him. This system is extended over larger and larger areas, each headman in turn recognizing some other headman who was in the area before him, until ultimately the primacy of the Invader chief over all his headmen is established by the same principle. There is no clear-cut district organization as among the Zulu and Bemba.[2]

[1] See also ' Preliminary Notes on Land Tenure and Agriculture among the Machinga Yao ', *Human Problems*, x (1950), 1–13. This system of land-holding has been called ' estates of holding ' by Gluckman. See his *Essays on Lozi Land and Royal Property*, Rhodes-Livingstone Paper, No. 10 (Livingstone, 1943), p. 29 ff.

[2] See the essays by Gluckman and Richards in Fortes, M., and Evans-Pritchard, E. E., *African Political Systems*, Oxford University Press for the International African Institute (London, 1940).

These headmen who are the centres of local social structure are the higher headmen that MacDonald mentions.[1] Many of them to-day are the descendants of the traditional councillors (*nduna*) who were sent out to the extremities of the chiefdoms to be the outer governors in these areas.[2] Their villages are social centres in that many disputes are taken to these important headmen before they are taken to the Native Authority's court. For example, the dispute between the women of Nampeya and Cikuwita was taken to Ntibwilibwi.[3] The chief usually orders headmen to assemble at the villages of important headmen when he has directions to issue to them. Very frequently the Administrative officers camp there for the night on their tours and call the headmen in to them for conference. The placing of mosques at the villages of these important headmen also indicates their significance as social centres. Most Moslem villages have small mosques which the more devout use for the morning and evening prayers during Ramadan only. At the villages of important headmen larger mosques have been built and these are used for the midday prayers on Fridays (*jumo*), when most of the Moslems in each area assemble in their best clothes for communal prayers. Large brick mosques have been built at the court villages of Jalasi, Liwonde and Kawinga. There are other large mosques at the villages of chieftains such as Chiwalo, Chamba, Mposa, and of important headmen such as Kangomba, Nyenje and many others. These chiefs and headmen were all Invaders and are, as I shall show later, almost by definition Moslems. They are also headmen of high rank so that the placing of the mosque, and the other features of local social structure, are largely derivatives of the system of ranking.

Rank therefore underlies the structure of local areas as well as the structure of the chiefdoms as wholes. It is, as I show later, closely associated with the historical origin of the headmen. Yet the correlation is not perfect and I shall show that other factors tend to militate against the fixed historical ranking of headmen. Nevertheless, the principle of primacy is the most important single factor.

[1] See Chap. II, p. 36.
[2] See Chap. IV, pp. 92–3.   [3] See Chap. V, p. 130.

THE CHARACTERISTICS OF THE THREE CATEGORIES
OF HEADMEN

In Table V I have set out the ethnic affiliation of the headmen in the three categories and also the dates of arrival of Newcomers in the Kawinga–Liwonde area. This table shows that

TABLE V

NUMBERS OF VILLAGE HEADMEN WHO ARE ABORIGINES, INVADERS AND
NEWCOMERS

| Tribes | Aborigines | Invaders* | Newcomers | | | | | | | Total |
			Pre-White	White Conquest—1907	1908–17	1918–27	1928–37	1938–47	Unrecorded	
Yao . . .	—	144	19	60	20	14	13	13	35	318
Mpotola . .	—	53	—	43	21	9	1	1	—	128
Nguru . .	—	5	2	46	58	49	27	14	17	218
Nyanja . .	25	3	1	4	6	1	1	4	1	46
Unrecorded .	—	—	—	—	—	—	—	—	6	6
Total . . .	25	205	22	153	105	73	42	32	59	716

* In Ngokwe area, 39 villages are classified as Invaders who came into Nyasa-land as refugees from the Portuguese military actions at the close of the nineteenth century.

easily the great majority of villages has come into the area since the White conquest. On the other hand, only 3·5 per cent are Aborigines. Just over a quarter (28·6 per cent) are direct descendants of the original Invaders or headmen of villages which have branched off from these. The remainder (67·9 per cent) are the Newcomers who have submitted themselves to the Invaders. Far more Newcomers came in during the decade following the White conquest than in any of the more recent decades.[1] We cannot argue directly from these figures that the greatest influx of Newcomers into Nyasaland took place before World War I. Newcomers in the more recent decades may be as numerous but may be passing out of the area more quickly, and therefore are not recorded in my survey. On the other

[1] Nguru immigration in 1908–27 was due to exceptional causes.

hand, all villages tend to disappear in time. We should therefore expect more of the headmen who came in during the
earlier decades to be forgotten, and the trend should be more
pronounced than it is. In fact we know from other sources that
immigration of the Nguru, who represent about one-half of
the Newcomers, was greatest before 1930, and it is almost
certain that the figures do reflect the change in the amount of
Nguru immigration, and that the factors which may operate
against the trend are not important. As a whole the set of
figures suggests that immigration is slowly coming to an end.

The Aborigines are all Nyanja. Among the Invaders, 70·2 per
cent are Yao, 25·9 per cent are Mpotola, and the remainder
3·9 per cent are Nyanja and Nguru. The Mpotola Invaders are
practically all in the Ngokwe and Chikweo areas, so that in the
other areas (i.e. in Liwonde, Kawinga, Chamba and Mposa) the
Yao represent 94·9 per cent of the Invaders ; the remainder are
Mpotola. Under Ngokwe and Chikweo who are Mpotola
chieftains, 54·5 per cent (48 of 88) of the Invaders are Mpotola,
and 37·5 per cent are Yao, and the remaining 8·0 per cent are
Nyanja and Nguru. Among the 486 Newcomers, 35·8 per cent
of the headmen are Yao, 15·4 per cent Mpotola, 43·8 per cent
Nguru and 4·9 per cent are mainly Nyanja. In general, therefore, we may say that the Aborigines are all Nyanja ; the
Invaders are Yao in the major area and Mpotola in the other
area ; and the Newcomers are predominantly Nguru from
Portuguese East Africa, though there is a fair proportion of Yao
who have come from other Nyasaland districts.

There are significant differences among the three categories of
headmen in their religious affiliations. In general there are more
Moslems (71·8 per cent) among all headmen than Christians or
Pagans. But there are more Moslems among the Invaders than
among either the Aborigines or the Newcomers.[1] There are
more Pagans among the Newcomers, but the proportion of
Christians among the Aborigines and the Newcomers is about
equal (25·0 per cent and 21·9 per cent). These differences in
religious affiliations are consistent with the different historical
backgrounds of the two groups. The Invaders are the descendants of the Yao slavers, who in the past had been in intimate

---

[1] Invaders = 91·1 per cent ; Others = 63·9 per cent ; Diff. of per cent
= 27·2 ; S.E. of diff. = 3·7 ; C.R. = 7·2 ; $p < 0.0001$.

TABLE VI

RELIGIOUS AFFILIATION OF ABORIGINE, INVADER AND NEWCOMER HEADMEN

Religious Affiliation	Numbers				Percentages			
	Abori- gine	In- vader	New- comer	Total	Abori- gine	In- vader	New- comer	Total
Moslem . .	17	184	296	497	70·8	91·1	63·5	71·8
Pagan . .	1	4	68	73	4·2	2·0	14·6	10·6
Church of Scotland .	3	10	59	72	12·5	5·0	12·7	10·4
Roman Catholic .	2	1	33	36	8·3	0·5	7·1	5·2
Other Christians .	1	3	10	14	4·2	1·5	2·1	2·0
Total . .	24	202	466	692	100·0	100·0	100·0	100·0
Unknown .	1	3	20	24				
	25	205	486	716				

Combining Roman Catholic and other Christian totals.
$n = 6$; $\chi^2 = 56·48$; $p < 0.00001$.

contact with the Arab slave-traders and had taken over Islam from them. To-day the chiefs are still frequently called ' sultan '. All the chiefs in the Machinga area are Moslems except possibly the Malemia who was installed in 1947. He was brought up as a Christian but the strong Islamic tradition behind his status is reflected in the star and crescent on his ceremonial headdress. The Nyanja, however, were influenced by the Missions from the start and the Nguru were not as directly concerned in the slave-trade and were therefore less affected by Islam. They have been easily converted to Christianity. Among them too there are more Pagans. The difference in religion here is largely a reflex of the political relationships of the headmen. In other words, the Yao stoutly maintain that they are Moslems merely because Islam is one of the distinguishing marks of the Yao and of the Invaders in particular. It would be difficult for some of them to maintain their point in face of strict Moslems, for many of them follow the tenets of Islam in only the most cursory way. An Nguru therefore admits to being a Pagan more readily than a Yao, because he cannot identify himself with the Invading group.

KINSHIP WITH THE CHIEF

The most important way in which the three categories differ, however, is in the degree to which they are associated with the chief. While the Invaders are identified with the chief because of their association with him in the invasion, they are also tied to him to a greater degree by various kinship links than the other categories of headmen.

Although the exact composition of the Invading groups will never be known, it appears from the accounts of old men, that the groups were made up primarily of the chief and his younger brothers, together with their sons and slaves, and some unrelated followers. Other chieftaincies and village headmen have sprung from the chief's lineage. For example, Kawinga was the leader who brought the present Kawinga–Liwonde group into Nyasaland. The first man to be called Kawinga left the Lujenda River where he was living with an elder relative called Nsanama, whose exact genealogical connection I have never been able to determine. Accompanying them was Liwonde, a younger brother of Kawinga. As they passed through the country just west of Lake Chiuta they encountered the Mpotola under Chikweo, and these joined up with Kawinga and his relatives and went to Kongwe on the west side of Lake Malombe (in the present Kalembo's area). From this place they were displaced by the Ngoni and returned east and south to the Chikala Range where they displaced Malemia and occupied the heights. Subsequently, Liwonde left the mountain and went to live on the Shire River where the old Government station used to be. From this point on, Kawinga and Liwonde seem to have acted almost independently. Nsanama seems to have stayed with Kawinga. Chamba who was the son of the first Kawinga now set himself up as a chief on the south side of Chikala and Chaoni. Mposa, the son of the first Liwonde, moved to the shores of Lake Shirwa and set himself up there. Chiwalo, a sister's daughter's son of the first Kawinga, set himself up on the northern fringe of the area. Recently Stora, a sister's daughter's daughter's daughter's son of the first Kawinga, has been recognized as a subordinate Native Authority. Village headmen also develop in the same way from the relatives of the chief. Among the 205 village headmen who are of Invader stock, there are 62 who are

TABLE VII

PROPORTIONS OF RELATED AND UNRELATED HEADMEN AMONG THE INVADERS

Chief's Relatives						Non-Relatives	Total
Direct			Clan				
Mat.*	Pat.	Aff.	Mat.†	Pat.	Aff.		
17 8·3	35 17·1	10 4·9	37 18·0	22 10·7	12 5·9	72 35·1	205 100%
30·3%			34·6%			35·1%	

* Includes the six chiefs themselves.
† Those who have the same clan-name.
Mat. = Matrilineally related ; Pat. = Patrilaterally related ; Aff. = Affinally related.

either chiefs, their direct matrilineal relatives or their direct patrilateral relatives. This represents 30·3 per cent of the total. Of these 35 or 17·1 per cent are patrilateral relatives.

The chief's sons occupied a very strong position in the early Yao chiefdoms. Most sons of the early chiefs were their children by slave-wives. Since there was no one on their mother's side from whom they could inherit rank, it follows that they could only expect to achieve status through their father, the chief. Yet they were not, as his younger brothers and his sisters' sons were, a danger to him, because they were not in the line of succession and had no reason to wish his death. On the contrary, the bonds that unite father and son in Yao society are strong but not formal. The chief's sons, the *acibwana*, therefore came to occupy some of the most trusted positions under him. They became his military leaders ; they led his caravans to the coast and back ; they were the messengers who represented him to foreign chiefdoms and to the Whites when they came. In these positions the chief could trust his sons, because he knew that they had no hostile axes to grind. Younger brothers and sisters' sons might have used the military forces against him, or they might have squandered the wealth of the caravans because they had a jural right to it. As the sons grew older they were given groups of slaves and slave-wives to look after, and so they became village headmen under the chief. Many of them came to have initiation rights and hold other positions of importance.

The chief was also connected to other Invader headmen through marriage. It is clear that affinal links become in time cognatic, but the marriage of the chief with a headman's sister fixes the relationship between that headman and the chief in perpetuity. The succeeding chief does not look upon the village headman who is his mother's brother's wife's brother as a father-in-law, as he would if he were a commoner, but instead calls him ' brother-in-law '. Also, all the successors of the village headman call all the succeeding chiefs by this term, so that the political structure of the area becomes phrased in a kinship idiom : the quasi-kinship of headman and chief in this context becomes suffused with political meaning. The number of village headmen who claim some affinal relationship to the chief is not great—only 10 of the total of 205 (i.e. 4·9 per cent).

TABLE VIII

PROPORTIONS OF RELATED AND UNRELATED HEADMEN AMONG THE NEWCOMERS

Chief's Relatives						Non-Relatives	Total
Direct			Clan				
Mat.	Pat.	Aff.	Mat.	Pat.	Aff.		
0	13	15	24	13	16	300	381
0	3·4	3·9	6·3	3·4	4·2	78·8	100%
7·3%			13·9%			78·8%	

Among the Aborigines and Newcomers, naturally, there are very few direct relatives. There are, of course, no matrilineal relatives. The patrilateral relatives amongst the Newcomers (3·4 per cent) are those of Kawinga who have moved into Chamba and Liwonde areas. There have been various marriages between the chiefs and Newcomers and as a result there are 3·9 per cent of the Newcomer headmen who are linked affinally to the chiefs. The proportion of affinally-linked headmen in the two categories is approximately the same. The major differences are among the proportions of headmen linked by matrilineal and patrilateral ties to the chief.

CLANSHIP WITH THE CHIEF

A more numerous category is those who are related to the chief, not by common descent but by clanship.

Informants tell me that before the Whites came to Nyasaland, each person took the clan-name of his mother. People who had the same clan-name were said to be ' of one kind ' (*lukosyo lwamo*). The word *lukosyo* had no other meaning but ' kind ' or ' sort ', and the word *mtundu* is frequently used as a synonym. If a man is asked his *lukosyo*, he is as likely as not to give the reply ' Yao ' or ' Machinga ', i.e. his tribal origin. By extension it follows that if two people have the same clan-name inherited from their mothers, and their mothers in turn have inherited it from their mothers, and so on, eventually there must be a common ancestress. The two people therefore call each other ' brother '. However, among the Yao there are no stories of the origin of clans and only vague traditions of a common clan ancestress. I often questioned Yao about their clan-names and joked with them that though they were Invaders they shared the same clan-names as their subjects. The clan-names I found among the Machinga Yao were *apiri*, *amilasi*, *ambewe*, *abanda*, *asimbiri*, *amwale*, *angoma*, and these clan-names also appear among the Maraŵi group of tribes (Cewa, Maŋanja, Cipeta, Mbo, etc.), the Lakeside Tonga of Chinteche district, and the Mpotola and Lomwe or Nguru from Portuguese East Africa. The Achisi Yao under Katuli, a group related to the Mataka Yao from Portuguese East Africa, do not have these clan-names, nor, as far as I know do the Yao in Tanganyika. Clan-names, therefore, may be a feature of the Machinga Yao in Nyasaland, acquired as a result of their contact with the Maraŵi and other indigenous peoples of that country. It is significant that the clan-names are not as a rule common Yao words for everyday objects in the same way that clan-names amongst, say, the Bemba of Northern Rhodesia, are names of plants, animals and other natural phenomena. The word *amilasi* is used for bamboos and once an informant when pressed told me a tale of a group of people who in dire starvation ate bamboo leaves and were thenceforth called after the bamboos. This story, however, was discredited by others and I pass it off as unimportant. There is, however, some evidence that the words *apiri amilasi, ambewe* and so on, are commonly used in Nyanja, and possibly amongst the Lakeside Tonga who were once part of the Marawî peoples, for objects other than clan-names.

Informants say that people with the same clan-name could not marry in the past,[1] so that the clan appears to have had the characteristics of an exogamous descent group. The position to-day is vastly different. Not only do people take the clan-names of their fathers, but many young people do not even know their clan-names at all.

At this point I should make it clear that the modern confusion about clan-names is no doubt partly due to the emphasis placed on patrilineal descent by the purveyors of White culture, the Administrators and the Missionaries, and also by the same emphasis in Islamic tradition which has influenced most Yao groups. Another factor in the situation is that slave descent still markedly affects social relationships in modern Nyasaland. Its significance here is that when a man took a slave-wife in the old days, his children by her took his clan-name, and not hers. Patrilineal descent of the clan-name therefore tends to point to the slave origin of a person. People who are able to point to a freeman ancestry are proud of this fact and are proud to be able to claim a clan-name associated with a long line of matri-lineal ancestors, particularly if there were some well-known men among them. On the other hand, I found it a fairly safe indica-tion that, if I could find no information about an ancestress, particularly her clan-name, then I was dealing with a group descended from a slave. A third factor is that some people explained their lack of knowledge of a clan-name by the state of social unrest and confusion at the end of the last century. As a result of the incursions of the Ngoni, Nguru and slave-raiding Yao and Arab groups, and finally the punitive expeditions of the British and the Portuguese, villages were destroyed and groups annihilated. People lost contact with their relatives, even

[1] Confirmed by Hynde, R. S., 'Marriage and relationship among the Yao', *Nyasa News*, vii (1895), 217-18.

their parents. Therefore many people who were children then, but adult to-day, say that their parents were 'lost running from the wars' and that they were never told their clan-names.

Whatever are the factors which have led to the comparative lack of importance of the clan-name in the social relationships of commoners to-day, the clan-name has preserved its significance in the political structure. I have already said that the clan-names associated with particular village headmanships and chieftaincies are well remembered, and this fact is not without significance. It seems likely that the clan-name was used in earlier times by groups as a method of claiming protection. The same set of clan-names appears throughout the tribes which surround the Machinga Yao. It seems likely that the adoption of clan-names facilitated their incursion into the country, and it is certain that insurgent Yao groups have used the clan-name as excuses to move into an area, and gradually to extend their dominance over it.

For example, in Malemia's area there is an Nyanja village headman called Nyani, who has the clan-name *amwale*. Stannus reports that when Malemia moved into this area he claimed brotherhood with Nyani because of the clan-name, and was able to obtain from him the land extending from the Likwenu River to the Namadsi River, a district 30 to 40 miles long.[1] Again when Kawinga fled from Chikala after the British raids on it, he went to the land of Nkanyela, an Mpotola chief in Portuguese East Africa, who is also an *ambewe*. That the clan-name is used essentially in this political field is illustrated by the relationships of Mposa to Mbande. Mposa, the son of Kawinga I, settled in the country of the Nyanja chief Mbande, who had the same clan-name as Mposa, viz. *amilasi*. Mposa calls Mbande 'brother' to-day and Mbande holds a position of honour and rank in Mposa's chiefdom. It is significant that other village headmen such as Cilombo, Mbalika and Mkwinda also have the same clan-name, but they do not claim kinship to Mposa. In modern times, when there is no longer any great danger to be incurred in moving from one part of the country to another, it seems likely that the necessity for some mechanism, whereby the friendship of otherwise hostile groups could be secured, falls away. In other words, the significance of the clan-name is gradually disappearing as its functions atrophy.

[1] Stannus, 'The Wayao of Nyasaland', 237.

Relationship may be claimed not only through having the same clan-name, but also by patrilateral and affinal clan ties. For example, one of the early Kawingas is supposed to have married an *abanda* woman. Therefore Chikweo, whose clan-name is *abanda*, calls Kawinga ' brother-in-law ' (*alamu*). Some of Kawinga's village headmen also call him brother-in-law because of the clan-name. Ngokwe, whose clan-name is *asimbiri*, had an *amilasi* father, so that many of his *amilasi* headmen call him ' son '.

Here, as before, there are more Invader headmen who claim to be clan relatives of the chief (34·6 per cent) than Newcomer headmen (13·9 per cent) (see Tables VII and VIII). Once again the proportion of headmen who claim affinal links to the chief is approximately the same in the two categories and the main difference is in the proportions who have the same clan-name and who are clan-patrilateral relatives in the way I have explained. I have mentioned that though many headmen have the same clan-names as the chiefs or the clan-names of the chiefs' fathers, they do not all claim to be clan-relatives of the chiefs. There is no reason to suppose that the distribution of clan-members is different between the Invaders and Newcomers, so that it seems likely that more Invaders claim the clan-relationship to the chief when they can, than do Newcomers.

UNRELATED HEADMEN

The striking difference between the two main groups of headmen is in the proportion not related to the chief. Among the Invaders only 35·1 per cent of the headmen cannot claim some kinship link to the chief. Among the Newcomers, however, roughly double that proportion (78·8 per cent) are in this position. Among the Invaders some of the unrelated headmen hold positions of importance by virtue of their independence of the chief. These are the *nduna* whose functions I describe later.[1] Among the Newcomers, however, there are no *nduna*, so that this difference between the categories is one of the most important.

In Tables VII and VIII I have omitted a total of 105 villages, 93 of which were small villages whose relationship to the chief I did not record. All these villages were settled in distant and inaccessible places and I asked about them from the chiefs and

[1] Chap. IV, pp. 92–3.

their councillors at the courts. If they were relatives of the chief it is almost certain that he would have mentioned them. We may assume then that the true proportion of unrelated headmen among the Newcomers is, as we would expect, very much greater than among the Invaders.

Of the total of 424 Administrative villages there were ten in which I did not record the formal relationship to the chief. In Table IX I set out the proportions in these categories among the Administrative village headmen, and there is no radical difference between these proportions and those for all village headmen.

TABLE IX

PROPORTIONS OF RELATIVES AND NON-RELATIVES AMONG ADMINISTRATIVE HEADMEN*

	Chief's Relatives						Non-Relatives	Total
	Direct			Clan				
	Mat.	Pat.	Aff.	Mat.	Pat.	Aff.		
Invaders . .	17 (12·5)	24 (17·6)	6 (4·4)	24 (18·4)	10 (7·4)	9 (6·6)	45 (33·1)	136 (100·0%)
Newcomers .	0 (0·0)	9 (3·5)	12 (4·7)	20 (7·8)	11 (4·3)	12 (4·7)	193 (75·1)	257† (100·1%)
Total . .	18	32	18	44	22	21	238	393

$n = 6$; $\chi^2 = 90·5$; $p = 0·0001$.

* This table excludes the 21 Aborigines.

† Excludes 10 villages for which I have not recorded this information.

To summarize, we may characterize the Invaders as Yao, Moslems, and associates of their chiefs by historical connections and kinship ties. The Newcomers and the Aborigines on the other hand are of different tribes. They have more diverse religions, are not connected to the chiefs by kinship ties as closely as the Invaders are, and do not share with them the strong bond of being co-Invaders. It is in the struggle for prestige and rank that these bonds with the chiefs assume significance.

CHAPTER IV

PRESTIGE AND RANK AMONG THE VILLAGE HEADMEN

THE POLITICAL PROCESS AS THE STRUGGLE OF HEADMEN FOR RANK

THUS far I have been describing the composition of the three categories of headmen : the Aborigines, the Invaders and the Newcomers. This classification is fundamental to the system of ranking among them, and is the most important single factor. But rank among village headmen is determined by other factors as well. We may summarize the most important of these thus :

A. *Rank from association with the chief.*
  1. Accompanied the chief during the Invasion.
  2. Kinship with the chief.
B. *Rank from opposition to the chief.*
  1. Prestige from another area.
  2. Large following.

The struggle of the headmen for power and prestige, both among themselves and against the chief, constitutes the political process. This is expressed mainly in the competition for various symbols of prestige. In this process, village headmen may use whatever connection with the chief they can, in order to gain his favour. They may use their direct kinship or clanship with him, or some more nebulous connection, such as the friendship of their fathers with him, or they may play upon the history of the association of their village with his ancestors in the invasion of the country. If they cannot exploit some link with the chief in their struggle for prestige, they may press their claims on the basis that their villages are large, and that if they are frustrated they may move their allegiance to another chief.

The historical fact of being of Invader stock is clearly a major determinant of rank. Invaders always have the advantage over the Newcomers because of their historical association with the chief. They are more closely bound to him : they participate in the ritual of the chieftaincy more than Newcomers do ; provide the chief's councillors ; pay rain-levies and in other ways express their closer tie with him. But there is no rigid class structure based on tradition. All villages are liable to break up. If for any reason the village's internal cohesion begins to weaken, its members scatter and it disappears as a political entity. Invader as well as Newcomer villages may thus disintegrate. The smaller sections of an Invader village which now set up villages of their own have to compete with the larger and more united villages of Newcomer origin. Another facet of the political process, therefore, is the continual competition of village headmen who are trying to maintain the unity of the villages under them, and to increase their following, so that their status against the chief and the other village headmen may be enhanced.

MARKS OF RANK

In the vernacular it is the *name* of the village which is said to be important.[1] This name is usually taken from the founder of the village and is assumed by a new village headman when he succeeds to the position : when a new village is founded the headman gives it his name to distinguish it from the parent village. But the importance that is ascribed to a name is clearly the importance of the corporate group which it represents. The headman is an incumbent of a social status, the prestige of which is drawn from the corporate group which he represents in his public dealings.

The prestige of village headmen is shown particularly in the degree of deference accorded to them by other village headmen. The headman with the highest prestige is of course the chief : the original leader of the Invaders. Below him may be ranked the rest of the village headmen in a relatively fixed pyramidal hierarchy, determined by a number of factors which I shall outline later.

The dress of important headmen is often an indicator of prestige but this criterion is not infallible nowadays when labour migrants, craftsmen and tobacco growers can afford to buy better clothes than many headmen. But it is usually a fairly safe guess that when a man carries a long stick and is dressed in long flowing

---

[1] *Lina lya kulungwa*—lit. ' the name is great '.

G

robes (a gown not unlike a woman's dressing-gown), wears a bright-coloured turban, and has one or two men walking behind him, he is a rather important village headman. One particular item of clothing in the Kawinga, Liwonde and Nyambi areas, is the scarlet headband which some village headmen may wear. I shall discuss this later in the context of the competition of village headmen for rank.

Another external characteristic of rank, which seems to have disappeared with the changing economic structure of Nyasaland, was the carrying of knives (*nsinjo*) by important village headmen. Previously, status was indicated by the type and size of knife carried in public. The chief usually carried the largest and most ornate. The knife taken from Kawinga on his surrender in Portuguese East Africa was about 18 inches long and had a decorated ivory handle. Smaller knives of similar pattern belonged to his headmen.[1] Nowadays, many young commoners carry knives two or even three feet long, made from the broken blades of motor-car springs.

The right of important village headmen to build fences [2] at the back of their huts is also a mark of prestige which seems to have lost its significance. About 50 years ago only important headmen had the right to erect a fence at the back of their huts. This fence, made of tall grass about six feet high, enclosed the grain stores and other food supplies of the household and formed a private compound in which the headman's wife and slaves carried on their daily tasks.[3] It seems likely that private compounds and slavery were positively associated, so that only the important village headmen who had many slaves found it necessary to build fences. All chiefs and most important headmen to-day still erect these fences. Those who hold initiation rights are obliged to build them because, when the initiands return from the seclusion phase of the initiation ceremony, they are supposed to spend one night in the headman's private compound before going back to their villages. But nowadays, minor village headmen and commoners also frequently build these

---

[1] See f.n. 4, Chap. II, p. 38.

[2] *Lutenje*, pl. *ndenje*. The enclosed space or 'compound' is *cimbundi*. Typical hut compounds are depicted on Plate IX (*a*) and (*b*), facing p. 206.

[3] MacDonald suggests that the common term *kusyeto* for woman is derived from the adverb *kusyeto*—on the other side (of the fence).

compounds, especially in areas where there are man-eating lions,[1] so that it is no longer an infallible indicator of the hut-owner's rank.

Minor village headmen always allow their superiors to sit on a chair. If village headmen of commensurate status are present, chairs may be sought for them all. But a minor village headman never occupies a chair, even if one is available, in the presence of his superior. At a meeting, for example, a chief occupies a chair and so may his most important *nduna* or councillor. The more important headmen sit alone on separate mats, for a man only shares a mat with his equals, and then only rarely. Junior headmen, however many there are, have to try to squeeze themselves on to one mat or squat on the ground.

Important headmen also have the right of walking in front of their juniors. If there are three or four headmen returning from, say, a court case, they arrange themselves in the pathway in an order which reflects their rank. As they file down the narrow field paths the leader is the most senior among the group. After him come the other headmen and last of all the commoners. This order of precedence is also followed when initiands pass through the tribal initiation ceremonies. The sisters' sons and other matrilineal descendants of important headmen precede those of the less important headmen. At Chiwalo's hut also, I have noticed that the more important headmen sit under the verandah while listening to private cases. The less important headmen sit with the commoners under a shelter or out in the sun.

I have been discussing the visible marks of prestige. But high rank also tends to carry with it some other privileges which are not immediately observable. The most obvious is Government recognition. I have already mentioned that under the 1912 Ordinance, village headmen were recognized by the Administration. These Administrative village headmen, who had certain duties to perform, were paid a small annuity and were in earlier days given a 'book' in which the tax payments could be recorded. To-day, the Yao still describe Government recognition as 'having a book'. Administrative village headmen derived more benefit from Government recognition than merely an

[1] The huts in Plate IX (*a*) and (*b*) are in Namwera area where there are man-eating lions. Most huts have compounds. A large proportion of huts in areas where there are no lions also have compounds.

annuity. This recognition publicly announced their superior status, because not all headmen could be Administrative headmen. We do not know exactly how the Administrative headmen were appointed when the Ordinance was introduced. The observable results, however, are that no headman, as far as I am aware, who was of superior status in the indigenous ranking system, is not an Administrative headman to-day. Being an Administrative headman is then in itself an indicator of rank.

Rather more important than this is the right to hold initiation ceremonies. MacDonald says that these rights were held by the chief only, but it is not clear whether the word ' chief ' used here refers to the village headmen or the ' chief of the land '. Nowadays, the rights are held by village headmen as well as the chief. The right to hold initiation ceremonies is signified by the possession of a small flat basket (*ciselo*) in which the oblational flour for the ceremonies is carried. When a chief grants a *ciselo* or oblational basket to a village headman, what in fact he does is to grant him permission to approach the spirits of his ancestors. The headman uses the basket on three occasions during the initiation ceremonies. First, before the ceremony is announced he pours a little cone of sorghum meal at the root of a special tree in or near the village. This tree is known as the *nsolo*, or the shrine-tree where all offerings to the ancestors are made. While he works the flour through his fingers to allow it to fall in a cone, he calls on his ancestral spirits and asks them to intercede on his behalf with the spirits of the chief's ancestors. He then formally requests permission to hold the initiation ceremony. This cone is left intact through the night. Should it collapse the interpretation is that the spirits are not willing that the ceremony should take place and it is postponed for some days. Offerings are made until eventually the cone, by remaining intact through the night, indicates that all is propitious for the ceremony to be conducted. The second occasion when the oblational basket is used is when the village headman or chief goes down to the grass sheds where the rites of segregation and aggregation take place. Here he pours flour over a twig and begs the safe conduct of the initiands through this physically and mystically dangerous period. Third, each individual initiand, and his or her mother, is touched on the forehead and forearm with the flour on the evening that the initiands leave for the grass sheds. During the last rite the owner of the oblational basket exacts a payment of threepence or so from each parent. The headman does gain financially from the initiation ceremony, but it would be wrong to imagine that this is the only reason why he should want to have the right to hold it. The competition for the rights, which are limited to a few, is part of the general political process whereby village headmen compete for privileges and advantages over their fellows.

Village headmen may hold either the boys' or the girls' initiation ceremonies, or both. Sometimes, when they hold both, they delegate the girls' ceremony to a younger brother or some other relative without referring to the chief. For example, Kawinga's clan relative and important retainer, Ngalawanga, had the rights to both initiation ceremonies, and he allowed his perpetual 'son' Isa [1] to hold the girls'. Also in Nyambi area, Majaja, who had both initiation rights, allowed his perpetual 'son' Nantunga to have the girls' ceremony. It is generally conceded that the right to hold the boys' initiation ceremonies is more valuable than the right to hold the girls'. H. L. Duff, writing in 1906, had also noticed this when he wrote :

The respective ceremonies seem to be considered as on a somewhat different footing, for the boys' *inyago* can properly be held only at the village and under the patronage of, so to say, the paramount chief of the neighbourhood, whereas the girls' initiation may take place under the auspices of an inferior headman. This distinction is still jealously observed and any breach of the chief's privileges is apt to lead to bitter dispute.[2]

The sanction the chief holds over the headmen in this respect is mystical. A village headman believes that the initiation will be a success (that is, that the initiands will be free from the harm of wild beasts and illness, or the circumcision wounds of the boys will heal quickly and well), only if the approval of the chief's ancestors is obtained. He cannot hold the initiation ceremonies, unless he has obtained the basket from the chief.

Most people still follow tribal initiation customs, but in the extremes of the area in which I worked, religious ideas are bringing about a change. In the north in Jalasi's area where Islam

[1] The first Isa was the son of Ngalawanga and this relationship is preserved by the modern incumbents of the headmanships. See Chap. V, p. 122.
[2] Duff, H. L., *Nyasaland under the Foreign Office* (London, 1906), 312.

is most powerful, there is a tendency for the Islamic initiation ceremony for boys, *jandu*, and the Islamic initiation ceremony for girls, *nsondo*, to displace the tribal equivalents, *lupanda* and *ciputu*. These Moslem initiations are conducted by Moslem teachers (*mwalimu*) and are not controlled by the chief. Though it also involves the circumcision of the boys, *jandu* is very much shorter and the boys are secluded for only a week. Some say it is becoming more popular because it is less expensive for the boys' parents. In Chiwalo's area the two ceremonies are run concurrently. The boys and girls go through the normal segregation rites at the beginning of the ceremony, but an *mwalimu* circumcises the boys according to Islamic practice. At the aggregation rites at the end of the period of seclusion, the star and crescent appears as one of the symbols along with the whale (*namungumi*), antelope (*mbalapi*), leopard (*cisuwi*), and the other tribal effigies which are shown to the boys. Christianity in the south has had a similar effect. The Missions actively discouraged initiation ceremonies in the past. Many of the people in Mposa's and Malemia's area have dropped the custom, or have integrated prayers and other parts of Christian ritual into the ceremonies, though circumcision is steadfastly retained. The effect of these changes is that the important ritual control the chief had over the ceremony has been undermined, and so the prestige attached to it has also begun to fade in these areas. What I describe about the prestige of village headmen and the rights they have to initiation ceremonies is only partially true, and is falling away daily. The correlation I seek to establish is also disturbed by the fact that among the Nguru there is a slightly different initiation ceremony (*cidodoto*) for boys. Most Nguru send their boys to the Yao initiations but there are still some who hold their own traditional ceremonies. These are not within the mystical control of the chief so that some Nguru headmen are outside the competition for the initiation rights. I should say, however, that most compete with the Yao for Yao initiation rights so that this factor is not as disturbing as appears at first sight. In addition, village headmen who move into a new area usually must obtain the permission of the chief before they may use the initiation rights they held before coming into the area.

There are other indicators of the general high rank of village headmen. Junior headmen, like commoners, must give a special

Arabic greeting to their seniors. This is done by placing the left hand on the chest and bending slightly forward to the village headman, saying, ' *Subaye* '. The senior should then respond, ' *Alaye* '. Also, important headmen are usually buried in the centre of the village, not in the common graveyard. The tomb of an important headman or personage, usually built of stones, concrete or brick, is called *nsati*. The right to bury in the village must be obtained from the chief ' because the land is his ', and in Kawinga's area a fee of 6s. must be paid to him.

THE STRUGGLE FOR GOVERNMENT RECOGNITION

Thus far, I have been discussing the ways in which the rank of village headmen may be expressed. I now describe the way in which these marks of prestige are associated in the three categories of headmen we have distinguished, and in what way the competition between them is phrased. I have already described how all the chiefs in the areas to which I am referring are all successors of the original leaders of the invasions, and are usually the present Government representatives or Native Authorities.

The people must recognize the rank of chief because mystical beliefs prescribe activities in one direction, and because the limiting structure of the White Administration does so in another. A village headman cannot hold initiation ceremonies without the permission of the chief because of the mystical sanction, but the chief also has legal authority over his subject headmen. He as Native Authority is recognized by the Government and is its representative to his people. The Native Authority Ordinance (1933) specifically imposes penalties on those who do not recognize the authority of the chief. Under Section 12 of the Ordinance, the Native Authority may arrest without warrant any person who is accused of failing to obey his order or direction, interferes with his lawful duties, professes to be a chief or assumes the duties of a chief without Government approval. Under Section 13(*i*) severe penalties are imposed on any person who conspires against or in any way attempts to undermine the lawful power and authority of any chief or Native Authority. His position is therefore greatly strengthened against the village headmen and I have been told of one or two prosecutions by chiefs under this section. Nowadays, the mere threat of action under this Ordinance is sufficient to cow his opponents. Therefore, the chief may also control the rise to power of his headmen because he is a Government official. At the same time a village headman may not move away to form a chieftaincy of his own : should he migrate with his followers nowadays, he will always find himself under a White system of Administration which upholds some other chief against him. The rank system must operate within a circumscribed framework and in reference to the chiefs.

I have already mentioned that being an Administrative village headman is a mark of prestige. Most of the struggle for rank revolves around this axis. Under the 1912 Ordinance, village headmen were only recognized if they had at least 20 taxable huts under them and they were paid a small annuity proportionate to the number of their taxable huts.[1] Before a headman could be recognized, therefore, he had to gather around him at least 20 tax-payers. After a headman had been recognized, the more villagers he could attract the higher his annuity. This situation is one with which the Yao headmen were long familiar. It is indeed the same process that went on before the Whites came, and that was outlined so clearly by Duff MacDonald, except that it is now cast in slightly different form. In consonance with the new money economy, superior status, marked by more dependants, brings a higher financial reward. But it would be false to imagine that the prospect of financial gain is the only spur to a village headman's attempts to enlarge his following. A headman of a large village as such, is still a ' big ' village headman.

A headman who has sufficient followers to enable him to press a claim for a ' book ' goes to the chief for it. The chief considers the merits of the case, but is unwilling to grant too many ' books ' in his area. If he supports the claim the matter is referred to the District Commissioner, who considers the application, not in terms of the indigenous struggle for rank, but in terms of general Administrative considerations, such as finance,

---

[1] A definite rate of remuneration was fixed in 1918 : it was computed at 10s. for every 300 taxes. See Murray, *Handbook*, 142. Under the 1933 Ordinance the remuneration was fixed at 4d. per Government tax of 6s. to a village headman and 2d. per 6s. to a Native Authority. *Report on Native Affairs for the Year Ended 31st December 1933*, Government Printer (Zomba, 1934), p. 5.

and the ease of administering groups with centralized authority. If he agrees, the necessary alteration is made in the tax-registers, and the new Administrative headman is paid his annuity and is called up by the District Commissioner whenever he holds a meeting. To the District Commissioner the chiefdom is made up of the villages on the tax-register, and in a situation of political importance he calls on the headmen of those villages for decisions. For example, when a chief was being installed, the District Commissioner called each Administrative headman forward and asked him whether he agreed to the succession. When the District Commissioner wishes to discuss any matter with a villager he calls forward the Administrative headman. The position of village headmen in the political structure becomes more effective after they have been recognized by Government.

I have no accurate measure of the proportion of all village headmen who are recognized by Government. From my records the percentage of Administrative village headmen out of the total of recognized village headmen is:

	No. Admin. Villages	% of Total recognized
Kawinga	160	84
Liwonde	104	71
Mposa	30	48
Chikweo	48	43
Ngokwe	21	40
Chamba	61	39

I have full records for the smaller chiefdoms, Mposa, Chikweo, Ngokwe and Chamba, but I know for certain that the figures for Kawinga and Liwonde are incomplete. My fullest and most reliable records are for Ngokwe and Chikweo, so that we may estimate roughly that less than half of the village headmen are Administrative village headmen.

Naturally the village headman, whose taxable population will be reduced by the granting of a new 'book', opposes this in the same way as his ancestor opposed the emigration of his village members in pre-White days. In 1947, in Jalasi's area for example, there was an argument hinging on this.

Mlima was a village headman of long standing and had been recognized as an Administrative headman. Ngwaya was a headman who had come to settle under Mlima.[1] After some years Ngwaya felt that because he had his own village he should be given a 'book' and receive money from the Government. Mlima however resisted the claim, saying that his 'book' had been given to him by Jalasi. Both went to Jalasi's court so that the difference could be resolved. Jalasi rejected Ngwaya's claim and upbraided him for being recalcitrant. Ngwaya was fined 9s. and ordered to pay £1 to Mlima in compensation.

A rather more complex case brings out the position of the chief, the Administration and the conflict of the prestige-giving principles of historical primacy and White recognition.

In 1948, an Administrative village headman, Kalonga, from Nyambi's area, decided to migrate down to the more fertile land along the banks of the Shire River. This land was in Jalasi's area, and it was partially occupied by a minor village headman called Malilo. Kalonga had already selected his site for the village when Malilo came up to him and told him that he was the first in that area and that Kalonga should have asked him to indicate a building site. Kalonga, on the other hand, pointed out that he was an Administrative headman and that Malilo was not, and there the matter rested. In time Kalonga, because of his official position, became better known than Malilo. Malilo was jealous of this prestige and in due course went to Jalasi and complained that Kalonga was 'getting too big for his boots'[2] and that he was only a Newcomer into that area. Jalasi sent for Kalonga.

At the dispute in front of the chief, Malilo reiterated his complaint. Kalonga merely pointed out that Malilo was jealous of his 'book'. Jalasi dismissed the case reminding the two headmen that it was he who was chief of the country. Shortly after this, Kalonga went to Jalasi alone and told him that Malilo had told him that he, Jalasi, was no chief because he should have taken the 'book' and given it to Malilo. Jalasi said, 'It is impossible to change over the "books" which are written by the Whites', and then sent a messenger to bring Malilo to court. When he came he denied the tale and said that as far as he knew the only reason for Kalonga's animosity could be that he had refused to give him the *subaye* greeting. Jalasi informed both headmen that they were to be independent of each other. Malilo

---

[1] *Kwakulipatika*—lit. one who had made himself a slave.

[2] *Kulikwesya*—reflexive causative of the verb *kukwela*, to climb, i.e. to cause oneself to climb or to exalt one's status.

was to report strangers coming into his village area independently of Kalonga. Nowadays, there is much tension between the two headmen and they summon each other to court on the slightest pretext. The peace is kept only by order of Jalasi. On the whole, however, it is Kalonga who has the higher status and superior prestige.

Unfortunately I have no figures to show how large a village becomes before its headman applies for Government recognition. The average number of tax-payers under village headmen who have just been granted 'books' might have provided this information, but I was unable to collect it. Formerly, they could become Administrative headmen only if they had more than 20 tax-payers under them. Nowadays, however, owing to differential fertility and the reduction in size of villages because of internal dissension, many of the Administrative villages (22 per cent) are smaller than the 20 tax-payer limit. They, however, retain their 'books'. I know that often within the Administrative villages of important headmen or chiefs, there are contained some minor villages bigger than some Administrative villages which are farther away. For example, in Chiwalo's own Administrative village, I know that the villages of Selemani, Ali Kasoka and Ntapasia are larger than many Administrative villages. It is not only the size of the village which allows a headman to apply for a 'book'. It is his relative status in the community. Men of higher rank than Selemani, Ali Kasoka and Ntapasia could probably approach Chiwalo and ask him for a 'book'. But these three are Newcomers. Selemani was a refugee from the Portuguese wars and went to live in Mlumbe area in Zomba district. He came to Chiwalo's area in about 1930. Ali Kasoka moved in about 1940. Ntapasia came about 1921. But they dare not approach Chiwalo himself to ask for a 'book'. Here Chiwalo's rôle of chief is compounded with his rôle of Administrative village headman so that they would be asking Chiwalo voluntarily to reduce the size of his Administrative village. It is only when their villages become conspicuously large that headmen may begin to force the chief's hand. They have always one sanction they can bring to bear on the chief—they can threaten to move out of his area into another chiefdom. The chief may not retain any of his subjects by force. If they express a wish to live in another chiefdom he cannot stop them. On the other hand, useful as this weapon is when it is used by an Administrative village headman, as I shall illustrate later, it will not serve a minor village headman much to move out of one chiefdom to another if his object is to become recognized as an Administrative village headman. If he goes to another chiefdom he is automatically regarded as one of the most junior of the headmen. If he goes to another chiefdom as an Administrative village headman already, he takes with him his ' book ' and to some extent the rank associated with it.

The size of Administrative villages as measured by the number of tax-payers in them is about equal in all three categories of village headmen. Table X sets out the distribution. The

TABLE X

DISTRIBUTION BY SIZE OF VILLAGES UNDER ABORIGINAL, INVADER AND NEWCOMER ADMINISTRATIVE HEADMEN

Tax-payers	Totals				Percentages			
	Abori-gines*	In-vaders	New-comers†	Total	Abori-gines	In-vaders	New-comers	Total
0–19	6	29	57	92	30·0	21·3	22·0	22·2
20–39	7	49	85	141	35·0	36·0	33·5	34·4
40–59	2	25	57	84	10·0	18·4	22·4	20·5
60–79	3	16	29	48	15·0	11·8	11·4	11·7
80–99	1	1	13	15	5·0	0·7	5·1	3·7
100–119	1	6	4	11	5·0	4·4	1·6	2·7
120–139	—	4	4	8	—	2·9	1·6	2·0
140–159	—	1	1	2	—	0·7	0·4	0·5
160–179	—	1	1	2	—	0·7	0·4	0·5
180–199	—	1	1	2	—	0·7	0·4	0·5
200–249	—	3	—	3	—	2·2	—	0·7
250–300	—	—	3	3	—	—	1·2	0·7
Totals .	20	136	255	411‡	100·0	99·8	100·0	100·1
Mean .	39·0	48·5	45·1	45·9				
S.E. .	8·7	4·2	2·8	2·2				

  * Excludes one village whose size was unknown.
  † Excludes 2 villages whose sizes were unknown.
  ‡ The total excludes an additional 10 villages for which full details were not recorded.

Administrative villages of the Aborigines, mostly Nyanja, appear to be rather smaller than those of the Invaders and Newcomers.

There were only 20 villages in that sample and the difference may not be significant though the distribution is skewed to the smaller villages. The mean number of tax-payers under Invader village headmen was slightly larger than that under Newcomers, but the difference was not significant.[1] Among the Invaders are included the chiefs and *ndunas* who usually have villages of over 100 tax-payers. Smaller villages are less likely to break away from chiefs and *ndunas* than they are from Newcomers and less important men.

Village headmen may exploit their connections with the chief in their competition with their fellows for Government recognition. In Tables XI to XIV inclusive, I have used the material I collected in Mposa, Chamba, Chikweo and Ngokwe areas only, because I know that my survey did not include many headmen in Kawinga and Liwonde areas. The total in these tables includes both Administrative and non-Administrative village headmen. From Table XI it is clear that there is a

TABLE XI

PROPORTION OF ADMINISTRATIVE VILLAGE HEADMEN AMONG ALL VILLAGE
HEADMEN OF THE THREE CATEGORIES IN CHIKWEO, NGOKWE, CHAMBA AND
MPOSA AREAS

Type of Headman	Abori-gines	Invaders	New-comers	Total
Administrative . . .	12	61	78	151
Non-Administrative .	1	37	111	149
Total	13	98	189	300
% Admin. Headmen.	92·3	62·2	41·3	50·2

$$n = 2 ; \quad \chi^2 = 21·34 ; \quad p = 0·00002.$$

significantly greater proportion of headmen of Invader descent than headmen of Newcomer descent who are recognized as Administrative headmen.[2] The percentage of Aborigines who are Administrative headmen is highest of all but it is based on such a small number that not much value can be placed on it.

[1] Diff. of means = 3·4 ; S.E. of diff. = 4·5 ; C.R. = 0·76 ; *p* = 0·4472.
[2] Diff. of per cent = 20·9 ; S.E. of diff. = 6·07 ; C.R. = 3·44 ; *p* = 0·00058.

TABLE XII

PROPORTION OF ADMINISTRATIVE VILLAGE HEADMEN AMONG ALL VILLAGE
HEADMEN WHO ARE RELATED AND NOT RELATED TO THE CHIEF IN CHIKWEO,
NGOKWE, CHAMBA AND MPOSA AREAS

Type of Headman	Relatives		Non-Relatives	Total
	Direct	Clan		
Administrative . . .	39	36	76	151
Non-Administrative .	16	24	109	149
Total	55	60	185	300
% Admin. Headmen.	70·4	60·0	41·1	50·2

$n = 2$; $\chi^2 = 17 \cdot 90$; $p = 0 \cdot 00013$.

Table XII shows that among the chief's direct relatives (i.e. those
who can trace some direct link, matrilineally, patrilaterally or
affinally to the chief) there are more Administrative headmen
than among the relatives who are related only through clan
links. Further, it shows that there are more Administrative headmen among the chief's relatives as a whole than among those
headmen who are not related to him at all.

It seems probable also that village headmen have used their
link to the chiefs through religion to prosecute their claims to
rank. From Table XIII we see that there are more Moslem

TABLE XIII

PROPORTION OF ADMINISTRATIVE HEADMEN AMONG ALL VILLAGE HEADMEN
OF THE SAME RELIGION AS, OR DIFFERENT RELIGION FROM, THAT OF THE CHIEF
(ISLAM) IN CHIKWEO, NGOKWE, CHAMBA AND MPOSA AREAS

Type of Headman	Moslem	Christian	Pagan	Total
Administrative . . .	112	25	10	147
Non-Administrative .	93	31	21	145
Total	205	56	31	292★
% Admin. Headmen.	54·6	44·7	32·2	50·4

$n = 2$; $\chi^2 = 6 \cdot 30$; $p = 0 \cdot 0439$.

★ Excludes 7 village headmen whose religion I did not record.

Administrative headmen than either Christian or Pagan. The chiefs, of course, are all Moslem.

Lastly, the same trend is seen among those headmen who are of the same tribe as the chief, against those who are of other tribes (Table XIV). Here, however, the difference is so small

TABLE XIV

PROPORTION OF ADMINISTRATIVE HEADMEN AMONG ALL VILLAGE HEADMEN OF THE SAME TRIBE AS, OR DIFFERENT TRIBES FROM, THE CHIEF IN CHIKWEO, NGOKWE, CHAMBA AND MPOSA AREAS

Type of Headman	Same Tribe	Different Tribe	Total
Administrative	89	62	151
Non-Administrative	76	73	149
Total	165	135	300
% Administrative Headmen .	53·9	45·9	50·3

$$n = 1 ; \quad \chi^2 = 1·91 ; \quad p = 0·1676.$$

that it may easily have arisen by chance. These factors, how-ever, do not operate independently. There are more co-tribes-men, co-religionists and relatives of the chief among the Invaders than among the other categories. In other words, the factors are all intercorrelated and it is possible to consider any particular factor as the independent variable. From the point of view of the people themselves, to be an Invader is to have one of the best claims on the chief to become an Administrative headman.

THE SIGNIFICANCE OF THE SCARLET HEADBAND

Government recognition therefore provides the means whereby headmen are ranked in two major categories. But Administra-tive village headmen themselves are ranked by a number of prestige-indicating characteristics. The most important of these are the right to wear a plain scarlet headband and the right to hold boys' and girls' initiation ceremonies.

Of these two additional marks of rank the more important is the right to wear the scarlet headband. This headband is wrapped round the head, turban fashion. Most village headmen wear a headband of some sort, either of white or coloured cloth, while most commoners do not. In Kawinga–Liwonde area, village headmen of high rank are entitled to wear a plain scarlet headband (*mlangali*). One informant suggested to me that the plain scarlet stands for blood, i.e. it indicates one of the most important elements in rank to-day—warrior ancestry. I do not know that this opinion is well supported. Among the 424 village headmen I enquired about, 24 or 5·7 per cent were entitled to this mark of honour. Of these, three were Aboriginal Nyanja headmen, 17 were Invaders, and only four were New-comers. Of the four Newcomers, one had the right to hold it before he had come to the area from Portuguese East Africa and that was before the White conquest ; one living in Chamba's area had brought it from Liwonde's area where he had been given the right to wear it ; and the other two were in Chikweo's area and were given the right by the present Chikweo. The three Aborigines who wear the scarlet headbands are Kuzumbu in Kawinga's area, and Mbeta and Mbande in Mposa's area. All three are settled around the shores of Lake Shirwa and they are said to have been the original Nyanja chiefs in this area when the Yao invaded. These chiefs also have boys' and girls' initiation rights. The rank they held in their own tribal communities is recognized by the Yao, who in any case ascribe superior status to the first-comers into an area. With the Nyanja chiefs the position became ambiguous. They had superior rank in that they were in occupation of the land before the Yao moved in. At the same time when they subjugated themselves to the Yao they accepted servility. Nowadays, the Nyanja are well inte-grated into the political life of the area and carry on their exist-ence along the lake shores, still going to their traditional chief for the settlement of most of the cases not involving heavy compensation.

All Invader chieftains have scarlet headbands. Some of their direct relatives such as Stora, their clan relatives such as Nsanama and Mapundu, or their patrilateral relatives such as Cibwana Liwonde, the son of the first Liwonde, also have them. After these the next important group who are entitled to wear them are the *ndunas*. Examples are Kangomba, Masinde and Cin-damba in Kawinga's area and Makaca in Ngokwe area. The *ndunas* are village headmen, usually unrelated to the chief, but who have been long associated with him, and who are his councillors. Long ago they held a most important position within the chiefdom. They were the loyal headmen and intimates of the chief, who could therefore be entrusted with the government of outer areas. They were posted to various parts of the chiefdom; kept the chief advised of war and attacks; maintained the peace among the village headmen in their areas; and collected the ivory to which the chief was entitled and sent it to him. Nowadays, the *ndunas* find themselves in competition with other officials who have arisen from the White Administrative system. The chief also finds advisers and councillors in his court clerks and his court sergeants, but the *ndunas* still have much prestige and advise and assist the chief in his administration of the area. Earlier, I mentioned that a senior headman was allowed to have a mat to himself, and only his own friends and people of his rank could occupy it with him. The only people in the chiefdom who could share the chief's mat, were the *ndunas*, and they called him *anganga* (my friend). Because the *ndunas* were not related to the chief they were in the peculiar position of being able to settle quarrels between the chief and his family: they were the arbitrators in arguments between the chief and his 'younger brothers' (junior male matrilineal relatives), or the chief and his wives. By Yao custom, rank is inherited by a village headman's successor, so that the relationship between the chief and his *ndunas* is perpetuated through successive incumbents. In Kawinga's area, for example, the *ndunas* to-day have the same name and the same relationship and relative position with regard to the chief as the *ndunas* who invaded the country nearly 100 years ago. This traditional ranking of village headmen emerges as soon as the Government alters its policy. Recently, when the idea of group headmen was reintroduced, the chief nominated the *ndunas* to become group headmen—a position not unlike that they held before the White conquest.

There is considerable difference between the size of Administrative villages under those headmen who have the right to wear the scarlet headband and those who have not. Table XV shows this clearly. The mean number of tax-payers under the former headmen is 80, while under the latter it is only 38. Among the village headmen with the right to wear the scarlet headband 70·8 per cent had villages of more than 40 tax-payers, while among other headmen only 41·4 per cent of the villages were in

H

TABLE XV

Size of Administrative Villages under Headmen with Scarlet
Headbands and those without

No. of Tax-payers	Without Scarlet Headband	With Scarlet Headband	Total	% Headmen with S.H.
Under 40	228	7	235	3·0
40–79	125	7	132	5·3
80–119	23	3	26	11·5
120–139	6	2	8	25·0
140 and over . . .	7	5	12	41·7
Total	389	24	413*	5·8

Combining villages of more than 80 tax-payers.

$n = 2$; $\chi^2 = 24·87$; $p < 0·0001$.

* Excludes 1 village in which the number of tax-payers were unknown.

this category.[1] The village headmen who are entitled to wear
the scarlet headband are mainly Invaders and people of high
rank. Their villages are large because of their rank as well as
vice versa.

I have never heard of a village headman's wearing a scarlet
headband without the chief's permission, and I am not sure what
sanctions the chief would apply to prevent it. I have heard men
say that village headmen who are not entitled to wear it do so
if they live far away, but take it off when they come near the
chief's court. However, this was only in casual conversation
and I did not have an opportunity to check it. From the point
of view of the people the right is so bound up with traditional
status that it is almost inconceivable that the custom should be
flouted. As we have seen, among the Newcomers only two
have been given the right within the last 30 years.

Yet the significance of the scarlet headband differs considerably
from area to area. In Malemia and in Jalasi areas the custom
seems either to have fallen away or never to have existed. In
Jalasi area Islam may have some effect. In Malemia area the
majority are Christians and most headmen have taken to

[1] Diff. of per cent = 29·4; S.E. of diff. = 9·61; C.R. = 3·06;
$p = 0·0022$.

European-type clothing. In Nyambi area, abutting on Kawinga–
Liwonde area in the north, there are 12 Administrative village
headmen out of 57 who are entitled to the scarlet headband
(21 per cent). For the Kawinga–Liwonde area the percentage
is 5·7. An informant explained why a large proportion of
headmen in Nyambi area had the right to wear the headband :
' The old Nyambis and the present one do not care. If a man
has many huts, and if he says that his uncle had a scarlet headband,
then he is given one too.' Even within the Kawinga–Liwonde
area there is some variation in the number of headmen who are
entitled to the scarlet headband. The following table sets this out.

Chiefdom	Total Admin. Headmen	% Scarlet Headbands
Kawinga	160	3·7
Liwonde	104	4·8
Mposa	30	10·0
Chikweo	48	8·4
Ngokwe	21	14·2
Chamba	61	4·9

Mposa area near Lake Chirwa shows such a high proportion
because of the Nyanja ex-chiefs who are entitled to the scarlet
headband. Chikweo and Ngokwe on the other hand are the
Mpotola chiefs and seem to have taken the same attitude as
Nyambi and his predecessors. In contrast to the statement about
Nyambi, one Administrative headman in Mposa's area said :
' The chief's scarlet band is good enough for us all. If each
had one it would be too gaudy ! '

THE STRUGGLE FOR INITIATION RIGHTS

Village headmen are generally outside competition for the
right to wear the scarlet headband. These rights have been
established largely by ancient custom and are almost confined to
the Invaders or to those who have had them before they came
into the area. The competition for initiation rights, however,
goes on steadily. H. L. Duff had noticed this as early as 1906.[1]
Newcomers may approach the chief and agitate for the rights,

[1] See p. 81.

pressing their claims on many grounds. They may stress that they have a large village under them and that they have many children to initiate, and argue that their villages are far away from the nearest headman who has these rights. Or they may use their rank and connection with the chief. If all else fails they may threaten to move to another chiefdom. Punyu threatened to do this.

In 1947, Punyu, an Administrative village headman in Chiwalo area, had 43 tax-payers under him and thought that he should have initiation rights. He had come to Chiwalo's in 1933 after the village had split in Chikowi's area near Zomba. He had relatives in Kapaloma's village in Chiwalo's area. He argued with Chiwalo that his uncle had had initiation rights. Chiwalo on the other hand, argued that Punyu village was so close to his own—a matter of under a mile—that he could not consider it. This argument went on for some months. Eventually Punyu told the chief that he was going to leave his area. Chiwalo then recanted to some extent and offered Punyu the permission to use the *ciputu* basket, that is, the right to conduct girls' initiation ceremonies. Punyu, after consulting his sister, took this and was satisfied.

But the chief is not always cowed by the threat to leave his area. He is sometimes able to draw on his official position to control his headmen. The argument between Makata and Ntimbuka illustrates this very well.

Makata was an Administrative headman of some standing in Chiwalo's area. He had been one of the invading headmen and was entitled to wear the scarlet headband. In 1947, he had 101 tax-payers under him and had been given the right to hold boys' and girls' initiation ceremonies at least 30 years ago. Ntimbuka on the other hand was a comparative newcomer. He came from Kawinga's area in about 1930. He is of Nyanja stock but has adopted the Yao language and customs. His village in 1947 had 23 tax-payers and was about 300 yards from Makata's. Early in 1947, Ntimbuka started quarrelling with Makata about the right to boys' initiation ceremonies. He felt that he ought to have rights as well as Makata. Eventually he told Makata that he would refuse to take the boys to his initiation ceremonies. Seething with discontent Ntimbuka went to complain about Makata to Chiwalo, and told him that he had had an argument with Makata and that he was going to leave the area because of it. Chiwalo called Makata and asked him what the trouble was. Makata told Chiwalo that Ntimbuka was jealous of the basket. Chiwalo then told Ntimbuka that he could not give a sacrifice basket to him because his village was so close to Makata's. Ntimbuka was not satisfied with this and continued agitating. Chiwalo, at last exasperated, threatened Ntimbuka that if he had any more trouble he would send him to Kawinga to be dealt with. Kawinga of course is the Native Authority in the area and holds the power of arresting headmen under Section 12 of the Ordinance. Ntimbuka was duly cowed by this threat and meekly agreed to send his boys to Makata's initiation ceremonies.

Chiwalo had to support Makata against Ntimbuka. Makata was a powerful headman : he had rank from his descent and a large village under him. Ntimbuka was a Newcomer and he had only a fifth of the followers that Makata had. If it meant losing followers it was better to lose the smaller village. As it was Chiwalo could use the power of the White Administration to keep Ntimbuka within his area and yet keep him subservient.

A Newcomer is unlikely to be given both boys' and girls' initiation rights. He is more likely to be able to get only one of the rights. Table XVI sets out the number of headmen in

TABLE XVI

Numbers of Headmen holding Boys' and Girls' Initiation Rights among Aboriginal, Invader and Newcomer Headmen

Type of Initiation Right	Aborigines	Invaders	Newcomers	Total
Both boys' and girls' init. rights . .	—	17	14	31
Boys' init. rights only .	1	6	10	17
Girls' init. rights only .	1	12	31	44
No init. rights . . .	16	84	198	298
Total	18	119	253	390*
% Init. holders . .	11·5	29·4	21·7	24·5

Combining Aboriginal and Invader totals.

$n = 3$; $\chi^2 = 6·48$; $p = 0·09254$.

* Total excludes the 24 headmen who have the right to wear the scarlet headband.

each category who hold initiation ceremonies. While more Invaders have the right to both ceremonies the proportion holding only one is roughly the same.[1] A Newcomer may approach the chief and ask for initiation rights in certain circumstances only. In general, these are that his village is a very large one, that he had the rights in the area from which he has just come, and/or that he is living in so isolated a part that it would be a hardship for his children to go to the nearest other headman who holds the rights ; but he may press his claim if he is related to the chief and can approach him as a kinsman.

There is little doubt that the rights are closely associated with the size of the villages :

TABLE XVII*a*

INITIATION RIGHTS AMONG INVADER AND NEWCOMER HEADMEN WHO HAVE VILLAGES WITH MORE AND LESS THAN 60 TAX-PAYERS

(The figures in brackets are percentages)

Type of Init. Right	Over 60		Under 60		Total
	Invader	New-comer	Invader	New-comer	
Both init. rights . .	10 (32·3)	9 (29·0)	7 (22·6)	5 (16·1)	31 (100·0)
Boys' init. rights only .	2 (12·4)	5 (31·3)	4 (25·0)	5 (31·3)	16 (100·0)
Girls' init. rights only .	2 (4·8)	13 (31·0)	10 (23·8)	17 (40·4)	42 (100·0)*
No init. rights	9 (23·2)	26 (9·3)	75 (26·8)	170 (60·7)	280 (100·0)†
Total . .	23 (6·2)	53 (14·4)	96 (26·0)	197 (53·4)	369 (100·0)

$n = 3$ ‡; $\chi^2 = 53·49$; $p < 0·0001$.

* Excludes 1 village whose size was unknown.
† Excludes 2 villages whose sizes were unknown.
‡ Combining Invader and Newcomer groups.

---

[1] Invaders with both initiation rights (17 of 119) = 14·3 per cent ; Newcomers with both initiation rights (14 of 253) = 5·5 per cent ; Diff. of per cent = 8·8 ; S.E. of diff. = 3·07 ; C.R. = 2·85 ; $p = 0·0044$.
Invaders with rights to only one of the initiations (18 of 119) = 15·1 per cent ; Newcomers with rights to only one of the initiations (41 of 253) = 16·2 per cent.

TABLE XVII*b*

INITIATION RIGHTS AMONG INVADER AND NEWCOMER HEADMEN WHO HAVE
VILLAGES WITH MORE AND LESS THAN 60 TAX-PAYERS
(Arranged to hold the influence of village size fixed)

Type of Headman	Over 60		Under 60		Total
	Init.	No Init.	Init.	No Init.	
Invaders . .	14 (11·8)	9 (7·6)	21 (17·6)	75 (63·0)	119 (100·0)
Newcomers .	27 (10·8)	26 (10·4)	27 (10·8)	170 (68·0)	250 (100·0)
Total . .	41 (11·1)	35 (9·5)	48 (13·0)	245 (66·4)	369 (100·0)

$$n = 3 ; \quad \chi^2 = 3·96 ; \quad p = 0·26667.$$

Among all headmen (Table XVII*a*) :

19 of 31 headmen who hold both initiation rights have villages with
more than 60 tax-payers . . . . = 61·3%
7 of 16 headmen who hold only the boys' initiation rights have villages with more than 60 tax-payers . . . . = 43·7%
15 of 42 headmen who hold only the girls' initiation rights have villages of more than 60 tax-payers . . . . . = 35·7%
35 of 280 headmen who hold no initiation rights have villages with
more than 60 tax-payers . . . . . . = 12·5%

When the influence of village-size is held constant the advantages of Invaders over Newcomers in the competition for
initiation rights is discernible, but the differences are so small
that they are of doubtful significance (Table XVII*b*).

14 of 23 Invader headmen with villages over 60 tax-payers have
initiation rights . . . . = 60·9%
27 of 53 non-Invader headmen with villages over 60 tax-payers
have initiation rights . . . . = 50·9%
21 of 96 Invader headmen with villages less than 60 tax-payers have
initiation rights . . . . = 21·9%
27 of 197 non-Invader headmen with villages less than 60 tax-payers
have initiation rights . . . . = 13·7%

As we may anticipate, relationship with the chief is an important factor in the competition for initiation rights. Among
the chief's direct and clan relatives for example, 36·4 per cent
(51 of 140) hold initiation rights, but only 16·8 per cent (39 of

TABLE XVIII

INITIATION RIGHTS AMONGST INVADER AND NEWCOMER HEADMEN WHO ARE
RELATED AND UNRELATED TO THE CHIEF

Type of Initiation Holder	Invader				Newcomer				Total
	D	C	N	T	D	C	N	T	
Both init. rights .	5	8	4	17	2	3	9	14	31
Boys' init. rights only	2	2	2	6	1	1	8	10	16
Girls' init. rights only	5	5	2	12	5	12	14	31	43
No init. rights . .	26	25	33	84	13	25	160	198	282
Total	38	40	41	119	21	41	191	253	372
% Init. holders .	31·6	40·0	24·2	29·4	38·1	39·0	19·4	21·7	24·2

D = Direct relatives; C = Clan relatives; N = Non-relatives; T = Sub-totals.

Combining Invader and Newcomer totals.

$$n = 6; \quad \chi^2 = 22\cdot24; \quad p = 0\cdot00112.$$

232) of his non-relatives hold them [1] (Table XVIII). There is a slightly greater proportion of the clan relatives holding initiation rights than direct kinsmen, but the difference is insignificant.[2] Slightly more of the chief's relatives among the Newcomers hold initiation rights than those among the Invaders,[3] but once again the difference is so small that it might easily have arisen by chance. A much greater proportion of Invaders is related to the chief than of Newcomers,[4] so that among the Invaders the relative advantage of their kinship with the chief, as against the unrelated, is somewhat reduced. There are very many Invaders who can claim kinship with the chief in their struggle for initiation rights. Among the Newcomers, conversely, because there

[1] Diff. of per cent = 19·6; S.E. of diff. = 4·58; C.R. = 4·28; $p = 0\cdot00002$.

[2] Direct relatives (20 of 59) = 33·9 per cent; Clan relatives (31 of 81) = 38·2 per cent; Diff. of per cent = 4·3; S.E. of diff. = 8·2; C.R. = 0·52; $p = 0\cdot6030$.

[3] Newcomers (24 of 62) = 38·7 per cent; Invaders (27 of 78) = 34·6 per cent; Diff. of per cent = 4·1; S.E. of diff. = 8·2; C.R. = 0·5; $p = 0\cdot6170$.

[4] Excluding those entitled to wear the scarlet headband. Invaders (78 of 119) = 65·6 per cent; Newcomers (62 of 253) = 24·5 per cent.

are so few of the chief's kinsmen among them, to be related to the chief is a distinct advantage in this struggle.

I recorded the origin of the initiation rights of only 38 of the 55 Newcomer headmen who hold these, excluding those who also have the right to wear the scarlet headband. Table XIX sets out these data. We cannot put too much reliance on these

TABLE XIX

The Origin of Initiation Rights of Some Newcomer Headmen

Type of Initiation Right	Given by Chief of present residential chieftaincy	Brought from elsewhere	Total	% Brought in
Both init. rights . .	8	5	13	38
Boys' init. rights only .	9	0	9	0
Girls' init. rights only .	15	1	16	6
Total	32	6	38	16

figures because they cover only about three-quarters of the village headmen in this category, and these, moreover, were not randomly selected. As they stand, the figures support my earlier conclusion that Newcomers are more likely to obtain rights for only one initiation ceremony, than for both together. While 38·5 per cent (5 of 13) of the village headmen who hold both initiation ceremonies had brought in their rights with them from outside, only 4·0 per cent (1 of 25) of those who hold only one of the rights had done so.[1] An analysis of the periods when headmen were given their rights reveals consistent results.

From Table XX we see that :

Of 11 Invaders who hold rights to both initiation ceremonies, recent chiefs granted 3 . . . . = 27·3%
Of 8 Newcomers who hold rights to both initiation ceremonies, recent chiefs granted 2 . . . . = 25·0%
Of 12 Invaders who hold rights to only one of the initiation ceremonies, recent chiefs granted 3 . . . . . = 25·0%
Of 24 Newcomers who hold rights to only one of the initiation ceremonies, recent chiefs granted 14 . . . . = 58·3%

---

[1] Diff. of per cent = 34·5 ; S.E. of diff. = 12·47 ; C.R. = 2·77 ; p = 0·0056.

TABLE XX

WHEN INITIATION RIGHTS WERE GRANTED TO NEWCOMERS AND INVADERS

Type of Initiation Right	By early Chiefs		By recent Chiefs*		Total
	Invaders	Newcomers	Invaders	Newcomers	
Both init. . .	8	6	3	2	19
One init. only .	9	10	3	14	36
Total . . .	17	16	6	16	55

* This is obviously a crude classification. I have taken roughly 35 years as the dividing line. As the early chiefs I have classified all the Kawingas before and including Kawinga V who died in 1913 ; all the Liwondes before and including Liwonde III who died in 1921 ; all the Ngokwes before and including Ngokwe IV who died in 1905 ; all the Mposas before and including Mposa II who died in 1913 ; and all the Chikweos before and including Chikweo II who died in 1914.

In other words, recent chiefs have been granting single initiation rights to Invaders in the same proportion as they have been granting both rights, but they have been granting Newcomer headmen the right to hold only one ceremony more often than the right to hold both. Of the six sets of rights to initiation ceremonies granted by recent chiefs to Invader headmen, three were rights to hold only one ceremony, while 14 of the 16 initiation rights granted to Newcomer headmen were for one ceremony only.[1]

Headmen do not make use of their bonds of common religion or tribe with the chief in their competition for initiation rights. Table XXI sets out the numbers of headmen of different religion. There is a substantially smaller proportion of Pagan headmen (9.7 per cent) holding initiation ceremonies than either Christians (25.9 per cent) or Moslems (24.6 per cent).[2] Most Pagans, however, are also Newcomers so that this difference is actually a reflex of the generally lower rank of Newcomers. Table XXII sets out the number of headmen of the chief's tribe and of other

[1] i.e. 50.0 per cent against 87.5 per cent ; diff. of per cent = 37.5 ; S.E. of diff. = 20.08 ; C.R. = 1.87 ; $p = 0.0614$.

[2] Pagans = 9.7 per cent ; Others 24.8 per cent ; diff. of per cent = 15.1; S.E. of diff. = 7.94 ; C.R. = 1.90 ; $p = 0.0574$.

TABLE XXI

THE DISTRIBUTION OF INITIATION RIGHTS AMONG HEADMEN OF DIFFERENT
RELIGIONS

Type of Initiation Holder	Moslem	Christian	Pagan	Total
Both init. rights . .	25	4	1	30*
Boys' init. rights only .	12	4	—	16
Girls' init. rights only .	32	6	2	40†
No init. rights . . .	212	40	28	280‡
Total	281	54	31	366

$$n = 6; \quad \chi^2 = 5\cdot12; \quad p = 0\cdot52934.$$

* Excludes 1 headman whose religion was unrecorded.
† Excludes 3 headmen whose religion was unrecorded.
‡ Excludes 2 headmen whose religion was unrecorded.

TABLE XXII

THE DISTRIBUTION OF INITIATION RIGHTS AMONG HEADMEN OF THE SAME
AND DIFFERENT TRIBE AS THE CHIEF

Type of Initiation Holder	Same Tribe	Different Tribe	Total
Both init. holders	20	11	31
Boys' init. holders only . . .	7	9	16
Girls' init. holders only . . .	23	20	43
No init. rights	157	125	282
Total	207	165	372
% Init. holders	24·2	24·2	24·2

$$n = 3; \quad \chi^2 = 1\cdot99; \quad p = 0\cdot57470.$$

tribes who hold initiation rights. Once again the proportion of
headmen of the same tribe as the chief who hold initiation rights
is the same as that of headmen of different tribes from the chief.
We may say, therefore, that membership of tribe is not an opera-
tive factor in the granting of initiation rights.[1]

[1] The factors contributing to the granting of initiation rights are obviously
all intercorrelated. Some aspects of this are examined in Appendix E.

For the purposes of analysis thus far I have treated the holding of rights to initiation ceremonies separately from the right to wear the scarlet headband. But the right to hold either boys' or girls' initiation ceremonies, or both together, may be held concurrently with the right to wear a scarlet headband. By common consensus the right to wear a scarlet headband denotes highest prestige and the right to hold a boys' initiation ceremony more prestige than the right to hold a girls' initiation ceremony. In the light of this knowledge we are able to rank village headmen according to the particular combination of symbols of prestige they possess. A headman, for example, who has the right to

TABLE XXIII

MARKS OF RANK AMONG ADMINISTRATIVE VILLAGE HEADMEN

Type of Headman	With Headband				Without Headband				Total
	Both	Boys only	Girls only	No rights	Both	Boys only	Girls only	No rights	
Aborigines :									
Direct rel.	—	—	—	—	—	—	—	2	2
Clan rel.	1	—	—	—	—	—	—	1	2
No rel. .	2	—	—	—	—	1	1	13	17
Total .	3	—	—	—	—	1	1	16	21
Invaders :									
Direct rel.	8	1	—	—	5	2	5	26	47
Clan rel.	4	—	—	—	8	2	5	25	44
No rel. .	3	—	—	1	4	2	2	33	45
Total .	15	1	—	1	17	6	12	84	136
Newcomers :									
Direct rel.	—	—	—	—	2	1	5	13	21
Clan rel.	—	1	1	—	3	1	12	25	43
No rel. .	1	—	—	1	9	8	14	160	193
Total .	1	1	1	1	14	10	31	198	257
Grand total	19	2	1	2	31	17	44	298	414

wear a scarlet headband and also the right to hold a boys' initiation right ranks more highly than a headman who has the right to wear a scarlet headband and who also has the right to hold a girls' initiation ceremony. We may give each of these prestige ranks an arbitrary score to enable us to compare the general prestige ratings of various categories of headmen with one another.

These rankings would be:

The right to wear a scarlet headband and to hold both initiation ceremonies 1
The right to wear a scarlet headband and the right to hold a boys' initiation ceremony 2
The right to wear a scarlet headband and the right to hold a girls' initiation ceremony 3
The right to wear a scarlet headband only 4
The right to hold both boys' and girls' initiation ceremonies . . 5
The right to hold a boys' initiation ceremony only 6
The right to hold a girls' initiation ceremony only 7
No rights of these kinds 8

TABLE XXIV

RANK SCORES FOR ADMINISTRATIVE VILLAGE HEADMEN OF DIFFERENT
CATEGORIES

Aborigines :		
Chief's direct relatives	8·00	
Chief's clan relatives	4·50	
Chief's non-relatives	7·00	
All Aborigines		6·86
Invaders :		
Chief's direct relatives	6·17	
Chief's clan relatives	6·61	
Chief's non-relatives	7·04	
All Invader headmen		6·60
Newcomers :		
Chief's direct relatives	7·38	
Chief's clan relatives	7·21	
Chief's non-relatives	7·65	
All Newcomer headmen		7·55
All chief's direct relatives		6·58
All chief's clan relatives		6·85
All chief's non-relatives		7·50

For purposes of comparing the social standing of different categories of headmen with one another we may compute the mean rank score of the headmen in any one category as a whole. The mean rank score of all Administrative Village headmen therefore from Table XXIII would be :

$$(19 \times 1) + (2 \times 2) + (1 \times 3) + (2 \times 4) + (31 \times 5) + (17 \times 6) + (44 \times 7) + (298 \times 8)/414. = 2983/414$$
$$= 7 \cdot 21.$$

Low values of this mean rank scores indicate high prestige rankings.

Using this method I have set out in Table XXIV the rank scores for headmen in the categories in Table XXIII. Table XXIV shows that on the whole the ranking amongst the Invader

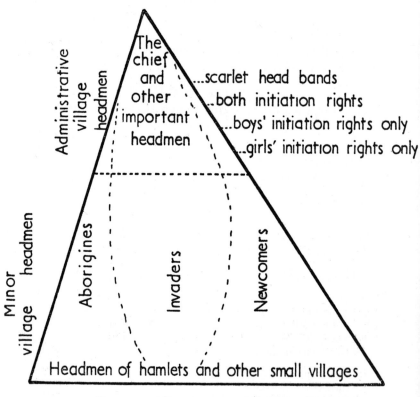

DIAGRAM 2. PARADIGM OF THE POLITICAL STRUCTURE.

headmen is higher than among the Aborigines or the New-comers. It also shows quite clearly that the chief's direct relatives hold more of the privileges associated with rank than his clan relatives do, and they in turn hold more than his non-relatives.

THE POLITICAL PROCESS AS A STRUGGLE OF HEADMEN AGAINST THE CHIEF

Modern chiefdoms appear to be organized on essentially the same principles as those described by Duff MacDonald. A chiefdom is headed by a chief and under him his subjects are organized in villages. Each village is represented by a head-man, who stands in a relationship to the chief and to other village headmen, according to the prestige of the group he represents. This prestige is determined partly by his historical association with the chief in his past military exploits, partly by the size of his village, and partly by the prestige he has had in other areas. These elements were significant in Yao polity before the advent of the Whites, as we have seen from Duff MacDonald's description. Village headmen then were continu-ally involved in a struggle for power among themselves and against the chief.[1] The struggle for power among village head-men continues to-day though in a changed context. Military power is no longer the object of the competition between them : the struggle for followers has become transmuted into a struggle for tax-payers. In harmony with the new political and econ-omic situation a successful headman is not rewarded by military superiority, but by Government recognition and an official emolument.

At the same time, the chief whose power in the pre-White days resided in his armed forces, nowadays draws on the power of the White Administration to exercise his authority over his village headmen. His position is strengthened by Government decree and he does not hesitate to threaten to use it if necessary. Although the prestige of chiefs is higher than that of any of the village headmen, the difference in prestige between any chief and his most important headman is not very great. They are treated with almost the same deference by the minor village headmen and commoners, and they are referred to by the same term (*mwenye* = chief). The chief or an important village headman

[1] See Chap. II, p. 34.

is usually addressed by a kinship term, either *baba* (father) or *ambuje* (master or grandparent). When he is referred to, his name is not used. Village headmen are owners or wardens of villages (*asyene misi*) but only those headmen of some standing are referred to as *mwenye*.

Important village headmen, like the chief, are in mystical danger from pollution by death. They cannot come to the hut in which a corpse is lying ; and they cannot eat the chicken which has been brought to them by relatives of the deceased to announce the death. Like the chief too, an important headman may be buried in a tomb in his village and not in the graveyard.

But an important element in their relationship nowadays is that the Administration will support the chief against a village headman when it comes to a trial of strength, and that a headman these days is precluded by modern conditions from setting up chiefdoms as he did in the old days. Village headmen therefore must struggle for power against their fellows and the chief within the modern Administrative framework. Some attempts are made to resist the power of the chief but these are rarely successful. The dispute between Liwonde and Ndenda illustrates this.

Ndenda was an Nguru headman, who in 1947 had 284 tax-payers under him (Liwonde, the chief, had 186 in his village). Ndenda had come into Liwonde's area before the White invasion and had surrendered with his relative Mlelemba, to Liwonde. The second Liwonde had given him both initiation rights but, unlike his relative, he did not have the right to wear a scarlet headband.

In 1938 or thereabouts, Liwonde decided to move his village site from the Shire River to its present site about half-way up the Great Rift scarp. He sent two of his young men to look for a suitable site, and to plant some mango trees there when they had found one. Ndenda heard of this and sent one of his men to take Liwonde's men into custody. He took their hoes away and then told them to go back to tell the chief they were planting in his (Ndenda's) land. In due course Liwonde moved up to his new site, and asked Ndenda why he had taken the hoes away and whether he owned the country, i.e. was the chief. Ndenda now argued that Mlelemba's ancestors had been given the rights of chieftainship over this area and that the first Mlelemba in the area had given Liwonde some elephant tusks for these rights. Liwonde replied that the chief has a right to tusks and that many had given tusks to him but were not entitled for that reason to rights of chieftainship. Liwonde handled this situation by calling a meeting of the village headmen in the area. They assembled and the claims of Ndenda were debated. The headmen supported Liwonde in his claim that the tusks were part of the chief's rights and that when Mlelemba had come he had come ' to get fire from the chief'. Liwonde then upbraided Ndenda for imagining that because he had so many followers he was a chief, and fined him 10s. for being insolent.

The struggle between Liwonde and Ndenda did not end however. Some years afterwards a man came to Liwonde and said that he wanted to live in his area. This man was a complete stranger and had no relatives there. Liwonde sent him to Ndenda's village. Later while living in the village, this man stole some cloth. He was arrested and Ndenda brought him to the chief saying that the chief was responsible for him. Liwonde told Ndenda that he was being insolent again and that the responsibility must rest with him because the man had married into his village. He ordered Ndenda to pay £1 to compensate the victims of the theft. This Ndenda did but in his view this was tantamount to being chased out of the chief's area. He therefore moved with his children across the boundary northwards into Jalasi's area, and told his unrelated villagers to follow him. They refused to leave Liwonde's area. He was helpless and could do nothing about it. He returned to Liwonde's area a broken man and died shortly afterwards. His eldest son took charge of the village affairs, but so far no successor has been found.

The struggle between Ndenda and Liwonde has some interesting features about it. The strength of the chief in his Government position is not as evident as it has been in other struggles, as, for example, between Jalasi and Kalonga, or between Chiwalo and Ntimbuka, in the cases I cited earlier.[1] It appears only indirectly. Ndenda did not appeal to the District Commissioner against the fine as he might have done if he had felt his position to be more secure. The case history also shows how Liwonde ranged his other important headmen, 47 per cent of whom were kinsmen or co-Invaders, around him against Ndenda who was neither. It shows also that Ndenda's reaction to what he felt to be an injustice, typically enough, was to emigrate and to try to injure the chief by reducing his followers. When this failed he was defeated and it was his downfall, for, like a chief, ' a headman without people is nothing '.[2]

[1] Pp. 86 and 96.

[2] *Mcilambo naga naganakola ŵandu ngawa mcilambo* : ' A chief who has no people is not a chief '—a saying frequently quoted to emphasize the dependence of the chief on his subjects.

I

CHAPTER V

THE VILLAGE HEADMAN

VILLAGES AS DISCRETE UNITS

THE village headman is a key personality in Yao social structure. Viewed as an organization of villages, the social structure may be described in terms of the positioning of village headmen in relation to each other and to the chief. But the village headman is a representative of a corporate group, the village. The position he occupies in the structure as a whole, the rôle he plays in his interaction with other village headmen and the chief, and the prestige that he has in the community as a whole, are all derived from the village of which he is the representative, and in particular from the history of the dominant matrilineage of that village.

I am now considering, of course, all village headmen, however small their villages are, and not only the Administrative village headmen, as in the previous chapter. Each group which sets up a village recognizes one man as the 'owner' or warden of the village (*asyene musi*). The word '*musi*' (pl. *misi*) in Yao, refers primarily to the physical concentration of huts, but it is impossible for the people to separate in their minds the dwellings in a village from the people who inhabit them. In Yao, a deserted village is no longer 'a village'. It is called instead *lisame* (pl. *masame*),[1] a word which refers now not to the village as a unit, but to the collection of deserted and individual huts. The word *musi* or its diminutive form *kamusi* may be applied to a cluster of only four or five huts, or at the other extreme it may be applied to a large concentration of more than 500 huts.[2] The essential point is that the cluster of huts is occupied by a group of kinsmen who are independent of their neighbours. For example, a stranger may see a cluster of huts and ask, 'Whose village is that?' The reply may be, 'That is no village, they are only homesteads.'[3]

---

[1] From the verb *kusama*—to migrate.

[2] Large complex villages may also be called *msinda*.

[3] *Maŵasa* (sing. *liŵasa*), which I have translated as 'homesteads', strictly speaking refers to the households set up by married men.

Further enquiries may reveal that this is only a section of a larger village, possibly a hundred or more yards away.

The boundaries of a village may not always be clear. Clusters of huts which are part of one village may be physically nearer another, but in the minds of the Yao, who see not only the huts but also the social relationships of the people occupying them, there is no confusion at all. As a general rule the villages are fairly compact and clearly demarcated from others, and even strangers have no difficulty in recognizing the autonomy of the group which is expressed in many different ways. MacDonald recorded that formerly a headman performed a certain amount of ritual which symbolized the unity of the village.[1] Much of this has fallen away, but the unity remains.

The ritual surrounding the foundation of a new village bears testimony to its persisting political significance. In this ritual the unity of the group, against other similar groups, including the village from which it has sprung, is expressed. On first arrival at a new village site the men build grass sheds, beginning with that of the headman. That night the headman pours a cone of sacred flour at the root of a tree on the site, and asks the spirits of his ancestors whether the site is propitious. Early next morning he examines the cone to see the answer. If a side of the cone has collapsed it does not augur well and another site is selected. If the cone is still whole it is taken that the spirits acquiesce, and permanent huts can be started. The headman then goes into the bush to find medicines [2] which he mixes with groundbeans. That night, with the medicated groundbeans in the hut, the headman has intercourse with his wife. In the morning those who are not sexually active come to the headman's grass shed to drink some water in which the medicine has been steeped and eat some of the medicated beans with a little porridge, which the headman's wife has prepared from the sacred flour. This medicine is called 'the medicine to strengthen the village' (*mtera wakulimbika musi*). Until then all members of the village should have been continent but after this sexual relationships may be resumed. The object of the medicine is to prevent those

[1] See pp. 31-2.
[2] *Nkulungutu* and *nkuta*, two plants commonly used for protection against *ndaka*. See f.n., p. 112.

who are sexually inactive from contracting *ndaka*.[1]　At the same time the headman gives each household a piece of the fire which has been newly kindled in the traditional way by rubbing two sticks together.

The mystical danger inherent in the act of setting up a new village is well brought out in the propitiatory prayer and the abstinence from sexual intercourse.　Once again it is the village headman who must make the offering to his ancestors ; and it is the village headman who has intercourse with his wife so that the effluvium from his sexual activity may permeate the medicine in the hut and so protect the villagers from *ndaka*.　Lastly, it is very important that the whole village cooks and is warmed by one fire.　' We are of one fire ' expresses the common origin of two villages ; though in fact every time a new village is founded a new fire should be kindled.　To bring fire from the village of origin is to bring sorcery, since the Yao believe that sorcery can operate between persons closely linked by kinship only.　To have one's own fire is to be autonomous from other groups.

THE BURDENS AND REWARDS OF HEADMANSHIP

MacDonald had the perspicuity to see not only that the village headman was the representative of a corporate group and that he represented this group to outsiders, but also that he represented external authority to his villagers.　The village headman who in his person stood for the unity of the group, performed certain ritual acts which emphasized this, such as praying to the village ancestors.　In spite of the decline of the ritual his position is still regarded as exceptional.　Much, however, depends on the rank of the village headman.　There may not be much difference in ritual observances and mystical dangers between a headman who has in his charge a meagre three or four huts, and a commoner.　In the larger and more important

---

[1] This is one of the most important mystical concepts of the Yao.　I have described this condition and its implications more fully in *Marriage among the Machinga Yao of Southern Nyasaland* (R.-L.I. Paper), forthcoming.　Briefly it is a disease characterized by œdema which affects those who are sexually inactive when they are suddenly brought into contact with a person, or an object which he has touched, after having intercourse.　The people most affected are the young and the old, i.e. those who cannot have sexual intercourse.　Those who are capable of intercourse are expected to have ritual intercourse with a stranger, and so fortify themselves against this dread disease.

villages, however, the headman's activities may be as circumscribed by ritual prohibitions as the chief's are.

The village headman is subject not only to mystical dangers but also to other dangers deriving from his position of authority. It is significant that villagers never go to a diviner to find out the cause of a village headman's death. When I asked informants why this was so, they said, ' Well, what's the use of it ? He has enemies on all sides in the village who are trying to kill him with their magic.' In harmony with this view of village headmanship, the symbolic object which represents the village headman in the diviners' gourds I have seen, is a small ring of grass (*singwa*), a copy of the grass cushion women place on their heads when they are carrying loads. This symbolizes the ring of enemies which surrounds the village headman. The saying ' the tortoise defecates on the one who carries it ',[1] usually applied to chieftainship, applies equally well to a village headman.

A village headman may expect little material benefit from his position of authority. If he is an Administrative village headman he may be paid a small annuity of 5s. or 10s.[2] Returning labour migrants may give him a blanket or a military overcoat, or perhaps a few shillings, but this is not usual. If he is not a strict Moslem he will almost certainly be given a pot of beer from every brewing made for sale in the local ' club house '. On the other hand, if an important stranger, particularly a White official, arrives in the village he feels he must give his guest a chicken. It is mannerly to reciprocate with another gift, but not all Whites know this, or, if they do, do not observe it. In particular if the chief comes to his village, he will be expected to entertain him and here can expect no recompense—the chief ' eats from his country '.

The Yao know that the position of headman is no sinecure. Frequently the one chosen to succeed refuses to accept the position, especially if he is well placed in employment. It is significant that the word for an heir is *litegwa* [3]—the one who is trapped. An

---

[1] *Ngoŋo jikunyela msyene iwajigele.*

[2] Until recently this was true. As I was leaving the field in 1949, I heard that the Administration had decided to abandon this system in favour of one in which only group headmen would be remunerated.

[3] Substantive form of the passive of the verb *kutega*—to set a trap as for animals. This word is not widely known, especially among the younger Yao.

heir has to balance up the difficulties inherent in his position of leadership, including his fear of sorcery, with its honour and rank.

Commoners respect village headmen in the same way as minor headmen respect their superiors. Headmen of important villages are given a special greeting by the commoners ; they usually wear a distinguishing headdress ; they sit on a mat alone or on a chair, while the commoners sit on the floor ; they walk in front of commoners on the road ; they sit under the chief's verandah while the commoners sit in the sun ; and they are buried in the village, while the unimportant commoners are buried in the graveyard.

Outside their villages too they are accorded deference. It is not only their own villagers who must treat them in this way : all commoners must do so. They are accepted by the chief as important men and are treated as such.

The Headman's Installation Ceremony

The peculiar position of the village headman is brought out particularly in the installation ceremonies. When a headman dies his heir should not assume the name until he has been formally installed. This is expressed as 'to enter the name' (*kwinjila lina*). All installation ceremonies are similar and there are only minor variations from one ceremony to another. The following is a description of a succession ceremony recounted to me by an informant. It concerns the succession to headmanship of Cimombo, a headman of some rank in Nyambi's area. Cimombo had a village of 30 tax-payers, wore a scarlet headband, and had the right to hold a girls' but not a boys' initiation ceremony.

Some time had passed since the death of Cimombo, and his heir, though commonly known by that name, had not been officially installed. Eventually he grew impatient and went to his perpetual [1] elder brother Kaukutu of Nyambi's area, who also wore a scarlet headband, and told him that he was going to Cholo to find work. Kaukutu told him that he might visit the men at Cholo but he himself must not enter employment there. The heir left for Cholo. As soon as he had gone Kaukutu collected his relatives and discussed the succession. They decided to get

---

[1] The relationship between some personalities in the social structure, originally kinsmen, becomes fixed and is perpetuated by their successors. See p. 122.

PLATE V

Village headman, Nyenje, at his installation ceremony. He is not entitled to wear a scarlet headband but wears a coloured one instead. On his right sits his sister, on his left his wives, adopting the posture correct for an initiand—head bowed, eyes downcast, hands in the lap. A villager is dropping a penny into the cloth at the headman's feet while the head-man's representative collects the pennies.

(July 1947)

Nyambi's formal permission to install the heir as Cimombo. Nyambi told them to start preparing malt for the ' beer of succession ' and to tell him when it was ready. Kaukutu then sent a man to Cholo on a bicycle to call Cimombo back to the village. One Tuesday, the day after Cimombo returned, Kaukutu reported to Nyambi, who told him to tell the women to prepare the beer, since the installation ceremony would take place on Saturday. Nyambi sent his perpetual sons Makoka and Ncimba to officiate on his behalf. These two men were important village headmen, Makoka having the right to wear a scarlet headband though Ncimba had not.

On Thursday, Makoka and Ncimbo came to a place about three miles from the village. They had four women with them, one of whom carried a sacred basket (*ciselo cambepesi*). Ncimbo sent a message to Kaukutu to say that they were waiting, and he told the heir that he was wanted along the road where a meeting was being held. When the women saw Kaukutu and the heir coming to the place where Makoka and Ncimbo were waiting, they ran to hide in the bush. The heir sat down under a mango tree and Makoka went up to him and begged for some snuff. Before he had time to take the snuff bottle out of his pocket, the women came out of the bush, Makoka got up and struck the heir on the forehead with his fist, knocking him to the ground, took some flour from the sacrifice basket and sprinkled it on the heir, shouting, ' This is Cimombo—he is risen from the dead ! ' [1] They put him in a hammock and carried him back to his hut in the village amidst wild exultation. They put him on his bed and made him stay there. Later, Mkoka and Ncimbo came in and started to deliver a series of homilies on his position as village headman.[2] They pointed out that from that day he was a chief (*mwenye*), a headman who had the right to wear a scarlet headband (*acimweni ŵambendera*). Thenceforth, he was not to go to funerals, or at least not into the hut in which a corpse was lying. If his child were to die while he was in the hut he must not move until other people had come in. It was only when a headman of similar rank died that he might go into the hut. They advised him particularly that he would have to look after his village and told him that he should

[1] *Ce Cimombo aŵoŵo—ajimwice kuŵaŵe.*
[2] *Kuunda misyungu*—to teach the customs.

neglect neither his sorority-group nor the husbands in his village,[1] that his sorority-group and his village were his garden and he must take care of the young plants in it. The husbands were the watchmen who look after the women in the village. A headman dare not take sides or be unfair, nor must he talk behind people's backs. He must take care to settle differences amicably by discussion at meetings. They advised him not to pay too much attention to his wives who may have quarrelled with his sisters and tell him that they have been insulting him. When he hears a report like that he may be unfair to his sisters and people will say that he has broken his village through listening to nonsense. This sort of instruction went on through the night.

On Friday when the beer was brewed, Mlamba and Mbalwe, both headmen and perpetual sons of Nyambi, came to the village and told the men to build a small grass shed for the successor to sit in. This the men did, and the women were told to plaster it and clean the huts out for the strangers who would be coming to the ceremony. On Saturday morning before cockcrow, Makoka and Ncimba got up and told the women to cook a big pot of porridge because they were taking Cimombo to bathe and when they returned they would want to find porridge ready. Makoka took some medicine called *mkulumo* in a bark container (*likungwa*) into the toilet enclosure. He put the medicine into two jars of water and told Cimombo to wash himself in it daily as he was an important headman, and it would strengthen his body.[2] After Cimombo had washed he went back into the hut where a mat was spread on the floor and on it were a dish of porridge and three dishes of relish. Makoka and Ncimbo told him to take a little porridge, dip it into one of the relishes—whichever he chose—and eat it. Cimombo did so. They did not tell him that one of the dishes contained human flesh.[3] When he tried the dish of human flesh he vomited and all the villagers cried with joy, saying that he was a good chief because he had

---

[1] *Mbumba jao ni akamwini wao*—the meaning and significance of this in the village context is explained on p. 183.

[2] This is a euphemism for protective medicine against sorcery.

[3] The immediate question is : Where did the human flesh come from ? No informant could tell me and I am inclined to believe that one of the dishes is 'ritually' made into human flesh for this ceremony. This special ceremony was always spoken about as if it were secret, especially from White people.

vomited human flesh.[1] They said that they had a strong headman and that they could trust him ; he was a good headman
without witchcraft. If he had been a sorcerer they would have
kept scolding him until the next morning.

About two hours after sunrise the people gathered and started
dancing. At about this time Cimombo was brought out of the
hut and put in the grass shed which had been built for the occasion.
This was the climax of the ceremony.[2] He sat on a chair in the
grass shed with one of his two wives on either side. Makoka
then started a chant, exhorting the visitors to come to throw
pennies at Cimombo's feet. Some of the people there made
speeches about the type of behaviour they would expect from
him. Then Nyambi arrived from the court village in a ricksha.
When the noise had subsided he told the people that if they
disobeyed Cimombo it meant that they disobeyed the chief.
He emphasized the importance of the rank of the new headman.
After the speech he presented 12s. to Cimombo which was
received on his behalf by Ncimbo. Nyambi then left and the
ceremony was over, but the people remained to dance and drink
beer.

This description of the procedure following the ' coming out
of the hut ' is somewhat sketchy. The interaction of the headman and his villagers on this formal and ceremonial occasion is
of great interest and importance. During the entire ceremony
the headman adopts the pose which is appropriate for any Yao
initiand. His hands are on his lap or on the arms of the chair
and his head is bowed forward with eyes downcast. He neither
speaks nor moves. His attendants, when necessary, wipe the
sweat off his face or chase away the flies. The other occupants
of the mat, who may be his wives, and sometimes his heir, adopt
similar postures. In contrast to this, is the behaviour of the
villagers who run about shouting wildly, the men discharging
muzzle-loading guns, and women ululating in the typical Central
African way.

Before the new headman comes out of the hut his mentors

---

[1] This is a test based on the witchlore of the Yao, who believe that sorcerers
kill relatives with magic and then share out the flesh of their victims with fellow
sorcerers in ghoulish feasts.

[2] Called the ' coming out from the hut ' (kukupoka nyumba). It is of course
the first public appearance of the headman in his newly assumed status.

impress on him the difficulty of his position, and when he is
taken outside some of this is repeated in public. At Nkacelenga's
installation ceremony in December 1946, which I attended, the
following incidents took place. Shortly after he was taken out
of the hut, Cigunda, one of the officiating headmen, said:
'Younger brothers of Nkacelenga, are you happy that Kambiri [1]
has an elder brother? You women, have you cooked beer so
that you can have your village headman?' In reply the men and
women clapped their hands and a few came forward to throw
some coppers into a cloth at Nkacelenga's feet. Cigunda went
on to say, 'From to-day no woman will be impudent to the chief,
because you are all of the same womb. All you men listen, only
this man is your village headman!' Cigunda now turned to
Nkacelenga who did not change his posture in the least. 'You
village headman Nkacelenga, don't listen to what your wife says,
because she will fight with your sisters and tell you that they have
been cursing you. You should make enquiries when you have
heard these things because you are a big man [i.e. important
headman]. From to-day onwards you are a big man. Every
person will be trying to spoil your name by saying that you are a
bad man. You need to be patient and easy-going.' Turning
to the public, Cigunda said, 'Even you husbands [*akamwini*] do
not listen to what your wives say if they try to traduce the village
headman, because some husbands can break the village.' Thereupon one husband got up feeling around for a penny, found he
did not have one, and with much ostentation borrowed one from
a fellow-husband sitting next to him. He then came forward to
where Nkacelenga was sitting and said, 'You say some husbands
can break a village. Is that true? But husbands build the
villages? They can't break the villages.' Then very deliber-
ately he threw the penny into the cloth at the headman's feet and
went back to his seat. His speech was greeted with acclamation
from the husbands. Cigunda said nothing after that and the
ceremony was over.

In September 1948, during the installation ceremony of Mapata,
one of Kawinga's less important headmen in the northern
part of his area, the significance of the relationship of the headman to his relatives for the continuation of the village as a
whole, was brought out more clearly. After the headman was

[1] A perpetual brother of Nkacelenga.

brought out of the hut, as always, songs were sung and speeches were made. One of the songs was : ' A tree when it grows, grows with its branches.'[1] This is a reference to the dependence of the village headman upon the increase of his relatives for an increase in his rank. The Yao compare kinship with a tree, the component segments of the maximal lineage (the tree) being the branches. Then one of the officiating headmen mentioned that there were many sisters' sons of the old Mapata but that Kawinga and Chiwalo had selected the one on the chair to be the headman. He then exhorted the others neither to be jealous nor to resort to sorcery, but to exalt the name [2] that it might live long. This was followed by a song which introduced a second theme, ' A husband however rich he becomes here, cannot climb high.'[3] This song emphasizes that the uxorilocal husbands of the village can never achieve rank outside their own matrilineal villages however rich they are. The officiating headman then went on to say that some women rebuke their husbands when they speak subversively, but others side with them against the village headman. He told the husbands and women that they were wrong to do this and that they must desist. After this followed a public rebuke of the village as a whole. One of the younger brothers of the new headman pointed out that when the mother of the previous Mapata had died she had been buried in the graveyard and not in the village. He rebuked the villagers and told them that, when the present chief died, he should be buried in the village. A man who had been charged with neglect by his wife (his cross-cousin) paid the headman the compensation which he had refused to pay to her. One of the headmen then exhorted the villagers to respect their headman ; to send someone to accompany him on his journeys to see to his wants ; never to allow the headman to carry a gift he had been given, and so on. The ceremony ended when Kapaloma, who was representing the chief, hinted that Mapata might be allowed to wear a scarlet headband in the near future.

Village headmen represented the chief at Nkacelenga's and

---

[1] *Mtera puukukula ukuwa ŵananyambi.*

[2] *Kwesya lina*—to cause the name to climb.

[3] *Tonde, tonde, mkamwini nasicila muno ngakwela iai.* Tonde is the word for billy goat and its use here emphasizes the procreative functions of the husband in the village.

Mapata's installation ceremonies. When an important headman succeeds, however, the chief himself usually makes a short appearance and talks to the people. When Nyenje was installed in July 1947, Kawinga attended. Nyenje has the same clan-name as Kawinga and is an Invader. In 1947, he had 109 tax-payers under him ; he held rights to both initiation ceremonies, but he did not have the right to wear the scarlet headband. Kawinga arrived at 11.18 a.m. before Nyenje had come out of the hut and he went straight to it and entered. He emerged at 11.45 and sat on a chair under a drying stand. Kangomba, his head *nduna*, came and sat with him. In the meantime the new headman was brought outside and seated on a chair. Sitting on either side of him on the mat on which his chair was placed, were his two wives. Nsanama,[1] a minor village headman of the same clan-name as Nyenje, officiated. The penny-giving now started. At 12.10 Kawinga got up and walked over to the crowd, and silenced them with a sharp whistle. They gathered round to hear his speech. He pointed out that the dispute about the succession to their headmanship had been going on for three or four years and that there had been two candidates, one of whom he had selected as successor because he knew he would be sensible and wise, and would look after his people in the village and in the smaller villages under him. He said that he had recommended this man to the District Commissioner who, with the Governor's sanction, had supported him. He did not therefore want to hear that the man had fallen ill ; he dealt strictly with sorcerers. He said that respect started with the relatives : brothers and sisters, the husbands and the boys and girls must also respect ' the chief'. They must not mention his name but refer to him as ' the chief'. Kawinga went on to say that some husbands were evil and could split a village like this one, by telling lies to the headman and falsely advising the headman that his sisters were talking behind his back and insulting him. When he hears this he may break the village by ill-treating his relatives, thereby causing them to migrate and leave him all alone. Kawinga told the people not to go talking in other villages about the man who was in the chair ; that sort of behaviour only led to sorcery. Finally, he warned them to help the headman in obeying the instructions of the White people who

[1] Not Kawinga's relative of the same name.

came to the village and in accommodating strangers while he was away. He told them that disputes were to be referred to the headman immediately. Turning to the new headman he said he had to report anything unusual that occurred in the village, and that he was authorized to arbitrate in small cases in his and surrounding villages.

Kawinga then left the centre of the crowd and went back to where he had been sitting. Then an officiating headman, addressing particularly the women, said, ' Only a few months ago there was a quarrel between the present chief and his elder sisters. These women ran away to Malemia's area in Zomba district without reporting the matter to anyone. This must stop. With effect from to-day any troubles must be brought to the headman without delay : he will settle them. A tree cannot grow without branches and a headman or a chief cannot be known without his people's respect. Do not behave as children. This man cannot do things alone : he must have your help. We leave him in your hands and we do not want to hear about any more trouble. Follow all the instructions the chief has given you.' He took his leave and Nyenje was taken back inside the hut. The people now dispersed to where there was beer and dancing.

THE STRUCTURAL REINCARNATION OF VILLAGE HEADMEN AND PERPETUAL RELATIONSHIPS

There appear to be a number of significant aspects of the installation ceremonies. First, there is the ritual death and rebirth of the village headman. The heir is ' killed ' by a blow with the fist on the forehead, but is reborn the headman. The Yao do not believe that the spirit of the headman is inherited by the heir ; [1] he has only eaten the name.[2] But socially he is born again and, logically consistent with this idea, he takes the wives of his predecessor without further marriage negotiation. He also takes over the property of the dead man, his clothes and his huts.

But this structural reincarnation of the headman has the important implication that the headman is immortal. He shares this characteristic with the group of which he is the leader. When

---

[1] As the Bemba do. A. I. Richards, ' Mother-right among the Central Bantu ' in E. E. Evans-Pritchard and others, *Essays Presented to C. G. Seligman*, Kegan Paul (London, 1933).

[2] *Kulya lina* is a synonym for succeeding to headmanship.

a village dies, so then does the headman die.[1] In his rebirth, he occupies the status that his predecessor held before he died, in both the kinship system and the political structure.[2] His mother's brother's children whom he formerly called ' cross-cousin ' he now calls ' my children '. His mother's younger brothers whom he previously called *akwelume* (mother's brothers), he now calls ' my younger brothers ' (*apwanga*), and so on. By the extension of this principle, an heir succeeds not only to the status of his mother's brother but also to that of the first of his name. Cigwaja VI, for example, calls the descendants of his mother's mother's mother's brother (Cigwaja IV) ' children '. In fact, he calls the children of any Cigwaja ' my children '.

Within the political field the same principle is used in establishing what we may call ' perpetual relationships '.[3] There are some village headmen who express their relationships to each other or to the chief by a kinship term. The headman Majaja, for example, is the ' son ' of Nyambi. In fact, the first Majaja to establish a village was the son of the second Nyambi. The present Majaja is the third incumbent and three Nyambis have died since Nyambi II. Nevertheless, by positional succession both of the present incumbents are translated to the formative phase in their relationships, which is thus perpetuated to-day, and will be, in their view, for ever. The present Liwonde calls Kawinga ' elder brother '. Kawinga is in fact his mother's mother's mother's sister's son. The first Liwonde was the first Kawinga's younger brother. They invaded Nyasaland together. At this significant point in their history their relationship became fixed and then perpetuated in the political structure. This relationship, though phrased in a kinship term and moulded to some extent by the norms of kinship behaviour appropriate to the term used, is in reality political, for it fixes the relative positions of two villages through their headmen.

[1] Sometimes after a village has broken up and the name has not been heard of for some years, some survivor revives it and resuscitates the village.

[2] Dr. Richards calls this ' positional succession '. See ' Some Types of Family Structure amongst the Central Bantu ' in A. R. Radcliffe-Brown and Daryll Forde (eds.), *African Systems of Kinship and Marriage*, Oxford University Press for the International African Institute (London, 1950), 224.

[3] This term was suggested by Dr. I. Cunnison's use of it for a similar practice among the peoples of the Luapula Valley. See his *Local Organization on the Luapula Valley*.

THE RÔLE OF THE CHIEF IN HEADMAN'S INSTALLATION CEREMONIES

The second significant aspect is the importance of the chief in the installation ceremony. In each ceremony the chief has to give his formal consent to the succession. Note that the chief is approached by one of the headman's relatives, so that at this level, in spite of Kawinga's statement,[1] the succession dispute is over and the heir is decided upon. The chief's formal consent, his formal fixing of the date of installation, his personal appearance or the appearance of his representative, and his giving of the gift, all serve to set his official seal on the installation and to recognize its political significance.

The chief recognizes the leader of the group, both in his actions and his words. He also sees in the headman his representative, as when Nyambi said, 'When you disobey the headman you disobey me,' or when Kawinga said, 'Nyenje, you are responsible to report to me any unusual thing which occurs in your village here.'

When a chief comes into a village it is the village headman who entertains him. I was told that if the headman or his representative were away, the chief would be given no hospitality at all, because the villagers only entertain him through their representative, the village headman. Though the chief himself may not frequently visit villages, his representatives are constantly coming and going on his errands. Where affairs of day-to-day administration of the chiefdom are concerned these representatives are usually the court messengers, who may be paid from Native Authority funds or from the chief's private funds. The chief's representative in his tribal capacity, however, is usually his *nduna*, but it may be practically any village headman whom the chief selects. For example, he may send his *nduna* or one of his satellites as his representative to a *mapeto*.[2] He sometimes sends his representative as a referee to divinations and to chicken poison-ordeals following accusations

---

[1] Kawinga had a say in Nyenje's succession because he was a clan-relative. I have evidence that some lobbying had been going on because the successor that Kawinga chose was not chosen by Kawinga's relatives.

[2] A meeting held shortly after a funeral to decide whether death has been caused by sorcery or is due to natural causes.

of sorcery, but the representative takes no part in the proceedings at all; he is outside them and is there merely to see that affairs are conducted fairly.

THE VALUE ATTACHED TO THE UNITED VILLAGE

The third aspect, the dominant theme in all speeches, is the emphasis on the position of the headman as a leader of a corporate group, and his duty to maintain its unity. The chief and the officiating headmen warn the successor about the possibility of conflict in the village. They advise him to settle differences at once lest these should lead to a split in the village. They also warn him that his wife's relationships with her sisters-in-law, living as she is, virilocally,[1] are a danger point and may lead to trouble. The danger from the 'husbands' who are members of other villages and whose loyalties do not lie directly with the new headman is made manifest to him. At Nyenje's ceremony the officiating headman remonstrated with Nyenje's sisters because some had left the village without giving him an opportunity to settle their differences. The frequent references to the danger of sorcery are also references to the fear of the breakdown of the village. The villagers are exhorted to respect the headman and to be obedient to him for the general welfare of the group as a whole. Regularly the image of the tree and its branches is invoked, and it is made clear that the headman is dependent on his people for his rank and status, and they on him for their unity.

The disintegration of a village in Yao eyes is a sad affair and the disruptive forces in it must be very strong before a section leaves it. People who want to leave a village are usually remonstrated with and told not to 'break' it. In the frequent conflicts between the headmen and their younger brothers the arbitrators usually try their utmost to prevent a migration. They always award compensation to the injured party and tell the disputants to live in peace, and not to leave the village. Frequently, however, the leader of the dissident group prefers to refuse the compensation money, which is often as much as £6 or £7, and

---

[1] i.e. living with her husband's kin. I use 'virilocal' and 'uxorilocal' in preference to the older but ambiguous terms 'patrilocal' and 'matrilocal'. See Richards, 'Some Types of Family Structure amongst the Central Bantu', 208–9.

strike out with his adherents to found a new village. A sum of £6 or £7 is a considerable amount in everyday Yao life where the annual cash income of the average individual is not much more. The leader of a dissident group is prepared to forgo this wealth to get one foot on to the lowest rung of the political ladder—that is by becoming a village headman.

Obversely there is a great deal of sentiment attached to the idea of a united village. To the Yao way of thinking a village is broken by fighting or death, and these evils are linked by witchcraft beliefs. The association of death and the break-up of the village is brought out clearly by the funeral ablutions of villagers after the burial of one of their number. An important ingredient in the medicine with which the mourners wash themselves after the funeral, is *cikula*. It is the earth from a particular type of termitary which is usually about 12 to 18 inches high, upright and almost cylindrical. The crust is very brittle and it is comparatively easy to chip off a piece. When this is done a mass of internal chambers and passages is revealed. The soldier ants, unlike those of other species that retreat into the darkness of their passages as soon as they are exposed, come into the open daylight and swarm in confusion over the fractured termitary. When I questioned my informant about *cikula*, he kicked the crust off the top of one of the hills and said, 'See all the houses in the village of the ants ? I have broken their village. So it is with death. It breaks the village.'

The Yao believe that death 'breaks the village' and that conflicts through sorcery lead to death. Therefore, conflicts are the real cause of village splits. Hence differences must be settled immediately if the village is to persist, because if they last too long one of the aggrieved parties is sure to start using sorcery against its opponents. Those who do move away, go to a distant place because they believe that sorcery operates only where there is social interaction. But the fear of sorcery on the other hand is just as strong a force in maintaining the physical unity of the village. It is while the migration is being planned that sorcery is most likely to be used. This is particularly so if the village break is taking the form of a lineage split. This happened, for example, in Lupunje village.

Kalambo, the sister's son of Lupunje, wanted to leave the village and had gone to seek a suitable site. When he returned he found that

K

his mother was ill and had gone with Lupunje's younger brother to the diviner to find out the cause of the illness. The diviner indicated that Lupunje thought that Kalambo was not showing him the proper respect. Lupunje knew that his sisters had lost their value in the lineage since they had stopped bearing children, whereas Kalambo's sisters were still reproducing. His malice had caused the woman's illness. When Kalambo got home he asked his mother's brother to blow water out of his mouth [1] and help him to prepare some medicine for the sick woman. This Lupunje did and the woman recovered immediately.

Shortly afterwards Kalambo remonstrated with his mother's brother for causing the illness of his sister, but Lupunje said that he had no control over it : the spirits had brought it on her. Kalambo knew that he could do nothing and abandoned the idea of building his own village. He knew that there was bound to be more illness if he carried on with his plan.

Clearly the belief in the mystical powers of the ancestors or of sorcery is a force which prevents sections from breaking away from the village. A break follows only when opposition within the village has reached sufficient pitch to force one of the sections to take the risk of illness, rather than to continue living in the village. Sometimes the dissident group comes back because further deaths at their new village site convince them that their action was wrong.[2]

EFFECTS OF THE HEADMAN'S PERSONALITY

Whether a village maintains its unity or not, depends very largely on the personality of the headman. This is why the officiating headmen and others at the installation ceremonies are so insistent that cases should be settled quickly. The main duty of a headman is to maintain harmonious relationships within his village and to see to the welfare of its members. All severe illnesses are immediately reported to him, and so are the results of all divinations. He usually sends his representative to divinations concerning kinsmen not related to him matrilineally. He is immediately notified of all deaths and he organizes the funeral rites. Squabbles are brought to him for arbitration and even where squabbles are settled by kinsmen in the village, usually the headman is formally told of them. Frequently marriage diffi-

---

[1] An act which recants malice. See Chap. VI, p. 139.
[2] See the case history in Chap. VI, p. 153.

culties are settled by the marriage sureties [1] who only report to him after the affair is settled. In disputes of unusual gravity, the headman may call in unrelated persons [2] to arbitrate, but he himself must be present.

His own behaviour is expected to be exemplary. Any deviation from the norm is likely to be strictly censured, not only by his own villagers, but also by other village headmen, who may say, 'Important men do not behave in this way.' A man who had an argument with his sister's son was told this. He had taken the dispute to a neighbouring headman who decided against the village headman and rebuked him for behaving in a way not consonant with his position. Village headmen should be above squabbling with their villagers. A village headman who was also a leech had virtually raped a woman whom he was treating. He tried to maintain this was part of the treatment. Her matrilineal relatives reported the matter to the headman of her village and he brought the errant headman in front of the chief who said, 'You are wrong to do this when you are an important man. You are a big man and you act as a commoner does. You ought to be able to show the commoners how to behave.' He was made to pay a compensation of £2 10s. and fined 10s. Had he been a commoner he would have been made to pay a compensation of only 30s.

The ultimate sanction to which all headmen are subject, is that their people will leave them if they behave badly. This was the fate of Cikumba.

In 1944 Cikumba had a village of about 30 huts. The son of the first Cikumba, Meya, had two wives who were living virilocally in Cikumba's village. Meya had enlisted in the army. While he was away, Cikumba, the village headman who was Meya's father's sister's son (though he called him 'father' because of positional succession), started taking Meya's two wives to beer drinks. Meya's sister one day asked Cikumba about his behaviour, but he only said that Meya could not do anything as he was far away. Things had gone too far, however, when one morning he was seen coming out of the

---

[1] The representative of a spouse in all affairs arising from conjugal relationships. They are usually senior matrilineal relatives. See Chap. VI, pp. 176–7. Their rôle is discussed fully in *Marriage among the Machinga Yao of Southern Nyasaland*.

[2] *Mundu juampambali*, i.e. a person from outside.

hut of one of Meya's wives. Meya's sister wrote a letter to tell him of this and he replied that he could do nothing until he returned. In 1946, Meya returned to be demobilized. The third night after his return he questioned his wives about their fidelity during his absence. They at first held out against him but before long he intimidated them into admitting that they had slept with the village headman. Meya now went to complain to Mapata, who was Cikumba's perpetual mother's brother, and he said that he would come to the village the next day.

When Mapata came he confronted Cikumba with the accusation. Cikumba denied it until Mapata called the women. When they confessed Cikumba was forced to admit his guilt. Mapata now decided to call in an arbitrator, Isa, an important but unrelated headman who lived close at hand. Isa said he would come the following day when the matter could be thrashed out. When Isa and Mapata came they asked the women about the affair in public. They admitted the charge and Cikumba did not deny it. Isa then remonstrated with him for being a bad man and said that he was ashamed to hear about it. Cikumba had to pay £6 10s. to the injured man, Meya, who, however, refused to take it. He argued that Cikumba ought to have behaved as a father to him. But Cikumba had not. He, Meya, could not remain living in the village because his wives would be as Cikumba's wives. Isa said that he could not object because Cikumba had caused the trouble and had broken the village himself. How could he complain? Meya took two-thirds of the huts in the village away with him.

THE HEADMAN AS A REPRESENTATIVE OF A CORPORATE GROUP

The headman is not only responsible for keeping the peace between the members of his village, but he is also supposed to control his members in their relationships with other villages. If members take corporate action against other villages, even if they do so without the consent of the headman, the chief will consider the village headman responsible. This was brought out clearly in the relationships between Cikoja, Mapata and Masimbo in Chiwalo's section.

Cikoja and Mapata are two of the more important headmen in Chiwalo's section. Masimbo is a minor village headman who lives in Mapata's village area. The quarrel arose over the question of fishing rights in a small pool lying between the two main villages. This pool was excavated by Cikoja and his villagers in 1924 during

PLATE VI

A typical village headman. He is dressed in white with a
cloth thrown across his shoulder. He wears a white cap.
This headman is not Government recognized, nor has he
the right to wear a scarlet headband. He has no initiation
rights.

(November 1948)

a severe drought, and he claimed the rights over it. One day in 1930, some boys from Mapata village came down to the pool with fish-poison. At about noon some boys from Cikoja's village arrived with their traps. When they saw the Mapata boys using fish-poison they told them to desist and tried to take away the fish. This led to a fight in which knives were drawn. One of Cikoja's boys ran back to tell him, and in anger he came down to the pool with some adults. The Mapata boys now ran back to Masimbo who immediately assembled some men and came to the assistance of the Mapata boys. The two groups joined battle immediately and there were casualties on both sides. Mapata heard about this and came running down to separate them.

The next morning they took the dispute to Chiwalo. He started by asking why Mapata had used fish-poison in someone else's pool without permission. Mapata replied that he did not know that his boys had gone down there. He said that Masimbo had told him about the conflict and that he had gone down to stop it. He was not aware of it before. Chiwalo now turned to Masimbo and said, 'Masimbo, you are in the wrong. You have caused the children to suffer. You went to make war because of your children. The people of Mapata, they are in the wrong because they did not report to the owner of the pool.'

When Cikoja was asked if he had anything to say he only replied that he was ashamed of what had happened because he was the first in the area, and until then they had been friends. The conflict had arisen because the children had done something which they did not know was wrong.

Chiwalo ordered Masimbo to pay 5s. and Mapata 6s. to Cikoja. He then told Cikoja that he should brew some beer and share it with the other two villages so that friendship might be restored and the children might go from village to village without fear. The chief's instructions were carried out and normal amicable relationships were re-established.

The way in which the villages acted as corporate groups is well illustrated by this incident. The responsibility of the village headmen for the activity of their members also emerges. The chief found Masimbo in the wrong for causing the fight, but he also fined Mapata because his boys had used fish-poison. The fines were paid by the village headmen, Masimbo and Mapata, to the village headman Cikoja, for they are the representatives of the corporate groups under them.

In no other field of village relationships is the corporate

identity of villages more clearly seen than in the arguments that arise over rights over waterholes. These are usually dug next to a stream or a marsh, or in some other place where the water will percolate into them. The physical labour of digging a waterhole establishes the rights to it, and a village retains these rights if at some time in the past any of its members had dug it.

In normal years, and of course during the rainy season, there is enough water for all and no friction arises, but in drought years difficulties arise. Friction between Nampeya and Cikuwita arose in this way in 1933.

During the dry season the waterholes that were normally used were drying up and the people of Nampeya decided to open up a disused one. When Cikuwita's people saw Nampeya's people using it they came to use it too. Nampeya's women saw this and told the other people they had no right to use the waterhole. Words passed between them and eventually there was a tussle between the two groups, during which a waterjar of one of Cikuwita's women was broken. Cikuwita's women said they would take the case up to Ntibwilibwi, a headman of local importance, and when they returned to their village they complained to their headman who took the complaint to Ntibwilibwi. He sent a message to Nampeya to arrange a date on which the dispute might be settled. On that day the members of the two villages gathered at Ntibwilibwi's hut. The dispute was settled amicably : the person who broke the waterjar was ordered to take a chicken and give it to the owner of the jar, and Cikuwita was told to gather his people the next day and make them dig a waterhole of their own.

The villagers in each of these situations had acted with regard to their fellows primarily as members of villages. They had seen themselves as members of corporate groups and had interacted as such. In the dispute in which the jar was broken, the individual responsibility was fixed and compensation awarded, but at the same time the village headman was instructed on behalf of his villagers to make a new well and thereby ensure peace in the future. In all these disputes, however, the headman had appeared as the responsible representative of his village.

CHAPTER VI

THE LINEAGE FRAMEWORK OF VILLAGES

MATRILINEAL KINSHIP

TO outsiders a village appears to be an undifferentiated whole and in interaction with other villages it acts as such. But within the village, social actions are determined by membership of kinship groups whose genealogical relationships to each other differ from one village to another. The village headman who represents the unity of the village is usually a kinsman of all the villagers, but the links to him are different and diverse. Yet he commands the leadership of the village, not so much by his kinship to the villagers, for a villager may have other mother's brothers and fathers in the village, but by his position in a political structure, where he represents the village to outsiders and to external authority.

Yao social groups are organized on a principle of matrilineal descent but we shall see that, although this is the main principle, it is modified by the general political mould into which villages are forced. We have already seen that, at least in the lines of important headmen, clan-names are inherited from the mother.[1] This is the simplest and most direct way in which matrilineal descent affects social relationships. The principle of matrilineal descent is far more important in organizing the smallest group which acts corporately within the village—the matrilineage.

A significant feature of Yao social structure is that the village organization tends to cut across lineages. In the process of segmentation of matrilineages, which I shall discuss in detail later, new villages are formed. When this happens the dissident kin usually set up their homesteads a good distance from the original or parent village. The links between different sections of the same matrilineage, therefore, tend to become lost, and the new village, conscious of its own identity and unity, gradually loses its links with the parent village. The general structural relationship between the villages as wholes, and their headmen as their representatives, is fixed at the time when the division takes place, and this is remembered. But the actual genealogical

[1] See Chap. III, p. 71.

links are usually forgotten, so that the two villages are known to be related, but it is not certain how. The matrilineages to which the two headmen belong recognize this forgotten link and they refer to this relationship as *ulongo ŵakumbana*, which I can only translate as 'distant relationship'. In Cikoja village, for example, the headman's matrilineage, or as I shall call it, dominant matrilineage, is related to at least two other villages. These are Mbande and Cibwana Kawinga, both in Jalasi's area. The links with these two groups cannot be remembered. The first Mbande and the first Cikoja, I am told, had the same mother. Neither the present Cikoja nor any of his villagers could remember the genealogy earlier than the fourth Cikoja. A section of Mbande village, nevertheless, lives in Chiwalo's area near Cikoja and there is a fair amount of co-operation between the two villages to-day. Cibwana Kawinga is by the same explanation a 'mother's brother' of the present Cikoja; he is called in whenever there are serious disputes in Cikoja's village, and brings the force of a senior relative to bear on Cikoja.

People who are thus vaguely and distantly related may express their kinship in many ways. For example, they say that they are 'the people of one founding ancestor or ancestress'. They may say that they are *acina Masumba*, 'the people of Masumba', or *acina Nkopo*, 'the people of Nkopo'. Masumba and Nkopo here may be either a woman from whom they are descended, or a man who was the leader of the group when they first moved into the area. Where a man is mentioned as the founder the term is used for the descendants of the man's sisters. But like most terms for social groups its meaning changes in different contexts. In another context, for example, *acina Cikoja* means simply the people of Cikoja village and has no reference to matrilineal descent at all.

Other terms are more specific. The word *mpago* may be used in the sense of one type or kind, as *pampago pamo*. An arbitrator at an intra-lineage dispute said, for example, 'You people who have a case are people of one kind [*ŵandu pampago*].' The word *cipapo* may be used in much the same way. But even here the reference may be to the entire span of matrilineal relatives whose relationship is vague and uncertain (*ŵakumbana*); or it may refer to a section of relatives having one known ancestress; or it may even refer to a segment within the section.

Among the relatives of the largest order of kinship (*cipapo*) there is a bond only slightly more intimate than that among people who have the same clan-name. There are none of the jural and moral obligations which characterize membership of a matrilineage which is a part of a village. The larger group, for which there is no exact Yao term, may be looked upon as a maximal lineage. It is characterized by a relationship of a more definite bond than that of having a common clan-name, but the members may still marry.

The Matrilineage

It is within the village that the matrilineage operates most clearly. The distant matrilineal link which connects villages such as Cikoja, Mbande and Cibwana Kawinga, is set in a context of inter-village relationships and is therefore part of the political system. Within the village the matrilineage becomes a corporately acting group of a different dimension. It is in this order of lineage within the village that we have the set of relationships described by Professor Fortes as applying to the inner lineage [1] among the Gold Coast Tallensi.

The depth of a matrilineage within a village is seldom more than five or six generations from the founding ancestress to the new-born children. The name of the founding ancestress is remembered and the descent of each member of the matri-lineage can easily be recounted. The ancestress is known as the *likolo* or *lipata*, words which also refer to the trunk of a tree. We have seen how at a headman's installation ceremony the image of a tree was invoked in describing the lineage.[2] We find it once again here, where the founding ancestress is seen as the stem or root from which all members of the lineage have sprung, and the various sections of the matrilineage are seen as the branches (*nyambi*). This symbol of the lineage appears also during offerings to the ancestors. The chief, or headman, in

---

[1] See Fortes, M., *Dynamics of Clanship among the Tallensi*, Oxford University Press (London, 1945), and *The Web of Kinship among the Tallensi*, Oxford University Press (London, 1948). The Yao system of lineages is not the clearly segmented type of structure characteristic of the Tallensi. I hesitate, therefore, to use Fortes's terms, and use *matrilineage* for the localized unit which is usually a component of a village.

[2] See Chap. V, p. 119.

making the oblation, pours the beer or sprinkles the flour at the root (*lipata*) of a shrine-tree. As would be consistent with this way of looking at the lineage, genealogically-distant ancestors are said to be ' below ' (*pasi*), so that if a Yao wishes to say that a certain person was a matrilineal ancestor many generations back, he would say that he was ' very much below '.

THE CONCEPT OF ' THE MOTHER '

The matrilineal descendants of the founder look upon themselves as having been fed from the same breast and may express this by saying ' we are of one breast '.[1] Deep sentiment is attached to the idea of the mother among the Yao. There is, for example, a sharp distinction drawn between those women who have had children and those who have not. When a woman becomes pregnant for the first time, she is given instruction in child welfare when she undergoes a special ceremony (*litiwo*). This is a ceremony which is publicly announced and attended by most of her matrilineal and other kinswomen and acquaintances. No woman may attend this ceremony if she has not herself had a baby. Thus her change in status in the community is clearly shown by the public recognition of her condition, and the fact that she is initiated into secrets which are shared by other mothers only. Her position in the lineage is much enhanced when she becomes a mother. It is the most important step towards becoming a village founder herself.

The concept of ' the mother ', in general, also appears in the boys' initiation ceremonies. Certain phases of ceremonies may be conducted only with the help of the women. They have to clap the rhythm to which the ' tailmen '[2] do their dances. Here all women are classified as ' mothers ' and without their co-operation the ceremonies could not be conducted. During the same ceremonies three women appear with baskets of food on their heads. The tailmen remove the baskets and sacralize the

---

[1] *Tuli pewele pamo.* The word *mlango*, a doorway, is also commonly used. The idea in essence is exactly the same. It is the concept of the children who come to settle around a woman's hut door. It is used as *wandu pamlango pao*, the people of his lineage section.

[2] The *m'mchira.* These are the functionaries in the initiation ceremonies. They carry medicated zebra tails during these ceremonies, and this gives them their names. See especially Stannus, ' The Wayao of Nyasaland ', 229 ff.

contents. Here once again the women, though they may have no boys in the initiation ceremony, are called ' the mothers '. The ritual co-operation of the mothers in the initiation ceremonies is paralleled by that of mothers and sons in political affairs : here sons are in charge of the villages, while their mothers and sisters form the nucleus of the localized kinship group, which in turn is the core of the village.

The ritual importance of the mother is nowhere more clearly seen than in the curse. The Yao believe that a mother may curse her child if he or she is disobedient or otherwise beyond control. Not many mothers do curse their children ; the threat to curse seems to be more often used. Informants have told me of some mothers who have cursed their children, and the procedure and the wording of the curse have always been very similar. It is usually not applied to young children who could be punished by other means, but to adults and particularly adolescents. Usually the mother lifts her breast and points the nipple upwards saying, ' If you have never sucked from this breast nothing dreadful will happen to you.' The consequences of this are greatly feared. Where I have been told of curses, each time the child has either died suddenly shortly after the curse, or at least it has gone mad. The curse is vaguely supposed to operate through the ancestor spirits, but I could get no clear statement on how this happens.[1] Whatever the cause, however, the symbolic action of lifting the breast and the dire effects which are supposed to follow from this, indicate the importance of the mother in the lineage.

The Yao attach this sentiment, in general, not only to the mother, but also to all senior matrilineal female relatives. In general speech all female members of the matrilineage in ascending generations are ' mothers ', and all members in the descending generations are ' children '. This fundamental relation of mother and child extends throughout the lineage. The Yao term *acinangolo*, used for the senior female members of the matrilineage, embodies this idea of ' the mothers '. More specifically, as far as men are concerned, the matrilineage is classified into

---

[1] Further evidence that the ancestor spirits are involved in the curse may be that madness is called *masoka*—spirits—and that it may be said of a madman that the spirits are beating him (*gakumputa masoka*). A curse may be revoked by blowing water out of the mouth, an act which is also vaguely connected with the ancestor spirits.

' sisters ' and ' mothers ' because alternate generations are merged in kinship terminology and in behaviour. A man's sister's daughter, for example, is called ' mother ', and her daughter (his granddaughter) in turn becomes ' sister '. A woman calls her male matrilineal descendants ' children ' (*mwanangu*), or ' grandchildren ' (*yisikulu*) ; her matrilineal male progenitors ' mother's brother ' (*akwelume*), or ' brother ' (*alumbwangu*).[1] By extension, therefore, another way of expressing common matrilineal descent is to say that two people are the children of one person, *ŵanakajumo*, even though that person may be their great-grandmother. A term which is almost synonymous with this is *mucitumbu cimo*, ' in one womb ', used as ' we were conceived in one womb ', though once again the reference may be to a common grandmother. But the inclusiveness of these terms varies in different contexts. Any may refer to the matrilineage of maximal span within the village, or to a section of the matrilineage seen as a segmented organization of parts. It is only by reference to the particular ancestress that the range of the term may be determined.

THE UNITY OF THE MATRILINEAGE

A person identifies himself most closely with the members of his matrilineage from whom he expects most help and whom he, in turn, is expected to help. If he is called upon to pay a heavy fine it will be the members of his own matrilineage who will club together to find sufficient money. They, more than others, support him in his quarrels. They come to his aid when he is ill or injured, by consulting the diviner and trying to find the sorcerer who is causing his illness, and by finding medicines which will bring him back to good health. They send him money if he has left the country and needs it to return. The goods he brings home from the labour centres will be shared mostly among his matrilineal relatives. They will find the food to be used at his funeral and also see that his burial is properly carried out. He owes these duties in turn to them. His property will stay almost entirely within the matrilineage after his death.

Relationship, unless qualified, is looked upon as being entirely matrilineal. This is well illustrated by the beliefs about the

---

[1] She more commonly addresses them as *acimweni*. See p. 147.

PLATE VII
A lineage elder in Citenjele village, Malemia area.
(*August 1949*)

disease *ndaka*.[1]   This disease, as we have seen, affects the sexually inactive when they are brought into contact with those who are sexually active.   But the disease will only affect the members of the matrilineage of the errant person.   For example, suppose a labour migrant is coming home from Southern Rhodesia and has, among other things, a few pounds of salt in his baggage for a gift to his relatives.   Suppose also that while he is returning he has promiscuous intercourse.   The salt becomes charged with sexual heat and if he gives it to any of his matrilineal relatives to cook with, they will contract this disease.   He must therefore give the salt to members of another matrilineage, even if they live in the same village.

It is when the unity of the matrilineage is threatened, by either death or division, that its mystical value appears most clearly. When a member of the matrilineage dies the whole matrilineage is thrown into mourning and remains continent for three days. On the fourth day they perform a ritual purification and some members resume sexual relations, but the closest matrilineal relatives, such as the mother and uterine siblings, remain continent for the remainder of the mourning period, which is about 36 days.

It is tension within the lineage which is most closely attended by dire results.   The most important reflex of this tension is accusations of sorcery.   Good relationships among members of a matrilineage are adjured, mainly because friction opens the way to sorcerers.   The Yao believe that sorcerers kill their matrilineal relatives so that they may share the flesh with other sorcerers.   The sorcerer is fundamentally a wicked person and may kill any relative but is more likely to kill those whom he hates. Hence it is most important that relationships are kept amicable within a matrilineage for fear that sorcery ensues.

An interesting variation of the dangers of sorcery is the belief that sorcerers take the opportunity of squabbles within a matrilineage to kill one of the members.   The rationale behind this is that the diviner's instruments are unable to detect the origin of the sorcery beyond the immediate cause.   A diviner will indicate that the cause of death of, say, a child is sorcery, but that the witch is obscured behind the quarrelling words of some relative. Consequently, danger to a matrilineage ensues when one of its

[1] See Chap. V, p. 112.

members goes to an outsider and grumbles to him about the family squabbles [1] and quarrels. The outsider then takes the opportunity of using this squabble to introduce his sorcery into the lineage. The Yao greatly fear backbiting because of their dread of sorcery and none dreads it more than a village headman, a warden of a sorority-group,[2] or a person in the position of having to keep a matrilineage or section together. These people are continually adjuring the women under them—for it is the women who are believed to be the main culprits—not to fight among themselves ; and if they do, not to take their complaints to an outsider but to the senior member of the matrilineage. The significance of this in relation to lineage unity is plain enough.

Apart from sorcery, strained relationships between members of a matrilineage are believed to be dangerous for other reasons. Malice may adversely affect people who are in mystically dangerous states. The most common of these states is pregnancy. If a woman has a quarrel with a matrilineage member while she is pregnant she is likely to have a difficult labour. The Yao say ' the womb has heard these bad words '. Another situation where malice or quarrelling will cause difficulties is in hunting. The luck of the chase is capricious and malice may easily bring bad fortune to an otherwise good hunter. For example, a successful hunter once gave each of his two sisters a piece of venison. Each complained that the other had been given the larger piece and quarrelled vehemently about it for weeks. The hunter now found that no game fell into his traps. He went to a diviner who indicated the quarrel of the sisters as the cause of his failure and told the hunter to get them to ' blow water ' (*kupesya*). He did this ; good relationships were restored and his traps were filled once more.

These deleterious effects, like the curse, are connected in some way with the ancestor spirits. This is sometimes expressed quite clearly when a person is called upon to ' blow water '. A mother who wishes to revoke a curse, a woman who wishes to recant her malice towards her matrilineal relative who is suffering in childbirth, or a man whose sister's son is ill supposedly because

[1] This is called *miseci*, which I have translated as ' backbiting '. This idea is extremely important, as we shall see later.

[2] i.e. those men who are responsible for their sisters and their descendants. See p. 145 ff.

of his malice towards him, might equally be called upon to do this. The person makes a statement to the effect that he bears no malice and hopes that the sufferer will be well. For example, a woman in Cikoja village who was called upon to ' blow water ' during the labour pains of her mother's younger sister's daughter's daughter,[1] because they had quarrelled over a sifting basket, put some water in her mouth, spat it out and said : ' Those words I spoke : the basket is mine. This is my child. Both are mine. When I spoke and asked my child about it, they were not words to place in my heart, so that to-day we should have to go to the diviner because my child is hitched [2] and be accused because of the sifting basket. These words I push aside. I do not know whether there are other words that we fought about, but if they are these, my daughter's child come out ! ' [3] Sometimes the ancestors are specifically invoked, ' *Conde, conde ŵamasoka . . .*' ' Please, please, O spirits . . .' This is a public confession of the tension within the lineage and it allows the lineage leaders to attempt to straighten out the difficulties, as they did in this case.[4]

These beliefs in mystical dangers of one sort or another which beset the matrilineage as the result of bad feelings within it, have the effect of constraining matrilineage members to maintain peaceable relations among themselves and are, therefore, conducive to maximum solidarity.

It is clear from MacDonald's writings that in earlier times the periodic offerings to the spirits of the ancestors was a valuable way in which the solidarity of the matrilineage was expressed. With the introduction of Islam and Christianity these sacrifices have disappeared. I have not worked in Christian areas long enough to be able to say whether the ancestor cult still persists. In the northern area, however, I can say that the ancestor cult survives as part of the practice of Islam. Periodically, feasts are held in

---

[1] See the history of the division in Cikoja lineage, pp. 165-6.

[2] *Kukolekwa*, i.e. the child cannot be born.

[3] *Une maloŵegala ciselo cila cangune. Aju mwanangu. Yosope yangune. Pinawecetaga nikuusya, kumbusya mwanangu, nginiwa maloŵe gakwika kuntima, gati mpaka lelo nikwenda kucisango cakolekwa mwanangu nikunkamula une ligonga lya ciselo. Celego ngututako. Kwalini nagapali gani getuwa kanganile nambo nagagaga maloŵe gakwe, cisukulu cangu cikopoce.*

[4] I have drawn attention to the cathartic effect of accusations of sorcery and public confession of guilt in a paper, ' A Note on the African Conception of Causality ', *The Nyasaland Journal*, v, 2 (July 1952), 57-8.

memory of the ancestors. These are called *sadaka*[1] and are similar to those held at the end of the mourning period. They are usually held when one of the lineage members has had a dream about an ancestor. The senior members are told of this and interpret it to mean that a feast in his memory should be held. The women cook a meal of mush and relish and on an appointed day the members of the matrilineage who live within a reasonable distance gather at the village of the senior section and share the feast. During this feast Islamic texts are chanted in Arabic. It is clear that in this situation the context of the meeting is exactly the same as that of the old offerings made by the lineage leader at the shrine-tree. The common ancestor is recalled and the matrilineage by meeting reaffirms its solidarity.

THE LOCALIZED MATRILINEAGE

The matrilineage may itself be localized in the form of a hamlet or small village, as in Ali Kasunka village. It has 9 huts situated about half a mile from Chiwalo's court house in Kawinga's area. The genealogy, hut plan and census are set out in Appendix B. I summarize the genealogy here to show how the hut owners in the village are related. The village is about 300 yards across and about a quarter of a mile from the main road.

Ali Kasunka (C6),[2] the warden of the village, formerly lived in a village known by his mother's brother's name Msilo (B1). Ali Kasunka is the son of the chieftain Mposa in Kawinga's area. The village of Msilo still exists in Mposa area. Ali Kasunka and his sisters moved out of Msilo village and established a hamlet in Malemia's area near Zomba township. While they were there Ali Kasunka went to work as a domestic servant in Zomba. One day the sister of the cook in the household in which he was working came down to visit her brother. She became Ali Kasunka's second wife (he was already married to a woman from Malemia area) and lived with him in Zomba. She was the daughter of the present chief Chiwalo, and was living at her

---

[1] Sanderson says that this is derived from the Arabic word *sadaqa* which means 'alms'. Sanderson, M., on 'Ceremonial Purification among the Wayao, Nyasaland', *Man*, xxii, 55 (June 1922), 91–3.

[2] The reference number is to assist the reader to identify the person on the genealogy in Appendix B.

(a) Women of a matrilineage preparing cassava together. A scene in a village in Malemia's area.

(*September 1949*)

(b) A hut in Ali Kasunka village (Bt. Ntuwa's hut, i.e. hut number 3 in the diagram in Appendix B). In the foreground are grainbins.

(*September 1948*)

PLATE VIII

village of birth in Chiwalo's before going to Zomba. After six years, when the land round Ali Kasunka's village in Malemia's had become exhausted, he decided to move the hamlet to Chiwalo's and selected a site about a mile from the hut of his second wife. This is where the village has been since 1940.

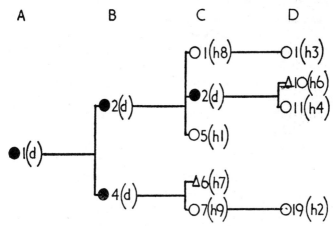

REFERENCE GENEALOGY. ALI KASUNKA VILLAGE.

Considering the matrilineage in detail : although Ali Kasunka's mother's mother is known, her collaterals are not, and Ali Kasunka's mother's mother's only sibling was her brother Kasembe. This genealogy is, therefore, built up from Ali Kasunka's mother's mother (A1). She had three daughters. One (B6) died before she had any children. Nyangu (B2), one of her other daughters, has two surviving daughters, Mbalasyao (C1) and Biti Kasembe (C5). Nyangu's other daughters, Amaliama (C2), Amwikonde (C3), and Amasingati (C4), all died when the village was at its present site. Amasingati died before she had any children.

Mbalasyao's (C1) daughter, Biti Mtuwa (D1), is in the village. Nalolape (D2) accompanied her husband to Cholo, where he went to work in 1947. Yahaya (D3), Ajida (D4), and Atwabi (D5) have all married uxorilocally. Taimu (D6) is unmarried and is away working for an Indian transport driver in Zomba, and Idi (D7) is working for a local Indian storekeeper as a domestic servant. Loni (D8), a girl of about 8 years, sleeps in her mother's hut.

L

Amaliama (C2) had five children before she died. The eldest Golosi (D9) is dead but he had married out before he died. The second, Mwanace (D10) has married virilocally and occupies hut 6. He has no children. Nyangu II (D11) has taken the name of her mother's mother (B2). She has gone to her husband's village with her five children, because he succeeded to a village headmanship in Mposa's area. Alieje (D12) is in the village and has three children, Kasonga (E9), Undeje (E10), and Amale (E11). All of them have not yet reached puberty and they sleep in their mother's hut.

Before she died Amwikonde (C3) had only one son, Mboga (D14), who is now about 5 years old and is cared for by his mother's elder sister, Mbalasyao (C1), in whose hut he sleeps.

Amasingati (C4) died before she had children.

Biti Kasembe (C5) is still living in the village (hut 1). She had only one daughter, Biti Sale (D15), who is in the village and who in turn had two sons, Taibu (E12), who died in infancy, and Rajabu (E13), who is an infant.

The other main section of the hamlet is made up of the descendants of Nyangu's sister Abeda (B4), who had six children. Ali Kasunka (C6), who is the warden of the village, is married uxorilocally about half a mile away at the village of his second wife. His first wife who was living virilocally has recently gone back to her village in Zomba to look after the children of her late elder sister. Ali Kasunka does not expect her to return. He had three children by her. They were Biliate (D16), who is married out, and two children who died in infancy. His children by his second wife live with her in her village. Ali Kasunka's sister Atawile (C7) had in all fourteen children of whom only Biti Mtemula (D19) survived infancy. She is living in the village (hut 2) and has had two children of whom only Wilson (E14), now aged 7, has survived.

Ali Kasunka's other surviving sister, Asausyeje (C8), with her 7-year-old child Mboga (D33), has gone to Zomba with her husband who is working there. Twalieje (C9) died before the village moved into this area and before she had children. Twalilemwapi (C10) also died before she had children. Andondonyeje (C11) died while living virilocally and her two sons married near her husband's village and have never lived in Ali Kasunka's village.

Table XXV sets out the disposition of the adult survivors of this matrilineage.

TABLE XXV

RELATIONSHIP OF ADULT SURVIVORS : ALI KASUNKA VILLAGE

Relationship to Founder	In Village	Married out	Labour Migrants	Total
D	—	—	—	—
S	—	—	—	—
DD	3	—	1	4
DS	1	—	—	1
DDD	4	1	1	6
DDS	1	4	2	7
Females	7	1	2	10
Males	2	4	2	8

In this hamlet Ali Kasunka is both village headman and the senior male member of the matrilineage. He brought the village into Chiwalo's area and he had the responsibility for the welfare of its members. He has to arbitrate in the disputes that arise within the village and he must at least appear at arbitrations where the members of his village have come into conflict with outsiders.

THE CONFLICT OF MALE AUTHORITY AND UXORILOCALITY

Although descent is matrilineal, authority still rests with the men. The senior man by generation and age is the leader of the matrilineage. It is true that there are a number of small hamlets under women. Biti Nkula village is one, Biti Cimeta is another. But even for these villages there is usually a man who can be called in to handle the affairs of the village. He may be a classificatory brother of the village headwoman, or he may be her own son if he is old enough. For example, in Biti Nkula's village, it is her own son Adam who goes to the divinations and finds the necessary medicine when people fall ill. He also attends the court cases involving a member of the village. Adam is married to a woman in Ndiwagani's village about three-quarters of a mile away from his home and he is therefore easily available when needed. When he became a labour migrant in 1945, his younger uterine brother Lipepeje took over the responsibilities. He is married in Ali Kasunka's village, which is about a mile from Biti Nkula's. In Biti Cimeta's village the minor disputes are settled by the headwoman herself. Her younger sister's son is married in a village ten miles away, and he would take over the duties if he could. He is married to his sister's husband's sister, and his sister's husband has threatened if he should try to take his wife home he will in turn take his wife to his home. Rather than stand the loss of a member from his matrilineal village he prefers to remain married uxorilocally. When more serious disputes occur he comes to Biti Cimeta's to settle them.

The principle of uxorilocal marriage is thus in conflict with the principle of male leadership of the lineage. If a man is living too far away he cannot attend to his numerous duties. The conflict can be solved in one of three ways. The first is that the man may marry in a village which is close at hand, and most marriages do take place between people who live near each other.[1] Second, he may marry a cross-cousin who is living in the village, albeit in another section of it. He need not then move out. Third, he may bring his wife into his village. The last two alternatives are from his point of view the best. He is then living with his matrilineal relatives, and among the group in which he has clearly defined rights and unequivocal status. But his wife's brothers will resist his attempts to take his wife from her village, especially if she is still capable of bearing children. He has to persuade her brothers to let her go with him and if they refuse, or if the woman herself refuses to go, he is helpless. If he wishes to live virilocally now his only course is to divorce the woman and marry a woman who will live virilocally with him. If he does bring his wife to his village she is kept there by only loose ties of marriage, and on the slightest pretext her male relatives will take her back to her village or she herself will run away home.

The larger the group of relatives to be looked after, the more urgent is the need for the senior matrilineal male to live with his lineage. All the villages headed by females are small. Table

[1] 75 per cent of marriages are contracted by people who live within 10 miles of each other. See *Marriage among the Machinga Yao*.

XXVI sets out the position of a casual sample of 36 villages in Chiwalo and Nyambi areas. Among the 23 villages which had

TABLE XXVI

Size of Villages under Headwomen and Headmen

Type of Village	Under 10 Huts	Over 10 Huts	Total
No matrilineage male resident .	13	2	15
Matrilineage male resident . .	10	11	21
Total	23	13	36

less than 10 huts each, 13 or 56·6 per cent had no male matrilineage members living in them. Among the 13 villages which had more than 10 huts, only two or 15·4 per cent had no matrilineage male members living in them.[1] The largest village in which there was no matrilineal male had only 11 huts. When the size of the village increases, the senior male matrilineage member tends to move in to live with his wards.

THE SORORITY-GROUP (*mbumba*)

But as the village grows and the duties of a senior matrilineage male become more onerous, a form of organization appears within the lineage which lessens his burden. This takes the form of the differentiation of sibling groups, and is part of the normal process of segmentation which is inherent in any lineage system. Consistent with the Yao idea that men should take care of the affairs of the lineage, sisters look to their eldest brother when they are in trouble. This group of sisters in the care of their brother is called *mbumba*. In the plural *acambumba* the word refers to women in general, but in the singular it refers to a particular group of women in the way I have explained. The word is always used in the sense of ' so-and-so's *mbumba* ', as *mbumba ja CeMayele*. The central concept here is the brother–sister link and I have accordingly translated the word *mbumba* as sorority-group.

The man who is in charge of the women, usually their eldest

[1] Diff. of per cent = 41·1 ; S.E. of diff. = 17·1 ; C.R. = 2·4 ; p = 0·0164.

brother, is called *asyene mbumba*, or ' the warden of the sorority-group '.   As one would expect among a matrilineal people, the link between a man and his mother and sisters is strong.   But it is the link with his sister that is strongest.   She relies on him for protection, particularly when she becomes ill, but also in her relationships with her husband.   Her brother will be her junior marriage surety, and he will give the consent which will allow a man to marry her.   Also a woman's brother will have to consult the diviner and find the medicines when she or her children sicken.   In times of distress, as, for example, if her crops have failed, she will appeal to her brother for help.   Similarly the man is dependent on his sister in a number of subtle ways.   He can always rely on her for hospitality, and is able to get a meal from her if he needs it.   But his dependence on his sisters for prestige is much more important.   The significance of this will emerge when we see the *mbumba* organization in the light of the segmentation and fission of the lineage.   A man can only found a new village if he has the full support of his sisters.   A sister also plays a most important rôle at the birth of his children.   She represents him both at the first fœtal-quickening ceremony and at the birth of his child, when she listens to the birth-pang confessions of his wife.[1]

At the same time the relations of sister and brother are restricted by custom.   A man must never appear too familiar with his sister, especially in sexual matters.   He may not, for example, sleep in the same hut as she does ; if she is away and he sleeps in her empty hut he must not make his bed in the place where she usually sleeps.   He may not even sit on her sleeping mat. Authentic cases of incest with a sister are extremely rare, whereas I recorded three or four cases of father–daughter incest while I was in the field.   Supposed cases of brother–sister incest are recounted and discussed widely.   This is understandable because a man who is suspiciously familiar with his sister is suspected of being a sorcerer, since it is widely believed that a sorcerer usually obtains the power that he needs for the performance of his dire deeds by sleeping with his sister.   The riddle of the initiands— ' What is the sweetest fruit which may not be tasted ? '   Answer, ' Your sister '—neatly reflects the attitude of the Yao.

The close link of brother and sister is also reflected in the

[1] The significance of this is explained in Chap. VII, p. 185.

kinship terminology. The common term used by both men and women to address sisters is *cemwali* and it is also applied to all women out of respect. But the term which is used descriptively and sometimes in address, cross-sexually, is *alumbwangu* (my sibling-of-opposite sex). It is self-reciprocal and thereby expresses the special relationship between the man and his sisters. Two sisters address each other in everyday conversation as *cemwali*. When it is necessary to be more specific an elder addresses the younger as *akuluwanga*. These are also descriptive terms. A man addresses his younger brothers as *apwanga* while they address him as *acimweni*. Women also address their elder or younger brothers as *acimweni*. This word is widely used as an honorific title but it is especially used for people who are in authority. The chief, for example, may be referred to as the *mcimweni*, and men frequently call their mother's brothers and other senior matrilineal male relatives by this term. An elder brother has the same duties towards his younger brothers as to his sisters, so that use of the term of address *acimweni* here indicates his position of authority over them.

From the point of view of a warden, his sorority-group is essentially made up of his sisters. We have seen that he is responsible for his younger brothers in exactly the same way as he is for his sisters, though technically they are not his sorority-group. He also has control over his sister's children so that ideally a warden sees his sorority-group as his sisters and their daughters and their daughter's daughters and so on. But a man's sister's daughters will probably have as their warden their own brother who stands in the same relationship to them as their mother's brother stands to their mother. The matrilineage is therefore organized internally in a system of inclusive sorority-groups extending from the eldest surviving member down to the youngest. However, a component sorority-group of a matrilineage does not begin to appear as a corporate group until the man who is to be its leader is old enough to take charge of the affairs of the women under him. Naturally, the age at which this happens is largely a matter of circumstance. Theoretically a man may not take charge until he has been initiated. But Yao boys nowadays are usually initiated at about 8 to 10 years of age. Obviously a child of this age cannot take over the affairs of his adult sisters, so that his mother's brother looks after them until he grows up. It is only when the boy becomes adolescent that he begins to take an active part in these affairs. This may begin in a small way. He may, for example, accompany his mother's brother when he goes to consult a diviner. Or he

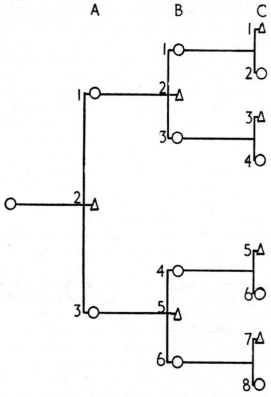

DIAGRAM 3. THE SORORITY-GROUP.

A2 sees his sorority-group as being composed of A1 and A3 and by extension *their* children.

B2 sees his sorority-group as B1 and B3 and by extension *their* children.

B5 sees his sorority-group as B4 and B6 and by extension *their* children.

may be given the charge of the conjugal affairs of one of his newly-married sisters. Gradually he assumes more and more responsibility. His mother's brother on the other hand falls more and more into the background and becomes rather a consultant than an active participant.

It is difficult to over-emphasize the importance of the sorority-group in everyday life. There is hardly a social situation in which the relationships of a man to his dependent female matrilineal kin are not involved. Probably marriage is the most frequent context in which his duties to and responsibilities for his sorority-group emerge. When a man wishes to marry a woman, he must get the consent of her brother. Ideally, it is a woman's brother who gives the consent, and if one asks a Yao how he gets married to any particular woman he will answer immediately, 'You go to ask her brother.' When consent has been obtained the woman's brother seeks out the man's brother and formally meets him, thereby setting the public seal on the relationships between the man and the woman. This gives the husband particular rights over his wife and her activities. After this, the difficulties of any of the marriage partners are the concern of the two sponsoring relatives (*acinamangoswe*) whom I have called 'marriage sureties'. They meet to discuss the illnesses of either of the marriage partners or their children and try to settle the differences that arise in the married life of their wards. They must be consulted before the marriage can end, and in fact they perform the act that ends the marriage, i.e. one pays a nominal sum of say 2s. to the other.

According to the Yao, women are quite helpless in their relationships with others, in illness or in any court cases, and must always have a man to look after them. They are seen to be as dependent on him as children are upon their parents. A statement made to me by old Naliwa, a man who has been looking after a sorority-group for years, reflects this attitude of the men towards the women in their care.

These dependent women (*mbumba*) are as annoying as children to look after. They are *miseci* [1] indeed. If a child is ill they go to tell their brother who says, 'Very well, I shall come to see the child.' If he is not very quick to do it they are likely to be backbiting. If he finds the child very ill he goes to tell the marriage sureties of its father, and they go to a diviner to look for medicine for the sick child. Then the sisters say that he is a good man because he gets on with the job when a person is ill.

Soon the child's mother becomes ill. Someone goes to tell her brother who says that he will come to see her. He visits her husband's

---

[1] Backbiting. See Chap. VI, pp. 137-8.

marriage surety and together they consult diviners and find medicine until she recovers. Then he goes back to his village.

He has no sooner got back when someone comes along to tell him that the child is ill again. He says, 'I am busy, I have some work to do. Tell someone else to go to the diviner.' The messenger goes back to his sisters and they say to each other : 'He is not a good man. He refuses to go to the diviner for the child.' Another says, 'Yes, it is so. Our brother is not diligent and when he comes here he will get no food from us. He eats our food but he does not work for us. Let us ask someone else to look after us. Our younger brother is a good man indeed.' Then everyone agrees that this should be so. The one that all said was a good man before, they all now say is bad. Then the sisters go along to tell the other brother who says, 'Go and tell my elder brother.' The sisters reply that he is not a good man and say, 'We want you to look after us.' He agrees and goes to the diviner to get medicine.

The next morning a husband goes off to his village without saying goodbye.[1] The wife now goes along to tell her younger brother who says that he can do nothing about it and that she will have to tell her older brother. She returns to her village crying, and tells her sisters that she told her brother about her husband's leaving and that he refused to have anything to do with it. Then one of the sisters says, 'Yes, the older one is a good man, not like that bad young one. If this one were the older one he would have already gone to get the man back.' Others say, 'Yes, that young one is not good at all. He is a sulky one. Is he not a sorcerer ? Go to the big one and tell him.'

Then the woman goes to the hut of the older brother and tells him of her difficulties. He tells her to go and fetch her husband and if he refuses to come back, to tell him. This she does and he refuses to return. She reports this to his elder brother. He tells her that his younger brother will return and if he does not they will come to talk matters over. The woman goes back to her village and goes to see her elder brother to tell him what she has done. He says, 'Very well, my sister, if he does not come to-day I shall go there to-morrow. Now go home and give the children some food.' When she gets back to the village she says, 'That brother is a good one indeed. He is diligent. He is going to fetch my husband back, if he does not return to-day.' If the man has not come by the next morning the woman goes to tell her brother. He goes to the husband's

---

[1] *Kuunduka*—to go off in a huff, to go off without saying goodbye. This is a sure sign that there is something wrong and that some action needs to be taken.

village and seeks out his marriage surety. They call him and tell him that the woman's brother has come to take him back to the village. He says that it is all right and that he will follow that evening. The brother goes back and tells his sister to cook porridge because her husband will be coming that evening, and then he goes home. The husband returns.

The woman now goes to tell her brother that her husband has returned and he says that he will come to visit him in the morning. Next morning her brother comes to the hut and asks her husband why he had left. 'You were cross about something and you did not come to tell me. Now tell me why you left.' The husband now tells him and they talk it over. If they fail to reach an understanding they go to tell the husband's sureties and discuss the case fully. If the woman is wrong her brother reprimands her and if the man is wrong his sureties reprimand him.

To live with a sorority-group needs courage.[1] You must not listen to backbiting. If you listen to the tales of others then you will not be able to live with your sorority-group because your heart has no fierceness. A sorority-group needs a man who has no fear. Then the women listen to what he says. He will say to his sister, 'Sister, hoe your gardens well. Do not have intercourse in the bush because it will finish your children with salt.[2] You must respect your husband and not tell him lies because he will not trust you and will be frightened of you. Listen to what I tell you. Things will be peaceful in your house if you come to tell us what is going on. If you do not tell us then there will be lots of friction.' Then the people say about a man whose sisters are not very happy, 'Who is that man who is not teaching[3] his sorority-group well?' Then the people will mention his name and they will laugh at him. If the sorority-group are living happily together he is a good man and he does not listen to the backbiting. His sorority-group are obeying him well and he lives happily with them.

In this account one cannot but be struck by the ambivalence of the relationship of brothers and sisters. Now they hate each other and now they love each other, depending largely on the fortunes of the moment. But the tie is the strongest in Yao social structure; while the relationships between the sorority-group and any particular brother may vary, the relationship between brothers and sisters in general is unassailable. When

---

[1] *Wakulimbika ntima*; perhaps more literally translated as 'a stout heart'.
[2] A reference to *ndaka*. See Chap. V, p. 112.
[3] In the sense of teaching them the right way to live, as their mentor.

one brother is unsuitable, they turn to another, uterine or collateral, and only if he too is unsuitable do they then turn to other relatives.

The attitude of Naliwa shows very clearly, too, the dependence of the women on the man. They have to wait for his action before they can settle their difficulties. This is part of the general process of internal differentiation within the lineage. The women become organized into small groups, each under the care of a man. These are siblings, so that their common descent, well expressed by the Yao *mucitumbo cimo*, 'in one womb', is the real unifying bond between them. When a Yao wants to express his close link with his uterine sister, that is to emphasize that she is not a collateral or classificatory sister, he stresses that they are from 'only one womb' (*citumbo cimpepe*). Naliwa says that a man who controls his sorority-group so that they live happily together is a happy man. He is happy also because his prestige is enhanced if he is a warden of a sorority-group. Being a warden is the first step on the ladder which leads eventually to independent village headmanship, and the man who has a large sorority-group under him can achieve this aim more easily. Therefore, the warden of a large sorority-group has even higher prestige than a man who has only a few sisters to look after. But the aphorism that 'chieftainship is slavery' [1] achieves significance when a man acquires more dependants.

SEGMENTATION AND FISSION IN THE MATRILINEAGE

The sorority-group organization in the matrilineage assumes most significance when viewed in its political setting. Segmentation and differentiation within the matrilineage consistently leads to splits, hence to village break-ups and the birth of new villages. Fission in the matrilineage usually appears when the wardens of the younger sorority-groups are over the age of 30. At that age each man is adult and therefore old enough to be responsible for his own and his sorority-group's actions and, usually, his mother's brothers, who when alive had kept their younger relatives united, are dead.

The events leading up to a split in a matrilineage usually follow

[1] From Smith and Dale, *The Ila-speaking Peoples of Northern Rhodesia*, Macmillan (London, 1920). For its significance, see Gluckman, Barnes and Mitchell, 'The Village Headman in British Central Africa', *Africa*, xix, 3.

a definite pattern. Very frequently indeed an accusation of sorcery is involved.[1] This usually stimulates a dissatisfied warden to gather his dependants together and to move off to found a new village. Elsewhere I have set out in detail the typical events which precede a village break-up when the lineage splits after a man quarrels with his mother's younger sister's sons.[2] These splits are not always successful because the seniority of the older relative, especially if he is a headman of some standing, may serve to reunite the village, and the leader of the dissident group may be unable to maintain its independence. This is what happened in Mwambajila village.

Mwambajila is one of the more important village headmen in Jalasi's area. The tension between him and his mother's younger sister's son Mbwana Somu reached a climax after a series of deaths among Mbwana Somu's children. He consulted a diviner and found that Mwambajila was the sorcerer causing these deaths. Mbwana Somu was very angry at this and told his sisters that they ought to leave the village and go to live in Liwonde's area, i.e. about 15 miles away. Eventually he persuaded them to move and they went to live on the Masanje river banks. But the deaths continued. The women now started to be worried because they had left Mwambajila's village

---

[1] The implication of this cannot be understood without some knowledge of Yao divining procedure. The type of divining is usually by gourd and object (*ndumba*). The diviner first of all establishes the reason for the visit, i.e. death, illness, theft, or whatever it is. He then consults his gourd and throws into his hand a variety of symbolic objects. He builds a story round these objects, and finally pronounces that he sees some person whom he vaguely defines. The consultor is then asked to mention who this could be. Though sorcery is supposed to be practised mainly in order to get human flesh for ghoulish feasts, it is not believed to act haphazard. In other words, a sorcerer is supposed to select his victims for revenge as well as for meat. The selective processes at work, therefore, when the consultor seeks to reconcile the diviner's findings with his own suspicions, are that he should select someone who is obviously evil, i.e. from his point of view, one with whom he has been quarrelling, and he should appraise the possible motivation for sorcery. After he has made the selection the name is tested by the diviner and the consultor may later submit a chicken to the poison ordeal to test the diviner's findings.
  This, of course, confirms Evans-Pritchard's analysis of Azande witchcraft and I here acknowledge my debt to him for stimulus both from his book and from the discussions we have had on the topic. I assume his analysis in my discussion. See Evans-Pritchard, E. E., *Witchcraft, Oracles and Magic among the Azande*, Clarendon Press (Oxford, 1937).
[2] In *Seven Tribes*. Case History II, 321.

as he was supposed to be the sorcerer. Suspicion fell on Mbwana Somu and eventually one of his sisters went back to Mwambajila and complained to him. Later the sisters consulted a diviner and found, as they suspected, that Mbwana Somu was the sorcerer. Thereupon, they returned to Mwambajila and left Mbwana Somu living alone with his wife.

Here is an example of a village which did not manage to maintain its identity but returned to be re-integrated into its village of origin.

Conflicts between collateral brothers are not frequent. This is for two reasons. Firstly, the opposition between lineage segments is usually expressed in a conflict between a man and his mother's brother, a fact which is no doubt related to the opposition of proximate generations. Secondly, lineages seldom persist long enough to contain within them several segments in which collateral brothers are leaders.

Conflicts seem to occur more frequently among uterine brothers, a fact which is significant in the light of the particularly strong bonds which unite them. The relationship between uterine brothers is much the same as that between sisters.[1] They are intimately linked by their bond of kinship and depend on one another for care and support. Usually the elder brother has his younger brothers in his care, in the same way that he has his sisters.

But at the same time they compete for the control of the sorority-group. A man, we have seen, can seek prestige in the indigenous political system only by becoming a village headman. He can become a village headman only by mustering his sisters and setting up a small hamlet with them. The elder brother prevents his younger brothers from doing this because the sorority-group is usually under his care. The younger brother can gain control only if he can persuade his sisters that the elder is a sorcerer, or incapable, or in some way unsuitable for his position. Hence the frequent accusations of sorcery among brothers : it is a rationalization of a hostility arising from the structural position of uterine brothers, which, in view of the commonly accepted strong sentiments uniting brothers, may not be otherwise expressed.

The break-up of Mponda's village in 1940 clearly illustrates

[1] I have dealt with this more fully in my essay in *Seven Tribes*.

how the opposition of brothers emerges in a situation where the lineage is concerned.

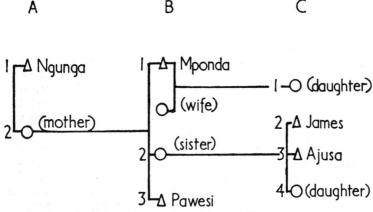

REFERENCE GENEALOGY. MPONDA VILLAGE.

Mponda, a village headman, was married virilocally. One day his daughter went to the pounding point in the village and found that her cross-cousin, the daughter of the headman's sister, was there. A quarrel arose between the two girls over the pounding mortar. Presently they started to fight. The wife of Mponda then came out and caught hold of her husband's sister's daughter and beat her. Mponda's sister had gone to draw water and was just returning. She heard her daughter crying out and ran to the place to find her sister-in-law beating her. The two women had a quarrel about this and separated with bad feelings. The next morning the quarrel broke out again. In the altercation that morning the headman's sister rebuked the headman's wife for behaving in a way which did not befit her position. The headman's wife on the other hand threatened to leave the village if this went on. The bickering continued for some time and eventually the two women came to blows. The headman's sister, who got the worst of this encounter, now decided to take the matter up to the headman. When she told him about it he refused to listen to her complaint. He told her that he had brought his wife to the village and that he did not want to have her treated like a slave. Another sister now chimed in and said that Mponda ought to invite his younger brother along to help him to settle the case. Another recommended their leaving him altogether because he was telling his wife to despise his sisters. To this Mponda replied that the village was his and that his sisters were only children and that he could not understand who could be inducing them to talk like this. He told them also that as far as he was concerned they could report the case to whomsoever they wished. The women came out of the hut and went straight to Pawesi who was the headman's younger brother. He told them to go back and to wait a while before they took further action.

After four days had passed the headman's sister who had fought with the headman's wife, became ill. In the morning the sisters sent a message to Mponda but he did not come. They sent another message to Pawesi who came and asked if they had told Mponda. They said that they had, but he had refused to come. Pawesi called James and Ajusa, the sister's sons of the headman, and told them that he would tell the headman that they were going to find out the cause of the illness. This they did. The diviner indicated that the headman had caused the illness by sorcery, because of the fight between his wife and sisters. Pawesi tested the divination by giving a chicken some poison. It died, indicating that the divination was accurate. He took the chicken's head to Ngunga who was Mponda's perpetual mother's brother.

When Ngunga heard this he refused to believe it. However, he agreed to send for Mponda and to ask him about it. When he did so Mponda denied the accusation. Ngunga now produced the chicken's head and accused Mponda of being a liar. At that moment a child came to tell them that the woman was dead and the interview ended. They went to the funeral and the next morning they decided to have a post-mortem meeting (*mapeto*) in order to decide the cause of the death. Mitomoni, one of Nyambi's perpetual sons, represented the chief. Ngunga opened the discussion by telling the meeting that the woman had been killed by the headman because of the fight between his sisters and wife. Mitomoni asked how they knew this and Ngunga told of the divination and the poison ordeal. He then asked Mponda if he had heard what had been said and what he had to say. Mponda replied that he knew nothing of it. Ngunga said that Mponda was a bad man and that the others would leave him and he would have to live alone. Mitomoni told Pawesi and Ngunga that they must not leave the village. Ngunga replied that it was impossible to stay there while Mponda was so bad. If the women stayed with him he would finish them all. Pawesi collected 30 of the 40 huts that made up the village and took them away to Chikweo's area, a distance of about 15 miles. Those who stayed behind with Mponda were his ' children ' and some unrelated people.

This case brings to the fore the position of the younger brother as a constant challenge to his elder for the care of his sisters.

The threat that lies over the head of an inefficient warden of a sorority-group is that of losing them to his younger brother, and it is scarcely possible to exaggerate the frequency with which this takes place in Yao society.

INTRA-LINEAGE TENSION AND SUCCESSION DISPUTES

The competition between brothers is heightened where the succession to an important name is involved. The rule of succession indicates a man's eldest sister's first-born son as the rightful heir. Informants in Jalasi's area told me that long ago the succession used to pass along the line of collateral brothers first, before dropping a generation to the sister's sons. It is true that in Jalasi's genealogy there are one or two early successions from a man to his most senior brothers, but recently the succession has passed regularly to sisters' sons. MacDonald, writing in 1880, quoted the succession rule for the Mangoche Yao to be ' from a man to his eldest surviving brother and then to the sister's son ',[1] but he describes in another part of the book the dispute for Malemia's name involving the deceased chief's younger brother and his sister's son, in which the sister's son's claims prevailed over those of the younger brother.[2] Stannus, writing of the Machinga in 1922, gives the rule of succession as I found it,[3] and suggested that MacDonald's interpretation of the Malemia succession dispute in 1875, was really a mistake, and that both disputants were sisters' sons of the head chief, but of different lineage sections. I cannot decide which account is true, but there seems to be no reason why MacDonald's general rule should be incorrect, especially since so much of the other material he recorded seems to be accurate. Also, as far as I could see, there are no differences in the Mangoche and Machinga Yao in successions to-day, so that it seems likely that there has been a change from adelphic succession to a straight system of matrilineal primogeniture. One is tempted to find a reason for this in the strong emphasis on patrilineal primogeniture in Islam, which was becoming widely accepted in these areas in the middle of the nineteenth century. Unfortunately I cannot bring direct evidence to support this hypothesis.

While the succession rule may indicate someone as having the

[1] MacDonald, *Africana*, i, 189.   [2] MacDonald, *Africana*, ii, 190.
[3] Stannus, ' The Wayao of Southern Nyasaland ', 277.

M

best claim to a headmanship or chieftainship, it does not ensure that he will succeed.   Succession to headmanship is not merely a matter of assuming control over the matrilineal relatives of the headman.   It is also taking command of the whole village as an entity in a political structure and keeping it together as a functioning whole.   The village as a whole, as well as the perpetual senior relatives, has a say in the selection of the new headman, and they select the man who is likely to be the most suitable for the position.   Here, as in most affairs, the women have an important say.   When they consider his suit the village members discuss in particular the ability of the prospective headman to hold the village together.   If he is unsuitable they may cite occasions when he is believed to have used sorcery, or sometimes they merely say that he ' has no mouth '.   This means that he is incapable of settling the disputes which arise in the village and therefore is unable to keep peace within it.   The attitudes of the villagers to suitors for a name are well brought out in the statements when the Misi name was considered.

There were two uterine nephews, Wadi and Mbulaje, whose claims were about equal though Wadi was the elder.   The chief Kawinga sent his representative Kasonga to call for a decision.   At a general meeting he asked the villagers whom they wanted.   Typically Kasonga's remarks were addressed particularly to the women.   There was a division of loyalties.   Some said that they wanted Mbulaje because ' he was of good heart, he gave gifts, he laughed and was not bad tempered, and he looked after the people when they were ill '.   Kasonga, however, asked the opinion of the women under Mbulaje, and they were apparently dissatisfied with him and supported his opponent.   Kasonga therefore announced that the new headman would be Wadi.   Mbulaje was dissatisfied with this decision and gathered about him his followers and went off to found a village elsewhere.   But the position for Wadi was an uneasy one.   He lived in dread of Mbulaje's sorcery.   When he was ill just before he died, he accused Mbulaje of putting poison in his beer.   After he died Mbulaje brought back the women he had taken away and adopted the attire of the village headman.   The people cynically accepted this, saying that he should perhaps take it because if any other should try to be headman he would not enjoy the fruits long before he too was killed.   But the women were not satisfied with this arrangement and led by Cilo, the headman's sister's son, migrated.   They said, ' We wonder that our chief should have died. The heart of the present chief is not good.   Those who will stay with

him will be other people, but for us the bush does not eat a person.' [1]
Mbulaje was left with a few personal adherents. My informant
assured me that 'He is a most unhappy man to-day because he is
forever accused of being the sorcerer who is causing the deaths of his
relatives. People are saying that Mbulaje had broken the village
because he wanted to be a chief when the people did not want him.
The one the people wanted was killed. Nowadays, no one visits him
because of his sorcery and the people are frightened of him especially
at beer drinks.'

Immaturity disqualifies many prospective village headmen. A
headman must be a man of experience and wisdom to take charge
of a village. Unfortunately I cannot present quantitative data on

REFERENCE GENEALOGY. CIKOJA VILLAGE.

the ages when village headmen succeeded to their title, but my
impressions are that unless a man is older than about 30 years
he will not be considered for the name. Difficulty arises when
there is a conflict between the principles of seniority and age.
The older women do not always bear sons before their younger
sisters, so that sometimes a man from a junior lineage section
(liŵelelyanandi) may be older than a man from the senior. If the
younger, but senior, is, say, over 35 it is likely that, other things
being equal, he will take the name, but if not the man from the
junior house stands the better chance. This is what has happened
in Cikoja village. The position is as follows. When Cikoja IV
(B2) died, quite regularly the elder sister's (B1) first-born son
(C1) succeeded. But many years elapsed between the birth of

[1] *Litinji liyangalya mundu.* In other words, if we go to live in the bush somewhere Mbulaje will not bewitch us. Yao sorcerers are supposed to eat their
victims. See p. 117, f.n. 1.

the children of Ncilaga (C5) and Bt. Mkwinda (C6). There was a big difference in the ages of these two women. Ncilaga died nearly 30 years ago but Bt. Mkwinda died in 1948. When Cikoja V (C1) died in 1936, Salimu II (D3), who was born in about 1914, was very much younger than the present Cikoja VI (E7), who was born about 1895. Ncilaga (C5) had no sons, nor had Atabiya (D1), her eldest daughter, so the succession passed to the only son of Amaliama (D2) who was the senior male in that generation. Salimu II, genealogically senior to the present Cikoja, is to be the next headman. He has married a 'cross-cousin' (his mother's mother's brother's daughter's daughter's daughter) and lives in the village. He has already taken over the affairs in one section of the village. The other section has moved out and built about half a mile away with the present Cikoja VI. Note that the junior house—i.e. the descendants of Citeleka (A2)—are completely out of the succession. Wegami's (E1) eldest son, Cilimba (F1), is living virilocally with Cikoja VI in his section of the village and is already opposed to the prospective village headman Salimu. He is likely to be the village headman after Salimu dies and may even push his claim when the present Cikoja VI dies, because Salimu has been accused of sorcery on several occasions.

The conflict between sister's sons and mother's brothers at successions has all but fallen away. The people oppose with some vigour the idea that a younger brother should succeed. Frequently the chief or headman would rather his younger brother succeed, and sometimes indicates him as his successor. Kawinga, for example, has given his pre-succession name of Mlomba to his younger brother and many say this is tantamount to announcing Mlomba as the next Kawinga. This is violently repudiated by most people I have spoken to and they indicate a sister's son as the likely successor. Jalasi too, before he died in 1941, indicated Mbawa, his mother's younger sister's son as the successor, but when it came to the point a sister's son succeeded. The weight of custom is in favour of the sister's sons and usually the succession is fought out among uterine or collateral brothers in the first descending generation.

A matrilineal relative is always chosen to be chief in preference to any other, but sometimes there is no heir. Other things being equal an unsuitable matrilineal relative will be chosen, or a woman will take the position, before the name will be allowed to pass to a non-matrilineal relative. While a matrilineal relative holds it there is always the chance that a suitable matrilineal heir will be born to a woman of the matrilineage, and will be able to take over the name. In Katuli's area the principle of primogeniture is so strong, I was told that rather than let a succession pass to a junior house, a woman is appointed to ' keep the name '. This happened before the succession of the present Katuli. Nkolojele was the present Katuli's mother, and when his mother's brother died Katuli was too young to become the chief. Instead Nkolojele took the name to prevent it from going to a junior lineage and held it from 1920 to 1936. Nkolojele was thus appointed Principal Headman under the 1912 Ordinance. In 1936, she retired in favour of her son who then took the name Katuli and became chief.

The name is kept within the matrilineage if it is at all possible. The history of the succession of Mpumbe's name is instructive in this context.

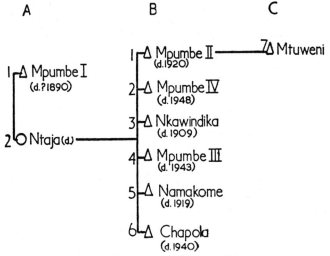

REFERENCE GENEALOGY. MPUMBE VILLAGE.

Mpumbe, it will be remembered,[1] came from Jalasi's area to Kawinga's after the White attack on Jalasi in Mangoche. The genealogical summary sets out the relevant data.

---

[1] See p. 59.

Mpumbe I (A1) died in Jalasi's area before the European attack in 1896. His sister's son (B1) succeeded. When he died in 1920 three brothers survived him. He had no sisters. His immediate brother (B2) was considered unsuitable for the headmanship and it passed instead to the next surviving brother Mpumbe III (B4). When he died in 1943 the only survivor in the matrilineage was Mpumbe IV (B2), and although he was by this time a very old man and had been previously considered unsuitable, he was selected as the next headman. In 1947, when I first visited the area he was blind, almost permanently bemused with beer and quite decrepit. At the same time Ntuweni (C7), the son of Mpumbe II by a slave wife, was about 50 years old and was the virtual village headman. All disputes were brought to him and he settled most of them. He also represented the village to the District Commissioner and at Kawinga's court house when the presence of the headman was required. Wadi, Mpumbe I's fifth wife's daughter's daughter's son, assisted him. The only thing that Mtuweni could not do was to make the sacrifices for the girls' initiation ceremony, but he took the old man to the shrine-tree and held his unsteady hand while the latter poured the flour on the ground and called on the ancestors. When Mpumbe IV died in 1948, the succession passed to a distant sister's son whom they found in Ngongondo's village in Liwonde's area. Mtuweni, who might have succeeded to the name, and for all intents and purposes was a village headman before the headman's death, was accused of killing the old man by sorcery so that he could press his claim to the succession. He consequently moved out with his sisters and founded a village of his own about 15 miles away.

When there are no heirs available one of two courses is open. The first is that a patrilaterally-linked relative may succeed to the name. I have heard, for example, of a chief's son who succeeded as Matola in the Makanjila dynasty. The son, of course, had the same clan-name as the chief.[1] In the Makanjila case there is some evidence that there were other heirs available and that this succession was the result of a clever piece of lobbying by the slaves with the Administration. I have on record a few villages where this has taken place, and where the name has kept to the slave lineage.

A more likely reaction to this situation is probably what would have happened in Mpumbe's village if no matrilineal relative could be found. Mtuweni would probably have taken the

[1] Slave-children took the clan-names of their captors. See p. 72.

village but called it Mtuweni and not Mpumbe village. The positions of the lineages in the village would have become inverted, and the patrilaterally-linked lineage become the dominant lineage. In this way villages may change their name or they may acquire two names, as happened to Mlungu village in Nyambi's area. Here a man called Masalu took over the control of the village. He was the son of the previous Mlungu and the village is known to-day by either of these names. The interesting point is what will happen when he dies, because there are now sisters' sons in a distant lineage old enough to take charge of the village. The rule is, as we have seen, that the matrilineal relatives always have the first claim.

PATERNITY AND SEGMENTATION

It is interesting to note that the paternity of brothers or sisters is not a differentiating feature in these social relationships. In the discussions which have hinged upon the care of sorority-groups I have never heard the paternity of brothers and sisters brought up as a reason why they should hold more or less closely together. The father is important in social life as I point out later, but while groups may be linked through paternity, it does not lead to a second principle of segmentation within the lineage.[1] This is manifestly the result of the fundamental difference in a system of matrilineal descent, where paternity is of less consequence than maternity is in a patrilineal structure. Among the Yao, unlike the patrilineal peoples of Southern and Northern Africa, no marriage payments are made ; divorce is easy and frequent, and there are no disputes about the custody of children, who always belong to their mother's group whether they are illegitimate or not.[2] This is consistent with the view of the husband as a mere begetter of children. Among the Yao, the

---

[1] This aspect of segmentation in patrilineal peoples, with different wives of men as points of fission, is brought out particularly in Evans-Pritchard, E. E., *The Nuer*, Oxford University Press (London, 1940), and *Marriage and the Family among the Nuer*, R.-L.I. Paper, No. 11 (1944) ; Fortes, M., *The Dynamics of Clanship*, and *The Web of Kinship* ; Kuper, H., *A Black Aristocracy*, Oxford University Press (London, 1947).

[2] This has been worked out in Gluckman, M., ' Kinship and Marriage among the Lozi of Northern Rhodesia and the Zulu of Natal ', in Radcliffe-Brown, A. R., and Forde, C. D. (eds.), *African Systems of Kinship and Marriage*, Oxford University Press for the International African Institute (London, 1950).

sisters are the points of cleavage in the matrilineage and the group of uterine sisters is seldom divided, unless their daughters are old enough to form a corporate group and to move off with their mother to found a new village under their brother.

THE SPATIAL REPRESENTATION OF LINEAGE SEGMENTATION

The segmentation of the matrilineage is also shown in the spatial distribution of the huts in a village. The daughters of the women of the matrilineage set up their huts near to their mothers', and as this continues over a number of years, the internal segmentation of the matrilineage is automatically reflected in the disposition of huts. Most Yao villages will show this spatial representation of social distance, some more clearly than others. The clearest example I have is in Meni section of Majaja village, Nyambi's area. The disposition of the huts is set out in the village plan in Appendix C. Here are five fairly distinct groups of huts in the village. Four are descendants of four uterine sisters, the children of the previous Majaja. The space between these four groups is cleared and paths reticulate among the huts. About 200 yards away, the fifth group is out of sight of the others and must be reached by a path leading through the fields. In this cluster of huts live the children of the uterine brother of the four sisters. The matrilineal relatives of Majaja live about half a mile away in a quite distinct cluster.

In Cikoja village the same principles are at work but the situation is somewhat obscured by the number of patrilaterally-linked relatives. A glance at the village plan in Appendix D shows that the major segments, denoted by the symbols Ma and Mc in the plan, are quite distinct in the old village site, the huts of Ma being separated from those of Mc by a broad path and by a patch of bamboos. In the new village site across the stream the same general segmentation is shown where the two sections, Ma_1 and Ma_2, are separated by a path.[1] The separation of the clusters of huts is difficult to represent on a diagram because not only are the huts placed in discrete clusters, but they face in towards one another and the space between them is kept clean. Between the clusters there may be rubbish heaps and small garden patches. I describe later how the village continually

[1] I describe how this section of the village came to be across the river on p. 169.

adjusts itself to the changes in its composition. At this point I wish only to indicate how the differentiation among the various segments of a matrilineage is reflected in the way the members site their huts in a village.

THE SEGMENTARY PROCESS

The segmentary tendencies within the lineage are countered by unifying forces, but the cleavages between the lineage sections show up at the slightest provocation. Once the cleavage starts it widens rapidly and charges of sorcery become more and more frequent between the two sections until eventually one moves out to found a new village. A cleavage of this type has been developing in Cikoja village for the last eight years. When I left the field in 1949, talk of migration was in the air but it had not yet happened. I summarize the major events which led to the present situation.

The cleavage first manifested itself in 1942 when Bt. Mbwana (F2) [1] fought with her mother's younger ' sister ' Ayesi (E8). These two were pounding at the same place in the village and Bt. Mbwana took Ayesi's flat sifting basket. She retained it for about four days without telling Ayesi that she had it. One day Ayesi saw it at the pounding point and asked Bt. Mbwana where she got it. They had a few words about it and Bt. Mbwana returned it and thought no more of it. She was pregnant at the time and was confined about a month later. It was her fifth child but she had a greatly prolonged labour. After labour had been going on for some hours, Cilimba (F1), her eldest brother, thought that there must be something wrong and sent his two younger brothers, Kausi (F3) and Gwili (F4) to a diviner. The diviner indicated that the cause of the difficult birth was that her ' younger mother ' Ayesi was bearing her malice,[2] and advised that Ayesi should blow water from her mouth and declare that she bore no malice. Kausi and Gwili returned and went to Bt. Amisa (E4) who was Ayesi's elder sister and told her what the diviner had said. Bt. Amisa did as she was advised and fetched Ayesi to the door of the hut in which Bt. Mbwana was lying, and made her confess. The child was born immediately. After a week Cilimba and Kausi brought a complaint to the village headman Cikoja (E7). They accused Ayesi of trying to kill their sister. Cikoja sent a message to

---

[1] The reference numbers refer to the genealogy in Appendix D.
[2] Difficult labour is usually assumed to be due to adultery, but it may also be due to sorcery or malice. See p. 138, and Chap. VII, p. 185.

his eldest uterine sister's first-born and second-born sons, Amidu (F18) and Kanyenga (F19), to advise them of this dispute, and told them that they would have to assume responsibility for the actions of their mother's younger sister, Ayesi. At the same time he sent to a neighbouring village to call in an unrelated man to act as arbitrator in the dispute. There was much argument and eventually the arbitrator awarded 15s. to be paid by Cikoja as leader of the junior lineage section to Cilimba as leader of the senior section. Amidu and Kanyenga found 10s. between them and gave it to Cikoja to give to Cilimba. The other 5s. they said they would try to find and pay later.

This payment formally settled the dispute but the tension was near to the surface. Amidu and Kanyenga said that there was separation in the group now that they had started to eat money. They were not wrong. Ayesi was pregnant and near to confinement. When she was confined her labour was as difficult as Bt. Mbwana's (it was also her fifth confinement). When her birthpang confessions seemed to be unavailing Bt. Bwana Isa (F16), her elder sister's daughter, went to Kanyenga to tell him that their ' younger mother ' was having a difficult childbirth. Kanyenga remarked that she had had many children before and had not suffered, so that there must be some reason for her difficulty. Then Kanyenga and his sister went to Ayesi's husband's sister's hut [1] to find a representative to go with them to a diviner. When they got there Ayesi's husband's sister told her son to accompany her brother's wife's representative to the diviner. The diviner indicated that the cause of the prolonged birth was the malice felt by Bt. Mbwana because the rest of the compensation awarded had not yet been paid. He said that the only thing to do was to call Bt. Mbwana and to get her to blow water from her mouth at the hut door where Ayesi was confined. Bt. Amisa went to find Bt. Mbwana and made her do this. Immediately Ayesi delivered a stillborn child.

The next morning Amidu and Kanyenga went to Cikoja and blamed him for the stillborn child.[2] Cikoja called Cilimba to listen to the complaint. Ayesi was inconsolable. She said that she had blown water for the sake of Bt. Mbwana who to-day had a child, whereas she was mourning her child. Once again Cikoja called in outsiders to act as arbitrators and the members of the two segments gathered to settle the dispute. At the end of protracted wrangling

---

[1] Ayesi was married to her MMMBDS (Katoli (D33)), whose lineage lived in another part of the same village. See genealogy and hut count in Appendix D.

[2] Cikoja is a representative of his lineage even to the lineage members. This accusation simply means that the blame lies within the lineage.

the arbitrators awarded 30s. compensation to be paid by Cilimba to Cikoja, less 5s. owing. This money was to be paid to Ayesi in compensation for the loss of her baby. Ayesi, however, refused to accept the money because she said she wanted to have her baby. The matter now became an intra-segment affair and Cikoja, Amidu, Kanyenga and Kaifa (F36), the son of Ayesi, with Bt. Amisa had a meeting on what to do. Ayesi was quite adamant about it. There was nothing to do but to drop the matter, and the state of tension between the segments remained as it was before.

The next incident occurred in 1943. Mpulula, the husband of Bt. Amisa, had some goats. One day two of them strayed on to the verandah of Bt. Madi's hut. Bt. Madi (F10) was the daughter of Asuna (F2) and a member of the senior lineage segment. One of the goats nosed its way into a basket of flour that was lying under the verandah and started to eat it. Bt. Madi came out and picked up a log that was lying nearby and threw it at the goat. It broke the goat's leg and the goat had to be destroyed. The owner, Mpulula, who was watching at that moment immediately rebuked the woman. He went and reported the matter to Cikoja and he sent a message to Mpulula's marriage surety who sent back to say that they would meet at Chiwalo's hut the following morning. The arbitrator in the case finally decided that the correct action should have been to take the goat to the owner and to lay a complaint against him. As it was he had to award compensation of 30s. to be paid to the owner of the goat. Mpulula, however, refused to take the money. He argued that although the goat was his, so was the offender.[1] He said that he was afraid of sorcery so he would take a token amount of 3s. only. Cikoja gave him this.[2]

A few months later the eldest child of Bt. Bwana Isa (F16) suddenly fell ill and died.[3] Kanyenga, Kaifa and Msusa went to the diviner. Kaifa, the son of Ayesi, went as the headman's representative. Kanyenga went as the warden of the sorority-group, i.e. the child's mother's brother. Msusa was the marriage surety of the child's father. Kanyenga consulted the diviner who indicated that Kanyenga's mother Bt. Amisa was responsible but that she was not a sorceress. Sorcery, he said, was introduced by an unknown person who was using Bt. Amisa's grumbling as a screen. Kanyenga refused to accept the finding of the diviner, saying that his mother had never been 'caught'

---

[1] His wife's collateral sister's child he also calls 'my child'.

[2] Mpulula is a stranger in the village and in this situation Cikoja represents both segments to Mpulula, even though the senior segment is guilty.

[3] Sudden illness, called *cikomo* or 'the hammer', is believed to be without a doubt due to sorcery.

by a diviner before. He went back and reported the matter to Cikoja who accepted the finding. Kanyenga, however, argued that the real sorcerer was using magic to confuse the diviner. After some argument Cikoja sent for the then senior living member of the matrilineage, Bt. Mkwinda (C6), who was living in Cholo district, for Mbande, a perpetual brother, and for Cibwana Kawinga, his perpetual mother's brother. A big meeting was held at which all the important local headmen attended. The case was argued on the point whether Bt. Amisa and her husband, who was implicated in the accusation, could be sorcerers. After some argument the court decided that it was impossible for Bt. Amisa to be a sorceress without Cikoja also being a sorcerer, so that the accusation now settled on Cikoja himself. The case was taken up to Chiwalo who refused to award compensation. He reviewed the various charges of sorcery that had been made in the village before and observed that after the death of one of the supposed sorcerers the village had lived peacefully. He deplored the new friction and warned that there was to be no migration from the village. He advised Cikoja to mollify his sisters if he could. Kanyenga, Cikoja's eldest sister's son, said that he did not think that it would be possible because the headman had virtually accused his sister of sorcery. Cibwana Kawinga now said that there was no question of whether it could be done or not. It simply had to be done.

About one month after this episode, Ajisa (F26), the last-born child of Bt. Amisa, who was about 2½ years old, died after two days' illness. When he was obviously very ill Kanyenga left with Mpulula to call Amidu. They went first to wake Cikoja who in turn sent for Gwili (F4) to be his representative. Kanyenga went off to a diviner at daybreak without waiting for the father's marriage surety. The diviner indicated that there was tension in the lineage which was at the back of the child's illness. Eventually, he indicated that Bt. Ntalika (E3) was the cause of the illness and it harked back to the dispute over the sifting basket and the goat. The diviner prepared suitable medicine and the two went back to the sick child. They got back about 8.30 a.m. and found the people congregated at the hut. In the meantime, Cikoja had sent off another divining party, Amidu (F18) and Jauma (F7). Kanyenga prepared the medicine and gave it to the child. It seemed to be getting no better and before Amidu and Jauma returned Cikoja sent Kanyenga and Gwili out to divine again. Then Amidu and Jauma returned and indicated that the same person was responsible, and almost immediately afterward Kanyenga and Gwili came back with the same result. When Kanyenga heard this he went to Chiwalo and reported the matter. Chiwalo sent a messenger to call Cikoja, Bt. Ntalika and her eldest sister's son Cilimba (F1), who was the senior male member of the senior lineage segment. They were to go to Chiwalo's hut the next morning. During the night the child Ajisa died, and Chiwalo remarked that Cikoja was bad at heart and that he merely killed his people like chickens.[1] Four days later after the funeral a meeting was held to decide the cause of death. The arbitrator and chief's representative was the local court assessor. The man's party opened the discussion saying, ' If Cikoja is tired of us he should tell us. To-day he is killing his child. We know that Mpulula [2] has begotten a sheep. The sheep pen is filled and when Cikoja wants to eat he merely eats these.' [3] The arbitrator said that Cikoja had done a shameful thing and that they should make up a divining party to find the cause of death. Kanyenga immediately demurred and said that they had divined three times with the same results. Further divination was a waste of money. He insisted that they called Cibwana Kawinga. The meeting broke up and Cibwana Kawinga was called for. He came a day or two later and the meeting was resumed. He said, ' Cikoja, you are evil.[4] You have found it impossible to keep the village. Now what are you going to do with your children? The man's surety says that he is going to take Mpulula away. Your brothers say that they are going to take their mothers away. Now what do you say to this?' Cikoja had no reply to make. Chiwalo then said that he would have to pay compensation to his sister. Kanyenga, however, said that they did not want money. They wanted to go away. Cibwana Kawinga here checked Kanyenga and told him that they would take Cikoja and give him a talking to, and instruct him on the traditional way of keeping a village together.[5] Chiwalo accepted this settlement of Cibwana Kawinga and endorsed his action.

When they got back, Cilimba told Cikoja and Mbande that he wanted to move out of the village because his ' mother ' had been called a sorceress by his ' brother '. Cikoja was anxious to avoid further trouble and told his lineage members that he was going to build a hut for his second wife some distance from the village because his first wife did not get on with her. He put up a hut about half a mile away across the Namwoce stream. Cilimba (F1) who was living virilocally, his mother Bt. Ntalika (E3), Bt. Mbwana (F2),

---

[1] This is a reference to the ghoul-motif in Yao witchlore. Cikoja here, of course, is a symbol of the whole lineage, so that this imprecation is directed toward the whole lineage and not to Cikoja personally, as in the last dispute.

[2] The father of the dead child.

[3] Mpulula had begotten eleven children. This is another reference to the ghoul-motif.

[4] *Usakwa*—this word is also used to mean ' polluted '.

[5] *Kala utawe wakwe musi*—' the building of a village of old '.

Kausi (F3), Bt. Madi (F10), Bt. Aliya (F11) and their children moved across the stream and built with Cikoja. One of Cikoja's wives stayed in the old village and the other moved across. Shortly after this Asimama (E6), Cikoja's sister, decided that she would like to move across to be with the headman. She reported to Kanyenga who sent her to tell Cikoja. Cikoja in turn sent her to tell Amidu. Eventually, Cikoja, Amidu, Kanyenga and Salimu (D3) had a meeting about it. Neither Amidu nor Kanyenga, nor Salimu, was enthusiastic, but they said she should follow her own wishes. She moved across with her children. Asimama's arrival on the other side of the stream was greeted with some suspicion by Cilimba because she was a member of the junior lineage. However, Cikoja assured him that he wanted one of Asimama's daughters to fetch water for him. Cilimba was satisfied with this explanation and accepted the situation as it was.

It was not easy, however, and there were continual quarrels between the children of Bt. Ntalika and those of Asimama. The members of the junior segment in the old village also looked upon this arrangement with some suspicion. The friendship of Amege (F28), Asimama's daughter, with Asubiya (E9), her mother's younger sister was particularly deprecated by the members of the junior segment. Asubiya was warned several times that this friendship could only lead to sorcery.[1]

In the meantime, Salimu (D3), who will be the next Cikoja and who was the senior lineage member in the old village site, undertook most of the duties of the headman in that section. He settled most of the minor cases and saw to the divining. However, he reported his doings to Cikoja who was still the village headman.

In 1948, another death took place and the tension became evident again. Bt. Ntalika's child died. Kausi (F3) and Jauma (F7) went to the diviner, who revealed that Amege had gone to Salimu to grumble about what was going on in the other village, and Salimu had taken this opportunity of bewitching the child. Cikoja refused to accept this explanation and said that the diviner was a liar. When the body was being washed, a knife was found under the mat on which it was lying, and the story went around that a piece of flesh was taken out of the dead child's buttock.[2] Cikoja interpreted this as meaning that Bt. Ntalika herself had bewitched the child. He felt it unnecessary to call a funeral meeting. Shortly after this there was some friction between Amisa and her younger sister Asubiya, arising out of jealousy because of the difference in their harvests. Bt. Amisa was convinced

---

[1] This is based on the fear of backbiting. See p. 138.

[2] Once a person is dead the matrilineal relatives do not touch him. They leave the hut and the undertakers (*awilo*) wash the body and prepare it for burial. They reported this finding to Cikoja.

that Asubiya in her jealousy had gone to grumble to Bt. Ntalika about this. Rajabu (F20) who had heard about this called Cikoja and they assembled Bt. Amisa, Bt. Bwana Isa and Asubiya in Bt. Amisa's hut, and spoke to them about the dangers of backbiting. Cikoja remonstrated with the women saying, ' I don't want to hear about this again. When you love people do not love people who are strangers. Do not talk behind people's backs and bring war in the knots of your body-cloths.'

A few weeks after this, in June 1948, Aluwinda (F47), a 3½-year-old daughter of Asubiya, died. When her mother saw that the child was seriously ill she took her to her patrilateral relatives in Liwonde area. She had barely got there when the child died. The headman of the village sent a message back to Cikoja to tell him of the death. He in turn sent a message to Amidu and Rajabu and they went to the village to attend the funeral. After the first mourning feast three days after the funeral, Kaifa, the child's mother's elder sister's son, and Malawago, representing the village in which the child had died, went to a diviner who indicated that the cause lay in the backbiting of Asubiya about Bt. Amisa, but that the sorcerer was Bt. Ntalika. The tension now had reached almost breaking point and after about six months Bt. Ntalika moved out into Liwonde area without announcing that she was going.

At the end of December, Asubiya's son Selemu (F46), aged 4½, suddenly became ill one night. In the morning Amidu and Rajabu and Nkatawila (D20), who was the husband's marriage surety, went to a diviner. He indicated that the cause was a girls' initiation basket which Ayesi kept. This basket, the diviner said, kept losing its strength and it was only on the death of a close relative that it would regain power. They returned and when they got near the village they could hear the women keening. They agreed that the diviner was a liar and returned and got their money back. The body was buried on January 3rd, 1949. Asubiya now left the village without announcing her intention and went to complain to chief Kawinga. Cikoja in the meantime, noticing that Asubiya was not present at the funeral, sent out men to search for her. After two days Kawinga's chief court assessor, Masunda, brought Asubiya back to the village. He told Cikoja that he had cross-examined her and found that she said her elder sister was causing death because of her jealousy over the food. Masunda returned and some days later Kawinga wrote a letter to Cikoja telling him to come to the court village. This he did and was told to hold the mourning feast, but to take the people to the court village to hold the funeral meeting. There a divining party would be arranged and the cause of the death determined.

After the first funeral feast the people of Cikoja assembled at

Kawinga's court village. Masunda reviewed the events leading up
to the calling of the meeting and asked Cikoja to give his statement.
Cikoja replied, 'You say I am finishing the people. I do not deny
it. If the people are being finished by my sister, then I am finishing
them.[1] You may speak what is in your hearts.' Asubiya now made
her statement. After this, Bt. Amisa was called out. She denied
knowing anything about the case. Masunda at this point was about
to send the case back to Cikoja when Matosa, a second arbitrator,
asked who the marriage sureties were. Amidu came forth as the
woman's surety. Matosa asked him to tell the court about Asubiya's
marriage relationships. Amidu then reviewed the history of Asubiya's
pregnancies. He pointed out that the first child had died.[2] The
second one also died. The diviner had indicated that she had broken
a sexual taboo and the child had died from *ndaka* as a result. The
third child was still alive. The fourth had died recently. The fifth
was the one about whom there was a case that day. He recounted
how they had gone to a diviner and how he had indicated that the
cause of the death lay in the backbiting which the person herself
had done. Masunda cross-questioned Amidu about the *ndaka* medicine
that was given and assured himself the complainant was satisfied that
the second child had died of *ndaka* and not sorcery. Masunda then
called Salimu since the woman was living at the old village site under
Salimu's charge. Salimu, who works as a tailor in an Indian store
some miles away, said that he did not have a great knowledge of the
case. Cikoja said he had nothing to say. Eventually, after some
hours of cross-questioning, Masunda decided that a divining party
must be made up and the results of the divination reported to the
court. Bt. Amisa now stood up and said she was prepared to undergo
the poison ordeal to prove that she was not a sorceress. She said that
she would go with them to the diviner to find out the cause of the
death of the child. Masunda said that they would leave the matter
at that. At the village they would have to decide on a divining party
and they would have to give poison to a chicken to make sure that
the divination was correct. After that Cikoja would have to report
the matter to Kawinga and the case would be re-opened. Nyenje
was at the inquest and said to Cikoja that if they were not relatives
he would have other words to say to him about this business. As it
was he did not see what he had to rejoice about. Cikoja said that he
did not know, but that Nyenje should ask the owner of the village.
Surprised, Nyenje said, 'Who is that?' Cikoja indicated Salimu.

---

[1] Cikoja is talking as a representative of his lineage here.

[2] The first death in a family is never divined for, because the Yao say that
if this is done, it 'would chase the father away'.

Salimu said that Cikoja ought not to speak like that because it only made things difficult.

Two days after this Cikoja called a meeting at Salimu's hut in order to choose a divining party. Eventually they chose Kanyenga, Asimama, Raisi and Musa. Musa was the witness for Kanyenga who represented the woman's party. Raisi represented the father's party, and Asimama went to be his witness. Cikoja gave them 5s. and they went to look for a diviner. Eventually they found one and Kanyenga opened the consultation. The diviner indicated that the cause of the death of the child was *litukula*.[1] The party paid him and looked for a place to sleep. The following day they sought another diviner. Kanyenga again consulted and was told that Bt. Ntalika and her son were sorcerers but that the mother herself was ill with *litukula*. Kanyenga rejected the *litukula* explanation and insisted on the sorcery of Bt. Ntalika and Cilimba. The diviner consulted again and said that the main cause of the death was the *litukula* and that the sorcery of Bt. Ntalika was added to the other. Asimama here insisted that the sorceress in reality was Bt. Amisa. The diviner rejected this. He said the best way to test the divination was to give poison to a chicken. The party was at a loss to know what to do. In two divinations, a *likango* was indicated twice, while sorcery was said to cloud the issue. They decided to give a chicken poison. They returned to Rajabu's hut in the village where he had married. Here they sent Rajabu to tell Salimu that they were about to test a chicken at the poison ordeal, but that he must not tell Cikoja. They gave two chickens poison, one for *litikula* of the mother and one for the sorcery of Bt. Amisa. The *litukula* chicken died, indicating that Bt. Amisa was innocent. When Cikoja was told this he refused to believe it and sent them to poison another two chickens. The result was the same. He now decided that he would take the divination to a distant place and chose to go to Ngokwe chiefdom. Kanyenga led the divination party again. They consulted the diviner and after much testing and retesting the diviner decided that the sorcerers were Bt. Ntalika and Cilimba and that the *litukula* had nothing to do with it. He also specifically excluded Bt. Amisa. The diviner now told the father's two representatives to stay behind while the woman's representatives fetched Cikoja. When he came, the diviner revealed the result to him personally. Cikoja was at a loss what to do in this situation. Two divinations including poison tests had indicated that *likango* was the cause, a third and very exhaustive one had revealed Bt. Ntalika and her son. Neither had indicated Bt. Amisa.

---

[1] *Litukula* is a type of pimple (the generic term for which is *likango*) which, when it comes to a head and bursts, causes the death of the last-born child.

Eventually, in March, he decided to take the case up to Kawinga's court. Cikoja was not willing to accuse Bt. Ntalika and Cilimba publicly. Accordingly he went to Kawinga but he did not send for Bt. Ntalika. When Masunda, the court assessor, heard this he refused to handle the case and told Cikoja that Bt. Ntalika had to be brought to court so that they could hear her statement. Cikoja and his people came back to the village and nothing more was done about it. In April, Rajabu wrote a letter to Cikoja telling him that he wanted to report him to Kawinga and to bring a charge for compensation against him because he had falsely accused his mother of sorcery.

I left the field in June and do not know what the result was.

The series of events are extremely complex. I have given only a summary of them. Nevertheless, the main themes in the history are clear enough. We see Cikoja as the representative of the lineage of any order whatsoever. We find in particular the opposition of the two collateral brothers, Kanyenga and Cilimba. They are the representatives of the two lineage segments in this situation. There is seldom any doubt about the affiliation of these two personalities. Consistently in the accounts of the divinations each rejects the diviner's finding if it accuses a member of his lineage segment. Note that the divination seance itself becomes a field in which the opposition of the segments is expressed. Kanyenga continued consulting diviners until finally he got the answer he wanted. His opponents rejected these findings and eventually even discounted the chicken ordeal. The diviners' findings and the results of the poison ordeals, therefore, are bandied about between the opposed groups, and though the whole procedure of divination and accusations of sorcery is directed towards the extirpation of discordant elements in the community, in fact, it is only a facet of the underlying cause of the tension—the opposition of segments in an ever-segmenting lineage.

In addition to the structural opposition of Kanyenga and Cilimba there is a certain amount of tension among Cikoja's uterine sisters. Bt. Amisa, Asimama, Ayesi and Asubiya have all had children. Bt. Amisa is the senior and the relationships between her and any of the other sisters are difficult. In addition to this there is the tension between the generations seen in the attempts of the sons of Amisa to bring a compensation claim against Cikoja himself. It is important that not once is a member of the junior major segment, that is a descendant of Citileka (A2), involved in the dispute. Only the descendants of Atabiya (D1) and Amaliama (D2) are involved, with the exception of Salimu who appears as the representative of the villagers on the old village site.

THE OPPOSITION OF THE GENERATIONS

Segmentation arises as more and more sorority-groups, the daughters of women, reach adulthood, and as the sons of the same women become old enough to undertake responsibilities for the care of the women. There is, in this situation, a fundamental opposition of generations. A woman is bound to her own sisters and at the same time she is bound to her daughters. These bonds come into conflict when her daughters want to express their unity against their mother's sister's daughters. The mother must decide whether she will go with her daughters to their new village site, or whether she will stay with her sisters and possibly with her own brother. I found consistently that a mother seldom stayed in a village when her daughters were moving out of it. The bond with her children is stronger than that with her sisters. Yet the conflict is clearly present. It finds expression in the kinship terminology. A daughter is usually identified with her mother's mother. A woman's daughter's daughter inherits her name, her position and her property in much the same way as a man succeeds his mother's brother.[1] When this has taken place the terms of address of her parental generation are now reversed. In other words her mother's brother instead of calling her, ' sister's child ' (*cipwa*), calls her ' mother ' (*amao*). Sometimes the qualificative *ŵamauja* (' who has returned ') is used to signify the difference. Her mother's mother's husband even before the succession has taken place calls her ' my wife ', and I have recorded one or two marriages between a man and his wife's daughter's daughter. A man's daughter's daughter must also perform some of the funeral rites for her grandfather after his wife has died.[2]

We have among the Yao, therefore, the familiar principle of

---

[1] See Chap. V, p. 121.
[2] She cooks the ritual meal which he eats at the end of mourning to protect himself against *ndaka*. Here she ritually fills her mother's mother's place.

the identification of alternate generations ; and this is particularly significant when we realize that the tension between the filial and parental generations is most likely to find expression in the situation where a group of young adult women wish to leave a village, and their mother, if she is still alive, must make up her mind whether to stay or to follow them.

The existence of rules of succession for men, different from those for women, presents an interesting analytical problem which I have not yet fully explored. Clearly men must succeed to positions in the first ascending generation, for they are the active leaders in Yao society and those who are to succeed must be sufficiently mature to take over the responsibilities of leadership. Women, on the other hand, are usually not leaders so that succession to positions in the second ascending generation involves no difficulties. A young woman may take her mother's mother's name without involving any responsibilities of leadership. Yet the interaction of the two systems of succession presumably has some reaction on the social structure. A man's sister's daughter who succeeds to her mother's mother's position becomes the man's mother and the man's mother's brother's sister. The man's own sister becomes his mother's brother's mother.[1] The effect of this presumably is to achieve some balance of power between a man and his mother's brother. By the rule of succession for women, a man's sister to whom he is tied by the closest possible ties of kinship, and on whom he is dependent for political success, becomes his mother's brother's mother, so forming a common link between two potentially opposed persons. By the same reasoning a man's sister's daughter who is part of his sorority-group and who is likely to desert her mother's mother's brother to go with her mother's brother if there is a conflict, by succession becomes the sister of her mother's brother's mother's brother, so forming a unifying influence within the lineage. This problem emerged after my fieldwork was completed so that I have no evidence to support these suggestions.

Among the men, because of the struggle for political power, the opposition of alternate generations is much stronger than among women. This emerges most clearly in the institution of marriage sureties.

The duties of the marriage sureties towards their wards are

[1] I am grateful to Prof. Gluckman who pointed this out to me.

part of the normal duties of a matrilineage leader to his kinsmen.[1] But ideally each marriage is supposed to have two marriage sureties. The first, or senior, surety is called *mkokowogona*, which was described to me as ' the log that lies at the doorway '. The picture here is of a wise old man who cannot move around too easily, but who sits at the doorway of his hut ready to give advice and information to his younger kinsmen. In contrast to this is the junior surety. He is called *mkupamame* or the ' beater down of dew '. He is pictured as a young man, who is vigorous about his daily tasks and who is waiting before the dew has evaporated in the morning, at the door of couples who have difficulties. He is essentially the ' one who walks about '.

The senior marriage surety is ideally supposed to be a mother's brother, while the junior marriage surety is supposed to be a brother. In fact, while the junior marriage surety is almost always a brother, though not necessarily an elder brother, the senior, for reasons which will emerge later, is frequently not a mother's brother. However, in the Yao mind the two are fixed in the relationship to each other as mother's brother and sister's son. The fundamental conflict of their positions is expressed by the opposition of the concepts of the ' recumbent log ' and the ' active man '. This view is consistent with the segmentation and internal differentiation that must go on within a lineage. As the segments of the matrilineage become progressively independent of each other, the senior relatives, who formerly held them together, become less and less active in their affairs. In Yao idiom they become ' recumbent logs '.

The relationship between mother's brother and sister's son therefore is fundamentally ambivalent. By the values surrounding the concepts of descent and relationship, a sister's son and mother's brother are close kin and bound together in their attachment to a common ancestry and to a common set of living women who are in their joint care. At the same time the mother's brother, belonging as he does to the parental generation, must be respected by his sister's sons. Recalcitrant sister's sons may be made to toe the line by a number of different sanctions. A mother's brother, for example, may take his case to an arbitrator and bring the force of public opinion to bear upon his

[1] I have described the rôles of the marriage sureties more fully in *Marriage among the Machinga Yao*.

sister's son. This, however, is not common because matters such as these, the Yao feel, ought to be settled within the matrilineage, or at least among kinsmen. The more usual procedure is for the mother's brother to take his complaint to some senior matrilineal relative who may be a perpetual mother's brother of the mother's brother, as say Cibwana Kawinga is to Cikoja.[1] Or if the matrilineage is part of a village, the mother's brother may take his case to his village headman, who is as likely as not his perpetual father. The senior relatives have the force of authority and public opinion behind them and frequently some agreement can be reached at this level. Where this is not possible, say because the perpetual elder relative lives too far away, the mother's brother may take the sister's son to court and bring the sanction of the Native Authority's punishment upon him. This is very rare.

There is still a certain mystical sanction behind the mother's brother's control over his junior relatives. This is based on the curse, which in turn draws on the belief in common ancestor spirits. A mother's brother may say to a sister's son or other junior matrilineal relative : ' If you have never sucked from the breast of my sister, nothing dreadful will happen to you.' [2]

The fear of sorcery is another force which operates to control the wayward activities of a sister's sons. People in senior generations are usually looked upon as having particularly wide knowledge of potent medicines. Though a sister's son may sometimes use sorcery against his mother's brother, the reverse is believed to be more likely to happen. I have recorded elsewhere [3] the details of a case where a sister's son left a village, against his mother's brother's wishes, to find work in town. He subsequently met his death in an accident while trying to get the honey out of a wild bees' hive in a treetop. At home his death was attributed to the sorcery of his mother's brother whose will he had frustrated.

On the other hand the sister's sons, while bound by an ethical code to honour and respect their mother's brothers, find that in fact these stand in the way of their own personal ambitions. A man's heir is his sister's son and it is quite understandable that there should be some tension between a man and his heir. But

---

[1] See p. 132.   [2] See Chap. VI, p. 135.
[3] ' A Note on the African Conception of Causality ', 54–5.

the opposition between mother's brothers and sister's sons in general has a much wider basis than this. Any man is likely to have more than one sister's son of whom only one is his heir. Yet his other uterine nephews are as much opposed to him as the heir is. The tension lies in the position of the mother's brother *vis-à-vis* his sister's sons within the segmenting lineage. The different sorority-groups within the matrilineage are held together through the authority of the mother's brother. This coercive force is undermined by the attempts of the wardens of the various sorority-groups to break away and form new villages of their own. In this way the segmentation and differentiation of the matrilineage is really a facet of the general political process in which groups are for ever trying at once to demonstrate their automony by setting up new villages, and their unity by remaining in large integrated villages. Conflicts between sister's sons and mother's brothers, therefore, are common.[1] For a typical example we need not go outside the village that I have chosen to illustrate the localized matrilineage.

Ali Kasunka (C6) fell out with his mother's sister's daughter's son Mwanace (D10). The trouble started when Ali Kasunka who had married the sister of the cook came to live uxorilocally in Chiwalo's area. While in Zomba he had asked Mwanace to come to live virilocally in his village to keep things in order. It soon became apparent that the women were not satisfied with Mwanace and every time that Ali Kasunka visited them they had tales to tell of his failure to keep the peace. Ali Kasunka then decided that he would move his village from Zomba area to Chiwalo's where he was married, so that he could stay married to his wife in Chiwalo's area and keep control over the village. Soon after the change had taken place the infant daughter (E15) of Biti Mtemula (D19) became ill and died. Ali Kasunka went to the diviner with Adusoni, the child's father's marriage surety, to establish the cause of the death. The diviner indicated that it was the sorcery of Mwanace. Ali Kasunka took no action on this at all, but he remembered it. Some time later he himself became ill and this time his sisters Asausyeje (C8) and Biti Kasembe (C5) went to the diviner. Once again he indicated that Mwanace was responsible because he was jealous of Ali Kasunka's authority in the village. Tension increased when the husband of Biti Sale (D15), Wayison, became ill. His wife immediately went to tell

---

[1] In 31 village splits involving matrilineal relatives, 9 hinged on MB–ZS conflicts.

Mwanace. He was the junior marriage surety to the marriage and it was his duty to go to the man's marriage surety, report the matter and arrange to take some action to get the man well again. Mwanace, however, refused to take any action. Instead he tauntingly said, ' Take the matter to Ali Kasunka, it is his village.' The woman did so, and Ali Kasunka asked immediately whether she had not taken the matter to Mwanace. She replied that she had and repeated Mwanace's words. Ali Kasunka took the matter up with Mwanace who now objected to being ordered about. Ali Kasunka, however, impressed on Mwanace that the village was his (Ali Kasunka's) and the authority rested with him. He then went to the man's home to tell them of Wayison's illness. The man's representative came and he and Ali Kasunka consulted a diviner. They found that the man was ill from *ndaka*, which he had contracted in his home village. They found medicine and treated him and he recovered.

Things came to a head in 1947. Mwanace's younger sister Nyangu II (D11) was married to a soldier who was away. One morning she came to her mother's elder sister, Mbalasyao (C1),[1] and told her that she had found semen on her pudenda and could not recall having had intercourse with anyone. Mbalasyao told Ali Kasunka about this. It was clearly a matter for divination and Ali Kasunka called Mwanace and told him that they ought to consult a diviner. But Mwanace's attitude, even in such a crisis as this, was hostile. He refused and said it was not his work to do this sort of thing. Ali Kasunka therefore went to a diviner with his sister Mbalasyao. The diviner said the semen was Mwanace's. He said that he had entered her hut magically and had sexual intercourse with her without her knowing it.[2] When Ali Kasunka got back to the village he called Mwanace and asked him what tricks he was playing in the village. Mwanace said that he had done nothing—it was not his village. Ali Kasunka then vaguely hinted at his crime. Mwanace pressed for more details and Ali Kasunka accused him outright of sleeping with his sister. He had hardly uttered the accusation before Mwanace had drawn a knife and attacked him. Mwanace was screaming something to the effect that Ali Kasunka had come to him with lies about having seen a diviner. Ali Kasunka beat off the attack and reiterated the accusation. Mwanace now turned his rage upon the woman and tried to catch her. Two of the men in the village then caught Mwanace and subdued

---

[1] Her mother, Amaliama, was dead.

[2] This is called *cigonecesya*. It combines the use of magic with sister-incest. To the Yao mind there could be no clearer proof of sorcery. I have already mentioned the importance of sister-incest in relationship to the beliefs surrounding the sorority-group. See p. 146.

him. The woman in the meantime had run to Chiwalo's hut half a mile away. Here she complained to the chief that Mwanace wanted to kill her. Chiwalo refused to listen to her complaint and sent for Ali Kasunka. When he had come and explained the sequence of events, he continued saying that he would like to take the case to court. Chiwalo, who was Ali Kasunka's wife's father's sister's son (hence a classificatory younger brother) and whose henchman Ali Kasunka was, refused to arbitrate in the case but referred it to Kawinga. On the day of the case the woman's husband came back from the Army. The case was tried and eventually the court assessors awarded a damages claim of £3 to be paid by Mwanace to his sister. The husband, at the same time, said that he could not remain married to her because whenever he saw her he would think that she had slept with her brother and in court he gave Ali Kasunka a marriage termination payment. The tension between Ali Kasunka and his ' sister's son ' did not end there however. When they got back to the village Ali Kasunka remonstrated with Mwanace saying, ' Are you not ashamed to have married your sister ? ' Mwanace said that he could not stand that sort of thing and went back to live uxorilocally.

A crucial point in this case history is that the women did not like Mwanace. Almost certainly there would have been a split in the village had the women had more confidence in Mwanace. The tension between Ali Kasunka and Mwanace, although the conflict is inter-generational, started, as it consistently does, from the relationships of a man to the women of his matrilineage. Without the support of the women, younger brothers or sister's sons are impotent against the power of their senior relatives. It is only when they can induce the women to follow them and to leave their rivals that they can found a new village and thereby begin to earn prestige. Therefore, although the men are the active agents in bringing about a physical act of fission, they are in fact only making manifest a situation which is latent within the lineage.

The position of the senior male matrilineal relative is of fundamental importance in questions involving segmentation. His position is seen most clearly in the dominant matrilineage, in which the name of the village is inherited. The Yao practise ' positional succession '. A man not only succeeds to his mother's brother's name but also to the position of the mother's brother in the social structure as a whole.[1] It follows that when the

[1] See Chap. V, p. 121.

successor takes over the name of his predecessor, he assumes the position in the structure of the village as a whole, which was occupied by the first of that name. For example, when Cikoja VI succeeded to the name he moved to the position of Cikoja IV (who founded the village), as far as the members of the village were concerned. He is therefore the senior male matrilineal kinsman in the dominant lineage in the village, and Salimu, in spite of being more senior by generation, must call him mother's brother. The man who succeeds to the name of the founder of a village, or to the name of any important matrilineage member, therefore represents its maximum span to the members. From one point of view he is founding ancestor of the dominant lineage and is, therefore, lifted above the conflicts of the component sections ; but from another, since he represents all other sections to any one segment, he is involved in all the conflicts. Cikoja, for example, is the senior marriage surety to all the members of the dominant matrilineage in his village, while the junior marriage sureties are drawn from the component lineage segments. In this way he unites the dominant lineage in that all difficulties are brought to him by the junior sureties. But the junior sureties accuse Cikoja of being a sorcerer when they see him as a representative of an opposed section. Whatever the degree of segmentation within a matrilineage, he is still a mother's brother to them all, and all the component segments are united through him. This is a concept aptly figured in the synonym for a senior matrilineage member, a village headman, or a chief *cikunje* = a bundle of grass ; that is, a person in whom many different members are bound into one.

CHAPTER VII

THE PATRILATERALLY-LINKED GROUPS

THE POSITION OF THE HUSBAND AND FATHER

MATRILINEAL descent provides the principle on which the smallest of villages, the hamlets, are organized. But not all villages are made up of huts owned by members of one matrilineage as in Ali Kasunka's village.[1] Most villages in fact have a more complex internal organization which may be epitomized as a dominant matrilineage which carries the village headmanship, and a number of subsidiary lineages linked to the dominant lineage by various means. The most common of these is the patrilateral link whereby the subsidiary lineage is connected to the dominant lineage through one of its men.[2] The subsidiary lineage develops in the village from the matrilineal descendants of the virilocally-married wife of one of the men of the dominant lineage, so that the subsidiary lineage, initially at least, are the 'children' of one of the men of the headman's matrilineage. Their peculiar position in the village must be seen in the light of the general position of the father in Yao society.

The father, obviously enough, is also a son-in-law; obvious as this may seem in English it is charged with meaning for the Yao. When parents-in-law refer to their daughters' husbands they use the term *akwegwe*; and they in turn are called this by their sons-in-law. But the *akamwini* are essentially men who are living uxorilocally and *ukamwini* is the general status of being a man in uxorilocal marriage. *Mkamwini* thus cannot be translated into English without periphrasis and I translate it merely as 'husband'. I emphasize, however, that whenever I speak of *husbands* or the *husband* in general I mean 'husbands in uxorilocal marriage'. The Yao assume that marriages as a rule are uxorilocal. Usually the young husband builds a house in his wife's village and is expected to live there for the rest of his life. But

---

[1] See Chap. VI, pp. 140-3.
[2] I have called this type of village structure the 'thorp' in my earlier essay, 'The Yao of Southern Nyasaland', *Seven Tribes*, 332 ff.

he cannot escape the fact that in his wife's village he is only a 'billy goat' and that his 'true home' is in his matrilineal village. The pull of the matrilineal village on him, therefore, is always very strong and he is constantly trying to return there. His wife's responsible relatives are constantly trying to avoid this because they know that in time they are likely to lose the children who will probably settle in their father's village if they grow up there. In general, therefore, a husband must have a very good reason before he can get his wife's kinsmen's permission to take her and her children to his village. His wife's relatives do not easily yield. But a headman must live in his own village so that nearly all headmen bring at least one of their wives into their villages. Other men sometimes succeed in doing so especially if their wives are past child-bearing, but it is typically the headman's wife who lives virilocally.

The husband's interest in returning to his matrilineal village is heightened by the fact that a man in his wife's village is looked upon as the typical man without prestige : a stranger, whose duty is largely procreative. The theme song at the installation ceremony where the husband was compared with a billy goat, and the common epithet ' chicken rooster ' for a husband, reflect the attitude of the Yao towards him. In the song I quoted, the husband was said to be unable to climb high in his village of marriage, however rich he may become.[1] He is, nevertheless, an essential member of the village and the Yao say that it can succeed neither economically nor physically without his aid.

A husband becomes more important when he stays in a village for a long time. He becomes known intimately to the villagers and is conversant with their affairs. He is, therefore, able to advise on many private intra-lineage and intra-village affairs and may even become a marriage surety if there is no more suitable person available. Also in time the husband's position in the village changes. As his children grow up and become active members in the matrilineage, his position of husband becomes supplanted by his position of father, which, in a matrilineal society like that of the Yao, is significant in the same way as that of the mother's brother is in patrilineal societies.

The Yao recognize the close bond between father and child. This bond is conceived to be both social and physical and is

[1] See Chap. V, p. 119.

rationalized in the Yao theory of conception.[1] They believe that after intercourse the semen clots and embeds itself in the womb. From this the child develops and is nurtured by the mother until it is due to be born. Subsequent acts of intercourse add semen to the body of the child and make it fat. Semen from other men may be used, too, to feed the child in its intra-uterine life, but its body and blood are derived from the semen which first clotted. In Yao opinion there can be one father only.

Not all acts of intercourse lead to impregnation because sometimes, for various reasons, especially in immature women, the semen fails to clot. There is therefore, to the Yao way of thinking, some difficulty in determining the ' father ' of a child. This difficulty is met by the belief that the intra-uterine child in some way knows about the doings of its parents and in particular knows who its father is. It therefore refuses to be born unless its father is recognized.[2] Hence if a child is born without undue puerperal complications it is assumed to be the offspring of the man who is currently living with its mother. If labour is prolonged, however, the relatives call for confessions (*kupaca*) from both husband and wife. The husband's confessions are usually formal and simple. The wife's confessions on the other hand are detailed and complete. She confesses the name of an adulterer, and her midwives, including the husband's sisters as his witnesses, wait for the next birth-spasm. If the child is not born at this spasm she is told to confess again. Only after she has confessed to a lover whom the Yao assume to be the genitor will the child eventually be born. After this the aggrieved husband summons the adulterer to court and he is made to accept the fatherhood of the child.

The act of formally accepting the paternity of a child, which is also done when a woman has a child out of wedlock, confers rights of two types on the child. The first set of rights is directly economic and physical. The father is expected to give the mother salt, money for relish, and cloth to help her rear the child. But this side of a father's duties to his child ceases as soon as another man marries the woman. The new husband than takes over the

---

[1] I have dealt with this more fully in *Marriage among the Machinga Yao*.
[2] It also refuses to be born for other reasons, but the first considered is always the adultery of its parents. See p. 138.

economic responsibility of all the woman's children regardless of whether he has begotten them or not. For example, gossips say that a woman married my clerk so that she could have her son initiated. The costs and fees for this boy's initiation amounted to over a pound.

The other set of rights that paternal recognition confers on the child are the moral rights against his paternal kinsmen. A person may turn to his 'father's people' (*kucitati*) in times of dire need, especially if one of them is rich. This right persists after divorce, though the children are adult and otherwise economically independent. For example, a woman who was married to a labour migrant needed clothes badly. She turned to Chiwalo her father, though he had been divorced from her mother for more than 15 years. People in trouble often run away to their father's village and find shelter there. A man who wanted medicine for success in gambling asked his father for it. Another who had broken a sexual taboo confessed to his father who found suitable medicine for him. In each of those relationships there was an intimate personal element.[1] A person has the moral right to appeal to his father or paternal kinsmen, but he has no legally enforceable right to demand help. He has to rely on their kindness and charity. There are few fathers who would deny their children's requests if they are reasonable, but they can if they wish to.

The divorce rate is high among the Yao [2] and a typical family of five uterine siblings may have three fathers. Furthermore, a man should not marry into the lineage segment where his brother has married, so that the patrilateral kinship ties of the members of matrilineages tend to spread widely in the vicinity of the village. The effect of this is that the members of the lineage as a whole have widespread connections with neighbours upon whom they may rely in times of distress. But of the individual members of the matrilineage only a few share the same group

[1] Compare Fortes's description of uterine kinship among the Tallensi: '[It] is essentially by a personal bond, a bond of mutual interest and concern uniting individual to individual', *The Web of Kinship*, 37.

[2] Eight of every ten men and women over the age of 40 have experienced a divorce at some time of their lives. Excluding the contingency of death a married couple have only 30 chances in 100 of living together for 20 years. For details, see *Marriage among the Machinga Yao*.

of patrilateral kinsmen, so that these bonds are personal and distinctive for each member.

THE DEVELOPMENT OF THE CORPORATE IDENTITY OF PATRILATERALLY-LINKED GROUPS

The parent–child relationship is reflected in the structural relationships of a patrilateral group to the dominant matrilineage. Children are less strongly tied to their father than to their matrilineal kinsmen. Usually when a woman dies or is divorced while living virilocally, her children return to her matrilineal village. If the children are too young to express their own wishes, their mother's brother comes for them and they are formally returned to their village of origin. Occasionally children who have grown up in their father's village, especially if they have married their cross-cousins there, refuse to move back to their matrilineal village. They prefer to remain in their father's matrilineal village where they know people more intimately. In time, as they grow older, the women have daughters who may marry uxorilocally and thus a section of a foreign matrilineage begins to develop in the village.

The village as a social unit is more closely integrated when the children who are living there with their father are still young. They do not yet form a corporate group within the village. Their affairs are supposed to be controlled by their mother's brother, but in fact the headman, who is usually their father or a paternal kinsman, may settle many of their minor difficulties and find medicine for lesser illnesses, without bothering their mother's brother. When the children become adults and begin to assert their own wills the position in the village becomes more unstable. As the daughters grow up and marry, their brothers become their junior marriage sureties. If the mother's brother lives far away, the father of the children may be the senior marriage surety. He still has a personal attachment to his children, but his sons' relationships with him may now become affected by structural elements as they tend to interact, with him and others, in certain situations as representatives of corporate groups. As the village develops a son takes over the position of senior marriage surety to the headman's wife's descendants and he becomes the senior male lineage member, while his sisters' sons begin to take over responsibilities for their sorority-groups.

The headman and father is now no longer directly concerned in the affairs of the linked lineage, and may only appear in their affairs formally as an adviser or an arbitrator in disputes. For example, he is advised of deaths in the village and of the disputes that have arisen and been settled. But this is part of his relationship to the linked lineage because of his headmanship. A fairly long-established village, therefore, contains two, three or four related lineages with complete autonomy in internal affairs yet together forming one community—one village under the leadership of the headman. As the village persists in time and successive village headmen and other men of the dominant matrilineage bring their wives into the village, related lineage segments develop from them, and the internal structure of the village becomes more and more complex.

An example of a village of this kind is Cikoja. It has 47 huts.

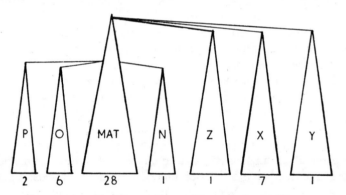

DIAGRAM 4. THE OWNERSHIP OF HUTS IN CIKOJA VILLAGE.

One of them is a dormitory for adolescent boys and we may ignore it in this analysis. Members of the dominant matrilineage live in 28 of the huts. Members of patrilaterally-linked groups are living in the remaining 19 huts. There are 6 of these patrilaterally-linked groups in the village and I have indicated them by the letters N, O, P, X, Y and Z. Their origin is as follows :

Z   A descendant of Cikoja IV's first wife   .   .   .   .   1 hut
X   The descendants of Cikoja IV's second wife   .   .   .   7 huts
Y   The descendants of Cikoja IV's third wife .   .   .   .   1 hut

N A descendant of Cikoja V's first wife . . . . 1 hut
O The descendants of Cikoja V's brother's first wife . . 6 huts
P The descendants of Cikoja V's brother's second wife . . 2 huts

All these wives were slaves. The present Cikoja has no children.

In this table I have counted huts owned jointly by a member of the dominant matrilineage and a patrilateral group (i.e. in cross-cousin marriage) as belonging to the matrilineage ; huts belonging to Z and X group as Z, etc. The exact ownership of the huts is set out in Table XXVII. It shows the number of

TABLE XXVII

OWNERSHIP OF HUTS IN CIKOJA VILLAGE

Origin of wife :	Origin of husband :										Total
	Mat.	Z	X	Y	N	O	P	Out-sid.	Wid.	Div.	
Mat. .	—	1	2	—	1	—	—	15	1	1	21
Z . .	—	—	—	—	—	—	—	1	—	—	1
X . .	1	—	—	—	—	—	—	7	—	—	8
Y . .	1	—	—	—	—	—	—	1	—	—	2
N . .	2	—	—	—	—	—	—	1	—	—	3
O . .	—	—	—	—	—	—	—	3	—	2	5
P . .	—	—	—	—	—	—	—	1	1	—	2
Outsid.	3	—	—	—	—	1	—	—	—	—	4
Wid. .	—	—	—	—	—	—	—	—	—	—	—
Div. .	—	—	—	—	—	—	—	—	—	—	—
Total	7	1	2	—	1	1	—	29	2	3	46

Mat. = Member of the dominant matrilineage.
Z, X, Y, N, O, P = Groups linked patrilaterally to the dominant matrilineage.
Outsid. = Outsiders or members of other villages.

men and women in the village who are married either to spouses from other villages or from this village, and the men and women who own huts but who are widowed and divorced. The distribution of these huts is set out in the village plan in Appendix D.

We have already seen that the social distance between sections of the matrilineage is reflected in the physical separation of their huts.[1] The social distance between the dominant matrilineage and the patrilaterally-linked groups is much greater than between

[1] See Chap. VI, p. 164.

O

sections of a matrilineage, and accordingly the huts of members of the dominant matrilineage are physically separated more distinctly from the huts of members of the patrilaterally-linked groups than from one another. As they develop their corporate identity the members of each matrilineage tend to build together and a little distance away from the main settlement of the other matrilineages. In Cikoja's village this tendency is seen quite plainly. There are two large patrilaterally-linked groups in the village. These are the children and matrilineal descendants of Cikoja IV's second wife (represented in the plan as N), and the children and matrilineal descendants of the first wife of Maperera, the brother of Cikoja V (represented in the plan as O). These two groups are situated quite separately from the main matrilineal block of the village. The huts of X matrilineage are hidden from the view of the rest of the village and must be reached by a path. The space between huts of O matrilineage and the remainder of the matrilineal block is clear, but in it there are some large trees and the grave of Cikoja V. The huts of the three women and the one man of N matrilineage are close together in the village but scarcely distinguishable from the huts of the main matrilineage. The huts of two women of Y matrilineage are set on the extremity of the village and are not yet separated from the huts of other lineages. Note how the huts of the villagers who have married their ' cross-cousins ' are placed within the village as a whole. Huts 32 and 33 belonging to the two women of X lineage have been placed between the main block of the X matrilineage and the matrilineage of Jauma (Ma$_1$), who is married to one of these women. Huts 10 and 11, where members of the dominant matrilineage and the patrilaterally-linked lineage N have intermarried, are placed on the mutual fringe of these two groups. The three men of the patrilaterally-linked lineage X who are married into the dominant lineage form a little block in the north-western corner of the village. As soon as the patrilaterally-linked groups develop their identity and are able to express their autonomy, they tend to build in separate sections and to form corporate but component parts of the village.

One of the clearest ways in which the autonomy of the matrilineage is expressed is in the arrangements made about marriage sureties. In Cikoja's village, Cikoja himself is senior marriage surety for only one member of the linked lineages. This is Naliwa (D39), who is the oldest surviving man in all the linked matrilineages and who is looked upon as the senior among them all. Naliwa is the senior marriage surety for most of the marriages in the linked matrilineages, but Katoli (D33) has taken over the duties for a number of his own lineage members. Table XXVIII lists the senior marriage sureties in all the

TABLE XXVIII

SENIOR MARRIAGE SURETIES IN CIKOJA VILLAGE

Surety	Rel.*	Lineage Affiliation						Total
		Mat.	Z	X	Y	N	O	
Cikoja . . .	Mat.	44	—	—	1	—	—	45
Naliwa . . .	Y	—	—	—	5	8	13	26
Katoli	X	—	3	12	—	—	—	15
Mbwana . . .	X	—	1	2	—	—	—	3
Suwedi . . .	X	—	—	1	—	—	—	1
Other† . . .	—	1	—	—	—	—	—	1
Total . . .	—	45	4	15	6	8	13	91

* This is the lineage affiliation of the senior marriage surety. Cikoja is the headman and automatically senior lineage member. Naliwa is the most senior surviving member of Y lineage. Suwedi is most senior in X, followed by his younger brother Mbwana and then his sister's son Katoli.

† This is Cikoja's own marriage. His perpetual younger brother Mbande is his senior surety.

Note : There were two marriages in P lineage for which I did not record the marriage sureties.

marriages I recorded in Cikoja village. Here, age is important. The male members in the lineage of Cikoja V's wife and of Maperera's wives are all much younger than the members of Cikoja IV's wives' lineages. The descendants of Cikoja V's wife and of Maperera's wives all have junior sureties from their own lineage, but so far none has become a senior marriage surety.

As time goes on, the affairs of the linked lineage, therefore, become regulated more and more within the lineage. The headman and perpetual father recedes from the picture but is never entirely obliterated even in his relation to a linked-matri-lineage which moves out to found its own village.

The father and headman is almost forgotten in those villages which, though founded by him, do not contain any of his matrilineage. Sometimes men who have a number of adult children move away and found small villages of their own. I have struck a few villages of this type on the outskirts of White settlement areas at Namwera and near Zomba. The man has been a servant of the Whites as, say, an estate labourer. After ten or fifteen years on the estates he decides to stop working. Local men have probably married his daughters and he has made acquaintances with local people, while his attachment to his home village has become attenuated. Consequently, with his daughters he sets up his own homestead somewhere near the estate. He is probably both senior and junior marriage surety for his daughters' marriages, and also responsible for the welfare of his children and grandchildren. He reports serious illnesses and deaths to his wife's brother or her male uterine kinsmen, but otherwise he runs the internal affairs of his village as if he were the senior matrilineal kinsman. But as his sons grow up the sorority-group organization exerts itself, and soon his adult sons begin to take over the more arduous duties concerning the affairs of their sisters. They now walk to a sister's husband's home to tell of the husband's illnesses, or trudge for miles to find a diviner when one of the babies is ill. Their father still retains control over the village land and other important affairs concerning the village as a whole. At this stage in its history the hamlet will be known by his name. When he dies the control of the hamlet passes to his eldest son, and now it assumes once again the pattern of the ordinary Yao village. For a while it may retain the name of the father, but in due course it begins to be known by the name of the son. Gradually the father fades into the background and the son comes to the fore. Eventually, when the son dies, his sister's son assumes control over the village and inherits the name. Now there are probably some of the original headman's sons' children living in the village and forming the nucleus of a linked matrilineage. In spite of the foundation of the village as an extended family, the lineage principle soon begins to mould the village into the typical Yao pattern. It is clear from many of my genealogies in Malemia area that when villages first moved in they were made up of a man and wife and children. Now after, say, twenty years the 'extended family' pattern has completely disappeared and we have in its place a straightforward localized matrilineage as in Ali Kasunka village.

THE HEADMAN AS THE LINK BETWEEN THE DOMINANT LINEAGE AND THE PATRILATERALLY-LINKED GROUPS

A headman's position when his own children or the children of his predecessor have started to operate as a corporate group in the village is clearly difficult. To the dominant matrilineage they are outsiders, and they are a source of tension in the more complex villages. This, in essence, is the situation about which the officiating headmen have almost certainly warned him at the installation ceremony, when they told him to beware of his wife's chatter, because it may bring about a split of the village. The headman occupies a position of jural authority over his matrilineal relatives. He has succeeded to the name of his mother's brother and is structurally the most senior matrilineal kinsman in the village. He is directly responsible in court and outside it for the behaviour and welfare of the matrilineage members. At the same time he is personally attached to his children by ties of intimacy and sentiment. Where there is a conflict between his own children and the matrilineage members he is placed in an invidious position. By legal right he should support his lineage members, by moral right he cannot spurn his children. What he tries to do as a rule is to browbeat his matrilineal relatives into submission to maintain the peace within the village. He runs the risk, however, of alienating the support of his sisters who may turn to his younger brothers and leave the village. This is what happened in Mponda's village, as I have outlined earlier.[1] Here, it will be recalled, a quarrel started between two young girls over a pounding mortar. It spread to the mothers of the girls, who were the headman's wife and his sister. The headman tried to browbeat his sister into submission, but she immediately turned to her younger brother. The result was that the headman lost his sisters to his younger brother.

The way in which the two opposed groups in the village crystallize out into opposed factions cannot be more clearly shown than in the sequence of events in Mpakata village, in January 1947.

Mpakata was the headman of the village, and he had three younger brothers, Walusa, Merison and Nanculuya. Ali Cibwana, Mpakata's

---

[1] See Chap. VI, p. 155.

adult son, went to Walusa one day and borrowed a chicken. Some days afterwards Walusa asked for payment for the chicken. Ali Cibwana took offence at the way in which Walusa asked for payment and told him so. Walusa remarked that Ali Cibwana was insolent and insisted on the payment for the chicken. Ali Cibwana now said that if his father's brother insisted on asking in this rude way he would not be paid back at all. The tempers of the two men became more and more frayed until at last Walusa threw Ali Cibwana to the ground. When Sanudia, Ali Cibwana's younger brother, saw this he grabbed up a stick and came up to Walusa and asked him why he had thrown his elder brother down. Walusa had hardly time to answer before Sanudia had struck him. At this Walusa's younger brothers joined in the fight. Mpakata now rushed up and started to support his sons against his younger brothers. When Mpakata's sisters and sisters' daughters, who were pounding, heard this, they took up their pounding pestles (poles about five feet long and three inches in diameter) and came running to Mpakata's younger brothers' assistance. When Mpakata saw these women coming with their poles he dashed into his house and emerged with a stick with which he defended himself. The noise and clamour had by this time attracted a number of strangers from a nearby village and they were able to pacify Mpakata's villagers. The matrilineal relatives of Mpakata gathered in one part of the village and Walusa told them they ought to leave. They decided, nevertheless, ' to say goodbye ' [1] to Kaumbwe, who was a perpetual elder brother of Mpakata. Kaumbwe called in an unrelated village headman named Idi, and they held a meeting in the village the next day.

The dispute was discussed in the presence of the arbitrator. Walusa said he wished to leave the village with his sisters. Idi, however, told him that he should not do this but that they should take the matter up to Chiwalo's court. On an agreed day Mpakata and his children and matrilineal relatives went to Chiwalo's court where the case was arbitrated on by Capola who lived near to Mpakata. He found Mpakata guilty and ordered him to pay 10s. to Walusa. At the same time he told Walusa that he was not to take the female members of the matrilineage away from the village. And there the matter rested.

A village headman in Yao ' binds the village ',[2] and when the village is made up of linked groups as well as his matrilineal kin,

[1] Ostensibly to say goodbye but in fact to air their grievances.

[2] *Akutawa musi.* The word *kutawa* may also mean to build. Yao houses are built by binding poles together with ropes and then filling the gaps with mud.

the significance of this formulation of his position is clear. It is when he shows partiality that the village under him is likely to break up. If he sides with his children his matrilineal kin are almost sure to move out ; if he sides with his matrilineal kin, his children are likely either to return to their matrilineal village or, if they are adult, split off to set up a village of their own. The situation is precarious for the headman and it is very difficult for him to avoid a split in the village if he cannot keep the two opposed groups at peace.

My investigations show that few villages have contained patrilaterally-linked groups through the lives of two village headmen, unless these groups were descended from slaves. When the headman dies his successor assumes his name and social rôle. He also assumes the position of father towards the remaining children, who are in fact his cross-cousins. But his relationship towards them is not the same as that of father to children. The intimate link of the blood tie has been lost and the relationship becomes formalized. As more and more headmen succeed the genealogical link between the patrilaterally-linked groups and the dominant matrilineage becomes more and more remote, and the relationship becomes more and more casual. What usually happens is that shortly after the death of the headman and father, the patrilaterally-linked group takes exception to what the new headman does or says and moves off to found a village of its own. The case history I quoted earlier [1] brought this out clearly. The new headman had had intercourse with the wives of his ' son '. The son complained to the arbitrators in the dispute that ' he should have been as a father to me, and he is not '. The result was that the son refused compensation, and moved out of the village with his sisters to build on his own. When this happens the father–son relationship between the two villages is preserved and perpetuated, but the link is entirely formal and co-operation between them is limited to mutual attendance at funerals.

PATRILATERALLY-LINKED GROUPS AS THE LEGACY OF SLAVERY

Slave-groups in a village are usually linked patrilaterally to the dominant lineage. This is because the headman who was usually the captor of the slaves kept the women as concubines. They were given quasi-child status in the village, so that their children

[1] ' The Split of Cikumba Village ', see Chap. V, p. 127.

were called *yisikulu* (grandchildren) by the headman, who in turn was called *ambuje* (grandparent or master) by the slaves. The grandchild–grandparent relationship became fused with the master–slave relationship as the use of the term *ambuje* for master suggests. The slave descendants as a rule have no relatives in the neighbourhood. The Yao always redeemed uterine kin whom they found in slavery by replacing them with other slaves, usually taken or bought from the Nyanja, Ngoni or Bisa. Where there are slave-groups in a village to-day, they have frequently been bought or captured in distant places, so that their kinsmen have been unable to trace them. How much this

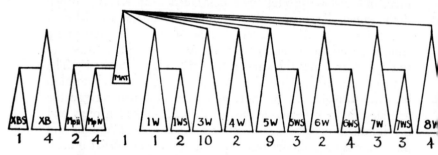

DIAGRAM 5. THE OWNERSHIP OF HUTS IN MPUMBE VILLAGE.

has prevented slave-groups from leaving Yao villages I cannot say. Certainly before the White conquest members of a slave-group could only leave their captor's village at the risk of death. But after the White conquest it seems that many of the slave-groups left to set up their own villages. Many, on the other hand, no doubt for personal reasons, stayed with their captors in their villages, and are there to-day. In Cikoja's village, for example, there are six of these groups. Some are not very large, but only 20 of the 46 huts are owned by members of the dominant matrilineage who are not married to descendants of slaves. Eight are owned by members of the dominant matri-lineage who have married slave descendants, and the remainder, 18 huts, are owned by members of the slave-groups who have married outsiders. This is a typical distribution of hut owner-ship. At one extreme is the pure matrilineal village such as Ali Kasunka's and at the other is the village in which the dominant lineage is barely represented. A village of this type was Mpumbe when I visited it in 1947.[1] The basic structure of this village is set out in Diagram 5. Here the headman [2] was the last surviving member of the dominant matrilineage. The founder of the village, his mother's brother, had thirteen slave concubines. Some of these were barren but others produced children to give this complex structure. In this village the 55 huts were arranged in 16 different affiliations. The details are set out in Table XXIX. These groups were held together by Mpumbe IV, old, blind and doddering as he was. The virtual leader of the village was his elder brother's son, a man in his late forties or early fifties. When Mpumbe died, late in 1948, the people said that it was because of the sorcery of his brother's son who wished to take over the name of the village. This led to a dispute, which ended in the brother's son's leaving to found a new village about 15 miles away. A distant sister's son, as I have said, succeeded to the headmanship, and the reduced village was reunited under this new leader.

However, this is an extremely unusual type of village as most villages, if they are not simple matrilineal groups, have only one patrilaterally-linked group living with them. The reasons for this are firstly, that if patrilaterally-linked matrilineages develop at all in the modern villages, they move out very soon after the death of their progenitor, and, secondly, that there are very few of the old slave-raiders' villages left intact.

CROSS-COUSIN AND OTHER KINDS OF INTRA-VILLAGE MARRIAGES

A most important factor in the welding of patrilaterally-linked groups to the dominant matrilineage is marriage. The tradition of cross-cousin marriage is very strong among the Yao. A person may marry either type of cross-cousin but in practice preference is given to a father's sister's daughter—i.e. the woman is married to her mother's brother's son. There is a special term for cross-cousins, *asiŵani*, which is used by either male or female talking to either sex. Between cross-cousins, especially cross-sexually, there is a joking-relationship which may vary all the way from ribald joking to sexual advances. Some of my male informants say that sexual intercourse may take place between cross-cousins

[1] See also Chap. VI, p. 161, and Chap. III, p. 59.
[2] He died late in 1948 and was succeeded by a distant ' sister's son ' from the village of his perpetual son, Ngongondo.

TABLE XXIX

OWNERSHIP OF HUTS IN MPUMBE VILLAGE

Affiliation of women :	Mat.	IW	IWS	3W	4W	5W	5WS	6W	6WS	7W	7WS	8W	Mpii	Mpiv	XB	XBS	Out.	Div.	Wid.	Total
						Affiliation of men :														
Mat.	■	–	–	–	–	–	–	–	–	–	–	–	–	–	–	–	–	–	–	–
IW	–	■	–	–	–	–	–	–	–	–	–	–	–	–	–	–	1	–	–	1
IWS	–	–	■	–	–	–	–	–	–	–	–	–	–	–	–	–	1	1	–	2
3W	–	–	–	■	–	1	–	–	–	–	–	–	–	–	1	–	4	–	1	7
4W	–	–	–	–	■	–	–	–	–	–	–	–	–	–	–	–	–	–	–	–
5W	–	–	–	1	–	■	–	–	–	–	–	–	–	–	–	–	5	–	2	8
5WS	–	–	–	–	–	–	■	–	–	–	–	–	–	–	–	–	2	1	–	3
6W	–	–	–	–	–	–	–	■	–	–	–	–	–	–	–	–	1	–	–	1
6WS	–	–	–	–	–	–	–	–	■	–	–	–	–	–	–	–	2	–	–	2
7W	–	–	–	–	–	–	–	–	–	■	–	–	–	–	–	–	–	–	–	–
7WS	–	–	–	1	–	–	–	–	–	–	■	–	–	–	–	–	3	–	–	4
8W	–	–	–	–	–	–	–	–	–	–	–	■	–	–	–	–	1	–	1	2
Mpii	–	–	–	–	2	–	–	–	–	–	–	–	■	–	–	–	–	1	1	4
Mpiv	1	–	–	–	–	–	–	–	–	–	–	–	–	■	–	–	3	–	1	5
XB	–	–	1	–	–	–	–	–	–	–	–	1	–	–	■	–	–	3	–	5
XBS	–	–	–	1	–	–	–	–	–	–	–	–	–	–	–	■	–	–	–	1
Out.	–	–	–	–	–	2	–	1	2	3	–	1	–	–	–	1	■	–	–	10
Div.	–	–	–	–	–	–	–	–	–	–	–	–	–	–	–	–	–	■	–	–
Wid.	–	–	–	–	–	–	–	–	–	–	–	–	–	–	–	–	–	–	■	–
Total	1	–	1	3	2	3	–	1	2	3	–	2	–	–	1	1	23	6	6	55

Notes. This table is on the same principle as Table XXVII. Here IW stands for the matrilineal descendants of Mpumbe I's first wife, 2WS for the matrilineal descendants of his second wife's son. Mpii stands for the matrilineal descendants of Mpumbe II's wife, and of course if she is alive she is included in the group. XB are the descendants of a classificatory brother of Mpumbe I. I am uncertain of his exact genealogical relationship to Mpumbe I. There are two huts not in this table. Hut 23 is occupied by Mpumbe II's late daughter's husband. Instead of moving back to his matrilineal village, this man has brought another woman into Mpumbe's. Hut 16 is occupied by the widow of Capola (Mpumbe I's ZS) and she has had no children.

In a village as complex as this the classification of the ownership of huts becomes arbitrary. Because of the amount of intermarriage between the component lineages most individuals can trace their descent from Mpumbe I by two or three lines. Here I have classified people into lineages by matrilineal descent as the first criterion. I have classified them into groups after that by one patrilateral link rather than by two, etc.

'if the women are stupid enough to allow it'. The kinship terminology is consistent with the assumption that every man marries his cross-cousin, except that the father's sister's husband is not called 'father-in-law', but 'father'. The mother's brother's wife is called *akwegwe* (parent-in-law). The husband of a cross-cousin is called *mpwao* (younger brother), on the reasoning that if a man does not marry his cross-cousin, then his younger brother will. Dr. Meredith Sanderson told me that it was once the custom for a man to ask a prospective wife's cross-cousin before he proposed marriage because it was assumed that the woman's cross-cousin had first right to her hand. As far as I could ascertain this politeness is no longer observed.

The children of cross-cousins are called 'my children'. In addition to this a person calls his mother's mother's brother's son or mother's father's sister's son, 'father', and his mother's mother's brother's daughter or mother's father's sister's daughter, 'female father', a term which he applies also to his father's sister.

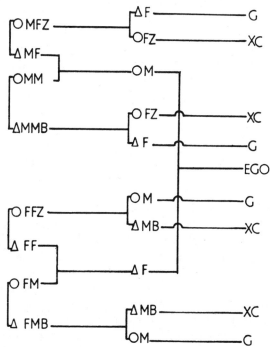

DIAGRAM 6. KINSHIP TERMS FOR PARENTS' CROSS-COUSINS.

A person calls his father's mother's brother's daughter and father's father's sister's daughter, 'mother'; his father's mother's brother's son or his father's father's sister's son, 'mother's brother'. Diagram 6 illustrates this. This is consistent with the assumption that each parent has married his cross-cousin.

Conversation with informants gives the impression that cross-cousin marriages are very common. They say, for example, that every man's first marriage ought to be to his cross-cousin. But in fact, of 103 first marriages, only 15 per cent were to real or classificatory cross-cousins, though 21 per cent were to other types of kinsmen. Marriages to other types of kinsmen are loosely called cross-cousin marriages, and often what has been called a cross-cousin marriage in conversation turns out to be marriage to a cross-cousin's daughter or something similar. This may be the reason why casual conversation leads one to imagine that cross-cousin marriage is so frequent.

But cross-cousinship is particularly significant when seen in relation to village structure. Typically, villages, if they are not built around a simple matrilineage, are composed of a dominant matrilineage and one or more lineages linked patrilaterally to it. Sometimes there are groups in a village which are connected by a patrilateral link to a matrilineage which is in turn linked patrilaterally to the dominant lineage. In other words, there are some lineages connected by a double patrilateral link to the dominant lineage. But this is not common. These linked groups have arisen because one or more of the men of the dominant lineage have brought their wives to live in their village. The set of kinship terms applied to members of the linked lineage by members of the dominant lineage are shown in Diagram 7. We have already seen that Ego, whether man or woman, calls his or her mother's mother's brother's son or daughter 'father' or 'female father'. This usage is consistent with the assumption that one's mother ought to have married her mother's brother's son so that the mother's maternal uncle's son should be called 'father'. On the same reasoning, one's mother's mother's brother's daughter should be one's father's sister and the appropriate term 'female father' is accordingly applied. Because uxorilocal marriage is the custom, Ego's mother's mother's brother's son marries out of the village and his children belong to another lineage. The children of Ego's mother's mother's

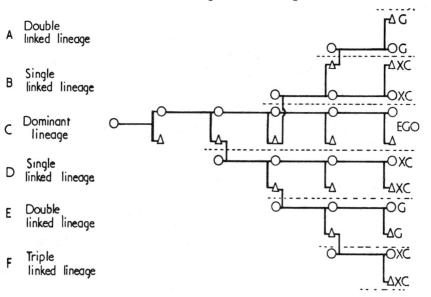

DIAGRAM 7. KINSHIP TERMS BETWEEN DOMINANT LINEAGE AND PATRILATERALLY-LINKED GROUPS.

brother's daughter, however, are members of the linked lineage and they are called ' cross-cousin ' by Ego and members of the dominant lineage in Ego's generation. The children of ' cross-cousins ' are called ' my children '. Hence, Ego and those in his generation in the dominant lineage call all those in the first descending generation in the linked lineage ' my children '.

I have used as an example a lineage which is linked to Ego's lineage through his mother's mother's brother. But the kinship terminology is unaltered if the link occurs in any ascending generation. In Diagram 7 I have set out the kinship terms applied by the dominant lineage to members in the linked lineage where the connection is through Ego's mother's mother's mother's brother.

The argument would run as follows :

Ego's MM calls Ego's MMMBD cross-cousin.
Therefore Ego's M calls Ego's MMMBD female father ;
therefore Ego's M calls Ego's MMMBDD cross-cousin ;
therefore Ego calls Ego's MMMBDD female father ;
therefore Ego calls Ego's MMMBDDD cross-cousin.

To Ego therefore, in a lineage linked through one patrilateral link :

> Any person in the first ascending generation is ' father ' or
> ' female father '.
> Any person in the same generation is " cross-cousin '.
> Any person in the first descending generation is ' child '.

Those in the second ascending generation are called ' grand-parent ' and those in the second descending generation are called ' grandchildren '.   By the merging of alternate generations, those in the second ascending and second descending generation may also be called ' cross-cousin '.

Where the subsidiary lineage is connected to the dominant lineage through two patrilateral links the kinship terms for siblings is applied to Ego's generation.   In Diagram 7 the linked lineage marked A is connected to the dominant lineage through Ego's **MMBS**. Ego calls his mother's mother's brother's son ' father ' and, therefore, calls his mother's mother's brother's sons' children by the appropriate sibling terms.

If a subsidiary lineage were connected through three patri-lateral links the kinship nomenclature would be the same as if there were only one link. Lineages connected to dominant lineages through two or more patrilateral links are very rare. Most subsidiary lineages are connected through one patrilateral link only. In any village the generation differences between members of dominant and subsidiary lineages tend to be obscured. The Yao tend to see the component lineages as wholes, and therefore speak of the relationships between members of the dominant lineage and members of the subsidiary lineages in general as ' cross-cousinship ' (*cisuwani*). It is only in special situations that the exact relationship becomes important.

The pattern of behaviour between cross-cousins is consistent with this view of their rôles in the make-up of a village. In the typical Yao village there are two or three groups who are united in their extra-village affairs but opposed in internal relationships. Their hostility to each other comes to the surface at the slightest provocation, but they are, nevertheless, co-villagers. They are kin and yet not kin, because the Yao look upon kinship as primarily matrilineal. They talk of the link through the father as ' not proper kinship '. The hostility between the members of the different cross-cousin groups in the village is dissipated in a joking-relationship which is more intense between men and women. Men and women in Yao public life always behave distantly to each other ; hence joking-relationships are most intense between male and female cross-cousins. The joking-relationships between cross-cousins of the same sex is much more subdued and limited. The village headman himself, if he is not the actual father of the cross-cousins, is likely to be the butt of most of this. His visits to the huts of his cross-cousins to give them irksome instructions is an especial occasion for this sort of joking. Cikoja ordered his female cross-cousins to sweep a site for my tent when I first went to his village. I was most embarrassed by the insults that were hurled at his head during this procedure, but he took it all calmly and said nothing. The hostility inherent in the headman–villager relationship, together with the opposition between the dominant matrilineage and the patrilaterally-linked groups, provided an opportunity *par excellence* for joking. Thus the joking between cross-cousins in the village context is a means whereby the hostility between the component groups is dissipated and the harmony within the village maintained.

The groups are, of course, welded more closely by cross-cousin marriages which are not only allowed but prescribed. By cross-cousin marriage a man from one of the component groups of the village may marry and yet not leave the village. He may in fact have to build a hut in another part of the village, but this is obviously not the separation that uxorilocal marriage entails. At the same time, in a village where the headmen have married their cross-cousins, there will be fewer patrilaterally-linked groups, so that the village will be less complex and consequently less liable to internal dissension. If cross-cousin marriages were not practised, and if the children of the headmen and senior members of the linked lineages did not return to their matrilineal villages on the death of one of their parents, the intra-village situation could in time become extremely complex. Assuming that each linked group had at least one male member married virilocally, the number of related groups would double itself in each generation.[1] However, because of limiting economic factors I describe later and the disruptive social processes within villages, this situation never occurs in practice, and Yao villages on the whole remain relatively simple in structure.

[1] See detailed argument and diagram in *Seven Tribes*, 333.

OTHER TYPES OF VILLAGE STRUCTURE

Linked groups in most villages are connected by patrilateral ties, but other kinsmen, or even unrelated persons, are also found in villages. I have been describing essentially the organization of groups. Some kinsmen do in fact come to live in villages because of personal links to the headman or some other villager. If a man or woman does this, he or she usually has a single hut which is placed close to his or her kinsman. If the person lives in the village long enough a related group may grow up around him or her, and when the children reach adulthood this group will become internally organized and corporate in its dealings with the other groups in the village. But this seldom happens, because the ties to the resident kinsman are usually too weak to hold the children, or the causes which drove the founder of the new group out of his or her original village have disappeared. Children may leave a village with their mother because she was accused of being a sorceress, and go to live in the village where her brother is married. When she dies, or the incident is forgotten, they may go back to their matrilineal village. For example, Bt. Mkwinda of Cikoja village ran away with her husband after her child was supposed to have been bewitched by her mother. But her children, as they grew up, came back to marry in the village of origin, or at least to contract marriages near it. In Chiwalo's, Nyambi's and Kawinga's areas, where I have recorded most genealogies of villages, I found few people who were neither matrilineal- nor patrilaterally-linked relatives. In Malemia area, which is nearer Zomba, the situation was somewhat different. The dominant matrilineage- and patrilaterally-linked groups of the typical Yao village were still quite easily discernible. But there were other related and unrelated groups and huts in the villages. An example of this is Citenjele village,[1] on the north boundary of Malemia's area. There the main village contained the following huts :

Dominant matrilineage	22
Groups linked through present headman	5
Hut linked through present headman's brother	1
Groups linked through previous headman . . .	5
Groups linked through previous headman's brother . . .	4
	37 huts

---

[1] See also 'An Outline of the Social Structure of Malemia Area', 36–40.

About 250 yards to the north-west is a single hut belonging to the sister of the husband of one of the present headman's daughters. In the middle of the group on the road is a single hut of a woman who has no connections in the village at all. Her husband works in a mission garden about a mile away. About 100 yards from the north-east edge of the main block is a group of 4 huts which are unrelated to Citenjele, but which had joined him about 25 years ago before he had moved into Malemia area. About 250 yards farther to the north-east there are 2 huts owned by the daughters of the sister of the wife of a man who had married one of the female members of the dominant matrilineage. Due east about half a mile away, there is a group of 6 huts which are owned by Yao. These are unrelated groups and are under Citenjele as Administrative Village Headman, but they are for all intents and purposes separate villages.

There are other types of villages. For example, in Namwera area I found a village composed of a number of unrelated sections. The huts of each could quite easily be distinguished from those of other sections though they were built very close to each other in some parts of the village. Each section was built up on exactly the same pattern as other Yao villages— that is, there was a dominant matrilineage and sometimes some patrilaterally-linked huts. Each section had its own leader who concerned himself with its internal affairs. He, nevertheless, recognized the authority in general of a village headman, who lived in one of the sections of the village. He was the Administrative Headman for the village and he was the first to come into the area. All the other sections had had to ask him for land when they had moved into the area. His authority was confined to his duties as Administrative Headman though he was much respected and the sections called him in regularly as an arbitrator in their affairs. But if the chief called all village headmen to the court, the leaders of the various sections went as well, so that he was not in fact their representative to outside authority in all situations. The relationships between the various sections, therefore, were very much like those between village headmen in Kawinga's area. The only difference seemed to be the amount of physical concentration of the huts.

I tried to find out why these sections lived so close to one another. My informants told me that there were many men away at labour centres and it was necessary to build the huts

P

close together so that the few men left in the village could protect the village against man-eating lions. This is certainly an area where man-eating lions are common and kill people every year. It is true also that man-eating lions have ceased their depredations in Kawinga and Nyambi areas. But I also found a similar type of village in Malemia area.[1] Here the explanation was that the villages had been made to live together by the Administration under the 1912 Ordinance. But the Ordinance was applied to the whole district, yet there are not many of these villages.

The relationships between the section leaders and the village headman are exactly the same as those between independent headmen farther south. The difference in the villages is the degree of physical concentration of the huts ; which brings up for review the concept of ' the village '. I have defined the village as a discrete cluster of huts occupied by a group of kinsmen [2] and hinted that the huts were not always clearly separated from neighbouring huts. In fact the Yao word for village, *musi*, may be applied to social groups of different orders. I have already mentioned that different sections of a village may be scattered in discrete groups. The term *kamusi* (diminutive) or even *musi* may be applied to any of these clusters of huts in a situation where the larger kinship section is not involved. A man may tell his friend that he has bought some maize at Meni's village. He means that he bought the maize at the group of huts under Meni in Majaja village. In a court case, however, he would say that he had married a woman in Majaja village even though he were referring to the daughter of Meni.

The expanded village—i.e. the groups of kinsmen who recognize the leadership of one man, but whose huts are relatively distantly spaced in discrete clusters—may give a stamp to the social organization in a small area of, say, a square mile or two. The dominant matrilineage of the senior headman and his patri-laterally-linked groups may all live in this area in physically separate groups, but their kinship is still dominant and they are for ritual purposes still ' of one fire '. In time any of these groups may move off and be replaced by complete strangers. The senior headman still retains his position of authority over the

---

[1] Ngalango village. It is described in ' An Outline of the Social Structure of Malemia Area ', 35–6.

[2] Chap. I, p. 3, and Chap. V, p. 110 f.

(*a*) Part of a village in Namwera area. The distinct group of huts on the right is not related to those in the left-hand corner, but is only one section of the village.

(*October 1948*)

(*b*) A slightly different view of the same part of the village. The fence encloses the grainbin, kitchen and latrine.

(*October 1948*)

PLATE IX

strangers. Meantime, the seceding group moves into some other village area at a distant place, where they are strangers themselves. The result is that kinship soon ceases to be the organizing principle in local areas, and the principle of primacy takes its place. Hence, primary [1] kinship provides the principle on which the relationships among village headmen, and therefore villages, may be organized in a local area, for only a relatively short time. Before long, for a variety of reasons, the smaller villages move away and their sites are taken by others.

Primary matrilineal kinship on the other hand retains its significance as the means whereby relationships are organized within villages. In other words, outside the lineages of the ruling families it is very difficult to record a genealogy which does more than link the component parts of a village. Beyond this genealogies are socially insignificant. Therefore, since villages are continually breaking up, genealogies are usually shallow. Once a group has broken away to found a new village, its exact genealogical link with the parent village tends to be forgotten and replaced by a formalized link of perpetual kinship between the two village headmen.

Yao society, therefore, is not ' organic ' in the way that Fortes describes Tallensi society : it is not ' governed by the same principles at all levels and in every sector of the social structure '.[2] Instead different principles of organization apply at different levels of Yao society. Thus the shallow lineages that form the cores of villages are internally segmented. Villages are composed of matrilineages linked to each other usually through patrilateral ties, ties which are initially primary but become perpetual. Chiefdoms, on the other hand, may be seen as organizations of villages ranked in relation to each other and to the chief in terms of their perpetual kinship links, their antecedents, and their strength of following.

The same groups of matrilineal kinsmen may interact in three different fields of social relationships. Firstly, they may form a segment within a matrilineage. Secondly, they may form a group in a village linked initially by a primary and later by a perpetual patrilateral tie to the headman. Thirdly, if they

[1] i.e. kinship that can actually be traced as against ' putative ' or ' perpetual ' kinship.
[2] Fortes, *The Web of Kinship*, 341.

should break away to found a new village they may become a Newcomer and relatively junior hamlet in political relationships with other villages in a local area of a chiefdom.

The group of kinsmen in each situation exhibits different degrees of corporate identity. As part of a lineage the identity of the group, except in unusual circumstances, is merged in the identity of the lineage. As part of a village the identity of the group appears clearly enough in intra-village affairs, but is merged in the identity of the village otherwise. It is only when the group can set up as a village of its own that its identity is finally established, that is, when the group becomes fully autonomous.

The identity of a group of matrilineal kinsmen therefore varies with the extent to which matrilineal ties with other kinsmen are attenuated. They can emphasize their independence of their kinsmen by playing down the link between them. A linked lineage in a village emphasizes its *patrilateral* link with the dominant lineage and so maintains its identity within its village of residence. The members do not consider themselves a part of a matrilineage which is dominant in some other village. By the same process a newly-founded hamlet does not emphasize its detailed and intimate links with its parent village, but tends to subsume these into a formal, perpetual relationship between the respective village headmen.

In Yao society, therefore, we may distinguish three orders or levels of social grouping :

1. The matrilineage which consists of ranked lineage segments.
2. The village which consists of ranked matrilineages.
3. The chiefdom which consists of ranked villages.

It is only at the most fundamental of these levels, i.e. within the matrilineage, that matrilineal descent provides a principle for organizing group relations. At the next level, i.e. within the village, matrilineal kinship gives way to other types of primary kinship between key personalities in the structure. At the third level, i.e. within the chiefdom, kinship appears only in the form of the highly formalized ' perpetual ' kinship—the actual links may well have been forgotten long ago. The same kinship term may be applied between personalities at all three levels of organization, but the content of the term changes according to the field of interaction.

CHAPTER VIII

THE VILLAGE THROUGH TIME

IN order to present my analysis of the internal structure of Yao villages and of the position of the village in the social structure as a whole, I have given static pictures of villages at particular moments of time. But it should be clear that this description of the enduring social relationships, which appear as a static social structure, is abstracted from a series of on-going processes in which certain social relationships appear as repetitive elements.

In reality villages are constantly changing. Their personnel is replaced, their internal lineage composition changes, and they change their sites from chiefdom to chiefdom. It is perhaps easiest to visualize these changes, and the way they affect the structure, by viewing them in terms of the slow ontogenetic development of villages. Villages pass through a cycle which leads from their inception, through internal differentiation out of a larger group, to final break-up through their own differentiation, and the resumption of their original simple form.

Let us consider the typical life history of a hamlet which has just moved into a particular area. It is composed of four or five huts belonging to the daughters of one woman. The mother herself may be alive, as an old woman and very probably a widow. The daughters are adults and have with them their husbands and children. The hamlet settles down to its life in its new area. The warden of this sorority-group probably lives some miles away and the women have to send the older children to call him when they need his help. As the daughters of the women grow up, young men come to marry them. Each couple may start to live in the girl's mother's kitchen at the back of the hut. In time the husband builds a hut next door to the hut of his mother-in-law. Yao huts as a rule are made from pole and daub and they last from five to ten years. White ants eat the poles away and the thatch always leaks a little in very wet weather. The winds and the rains erode away the plaster.

When a villager died in pre-White days, the hut and personal effects were destroyed. Nowadays, with the improving type of dwelling, which frequently includes well-timbered doors and glass-windows, huts are treated with medicine to cleanse them of the harmful effects of the death and they are used again. But all houses must be repaired continually if they are to remain habitable. Eventually most houses fall beyond repair and new houses must be built. The women pull the poles out of the ground and use them for firewood and the site is planted with pumpkins or maize by the nearest relative.[1] A new hut site is then chosen according to the wishes of the owners. As a rule outsiders are neutral about this, and a village member selects a site in accordance with his or her social position in the village. The women still stay near their mother, but they may build on the outside fringe of a group of huts. When the mother's house collapses she may in turn build her hut on the outside fringe of the group near her daughter's hut. In this way the spatial distribution of the huts gradually comes to reflect the segmentation of the lineage.

As the woman's daughter's children grow up and marry, the woman's son persuades his wife's relatives to allow him to take his wife to live in his home village. If he is a polygynist he usually takes the senior wife, but he may take the other or others as well. His own daughters now marry uxorilocally in the village if their mother is still alive. If the parents live long enough their daughter's daughters in turn marry and build their huts there. A crisis comes when either the man or his wife dies. The children have to decide whether to stay where they are or to move back to their own matrilineal village. If they do stay at their father's village they form the nucleus of a patrilaterally-linked group. As they grow older the senior male of their matrilineage may come to live with them. Through the years while this internal differentiation is developing within the village, the huts are decaying and being rebuilt. While new hut sites are being selected the physical form of the village is reflecting the continuing social differentiation.

At the same time gardens are being planted and crops reaped each year. The soil in the first garden sites has probably been depleted already and is either lying fallow or is under cassava.

[1] Usually the name-heir of a woman, i.e. her daughter's daughter.

As garden land becomes scarcer, members of the village have probably approached patrilateral or affinal kinsmen in other villages for personal grants of land. The lands immediately surrounding the village have long since become depleted and crops will only thrive on lands some miles away ; then the village moves its site. How long it will be before this becomes necessary, depends on the fertility of the soil. Most villages must move eventually. When they do they may move a few hundred yards only, or on the other hand, they may select a site thirty to forty miles away. Whether the site is far or near, the migration is not a mass movement of the village as I have so far assumed for the purposes of analysis. As a rule a few villagers, including the headman, move first. The headman may be there a year or more before the second lot of villagers move. They usually move in sorority-groups so that when they build at the new site they place their huts in sections. Thus, the internal social organization of the village is reflected in the same way as before. The whole move may take three or four years before it is completed.

This process of development of the village and its gradual and continual reformation is sometimes hastened by the conflicts that appear within it. I have from time to time mentioned various conflicts that have led to the split of a village and the subsequent migration of one of its sections. The new section sets up a small hamlet in a distant locality, especially if the reason for its secession was sorcery. Here the general process of evolution is started anew. Its parent village, however, is strengthened by the migration since the dissident elements have left it. It continues to carry on its existence and to throw off other villages from time to time.

The number of villages, in the area I studied, is increasing with the increase of population, but the average size of each village remains constant and appears to have done so for many years.[1] But at the same time some villages as entities are disappearing while new ones are being formed. A few new villages become resorbed by their parent villages when for some reason they cannot continue their separate existence. Other villages fragment and do not split. The individual village members leave the village and go their separate ways. Very frequently when

[1] See the argument in Chap. II, p. 40.

this happens the husbands take their wives to their several villages with them.

Throughout this general process the links between groups of any particular area are constantly changing but the general pattern remains constant.   A village expands outwards, and the various patrilaterally-linked groups, and often some of the segments of the dominant lineage, form hamlets separate from each other.   The dominance of one of the local headmen over the others is still recognized and the general pattern of primacy is maintained.   Some of the earliest villages in the area remain intact through many years.   Villages which were small hamlets twenty or thirty years ago, when they had just moved into the area, have become relatively senior.   Many headmen who were senior then have moved, or their villages have disintegrated, or ceased to exist.   Other villages have moved in and are ranked lower.   Thus through time the rank of any one headman may have changed, but the ranking system and the relationships of senior to junior headmen remain unaltered.

The general process is the same for the whole chiefdom, though there is less overall structural change than in smaller areas.   The more important a village headman, the less likely is his village to disappear entirely.   The most important village headmen, therefore, have long histories of association with the chief.   Thus while there is considerable change going on at the lowest levels of the social system, the social structure of the whole chiefdom is remarkably stable.   In other words, the rate of change taking place within the structure varies directly with the level of organization within that structure.   The names of the *nduna* of Kawinga, Liwonde and Malemia are the same as those of the *nduna* who accompanied these chiefs into Nyasaland in the middle of the nineteenth century.   Relatively few of them have disappeared.   And so it is with important village headmen. The links between them, fixed by their rank and status relative to each other in perpetual kinship and other ties, form the political structure of the chiefdoms.   From chiefdom to chiefdom the same pattern of organization is concealed behind an apparent diversity of actual links.

But, as a result of their contact with other peoples and their absorption into the economic and administrative framework of the British Empire, new social relationships are developing amongst the Yao. The religious sanctions behind tribal initiation ceremonies were weakened when many of the village headmen adopted Islam, and the rights of holding the Islamic equivalents fell to commoners who were leading Moslems. Thus for many village headmen the significance of the holding of initiation rights fell away. The White Administration has introduced new political personalities into the field, such as the court clerk, the court sergeant and other members of the chief's bureaucracy. These persons have been able to acquire peculiar positions of power in competition with the chief's traditional advisers.[1] Some wealthy individuals are able to wear better clothes, build better houses, and have more personal attendants, than the chiefs. For example, there is a carpenter in Kawinga's area living near an Indian store,[2] who is wheeled about in a garetta (ricksha) as the chiefs are, and who dresses far better than any of the chiefs.

But these changes have not yet affected the pattern of social relationships appreciably. Up to the present as new elements were introduced into Yao social structure they have been absorbed in terms of the traditional structure. The traditional chiefs, therefore, became the Principal Headmen when White Administration was imposed on them. Village headmen, no longer able to compete with each other in terms of followers and slaves, now began to vie with each other for 'books'. Important village headmen became the Moslem leaders, and the larger mosques were built at their villages. The chiefs, by virtue of their annuity from the Government, are able to maintain a higher standard of living than most of their subjects : they build burnt-brick houses, they wear finer clothes, they are wheeled about in garettas or, latterly, are pillion passengers on bicycles pedalled by retainers. By using their annuities as capital, they have been able to grow more tobacco than most of their subjects and so still maintain economic ascendancy over them.

So that until 1949, at least, in spite of the introduction of

[1] cf. my ' The Political Organization of the Yao of Southern Nyasaland '.
[2] He does not live in a village as most people do ; he is an Nguru, and has none of his relatives near him, which is significant. His relationships with his clients are formal and transitory and he is not bound by traditional kinship ties. He therefore attempts to achieve prestige through conspicuous expenditure.

new personalities into Yao society, the social structure remained
little altered. There were not enough Government officials, or
officials in the chief's bureaucracy, or rich individuals in Yao-
land to be able to represent significant elements in the social
structure. In the years 1946–49 Yao social structure was still
organized in terms of ranked lineage segments at one level,
ranked matrilineal groups at a second, and ranked villages at a
third.

APPENDIX A

ECONOMIC DATA

AMOUNT AND VALUE OF TOBACCO BOUGHT IN JALASI–KAWINGA AREAS 1942–49

Year	Growers	Amount in lbs.	Cash Value £	Av. Price per Grower (pence per lb.)	Lbs. per Grower	Cash per Grower
						£ s. d.
1941/2 .	1055	393,964	6695	4·08	373	6 6 9
1942/3 .	2106	465,477	7044	3·02	221	4 0 0
1943/4 .	1792	464,929	8025	4·15	259	4 8 5
1944/5 .	1246	269,212	3067	2·84	216	2 9 3
1945/6 .	1074	127,237	6471	12·41	119	6 0 6
1946/7 .	918	116,590	4020	8·28	127	4 7 5
1947/8 .	1570	132,832	5035	9·18	85	3 4 3
1948/9 .	1315	171,865	5206	9·60	130	4 0 0

AGRICULTURAL PRODUCE BOUGHT IN KAWINGA–JALASI AREAS AT NAMWERA, LIWONDE, MLOMBA, NTAJA, NYAMBI, AND MASUKU MARKETS. AVERAGE FOR THE YEARS 1945–47 INCLUSIVE

(in 1000 lb.)

Year	Maize	Groundnuts	Rice	Beans
1945	23·6	1395	94·0	31·0
1946	101·4	1268	60·4	34·6
1947	nil	1465	122·8	2·8
Total	125·0	4128	277·2	68·4
Average . . .	41·6	1376·1	92·4	22·8

LIVESTOCK CENSUS IN KAWINGA–JALASI AREAS, 1947
(Jalasi, Kawinga, Liwonde and Nyambi, and Malemia areas)

Goats	Sheep	Pigs	Cattle
4319	2498	4	225*

* Most of these are owned by White settlers.

STOCK HELD AT AN INDIAN-OWNED STORE IN CIKOJA VILLAGE, 1948

(Prices where I recorded them)

Cloth at 2/- to 4/6 a yard.
Blankets at 8/- to 20/- each.
Women's blouses, 6/9 each.
Men's vests.
Shirts and shorts (together 18/-).
Moslem men's caps.
Scarves.
Sewing thread.
Cooking utensils—Pot diam. 6 in., 7/6.
Tin plates, 2/- each.
Hoes, 2/10 to 3/6, according to size.
Salt (1d. a cup holding about 4 oz.).
Soap (1d. or 2d. per tablet, according to size).
Tobacco (1d. and 6d. a packet).
Cigarettes at 1d. a packet of 10.
Tea, 1/6 lb.
Dark glasses.
Ink.
Exercise books.
Playing cards.
Shoe polish.
Shoe whitening.
Pads.
Envelopes.

STOCK CARRIED BY AFRICAN CANTEEN, i.e. SMALL SHOP HOLDER

12 jars of solid brilliantine.
80 cakes of blue soap.
120 cakes of red soap.
100 packets of 10 cigarettes.
100 packets of tobacco.
6 small mirrors.
25 strings of beads.
60 lb. of coarse salt.

APPENDIX B

GENEALOGY, HUT COUNT AND VILLAGE PLAN: ALI KASUNKA VILLAGE

Hut numbers in brackets after the names in the genealogy.
Other symbols: d = dead; mo = married out; lm = labour **migrant**;
u = below age of puberty; k = kitchen.

HUT OWNERSHIP

Hut No.	Owner	Gen. Ref.
1	Bt. Kasembe	C5
2	Bt. Ntemula	D19
3	Bt. Ntuwa	D1
4	Alieje	D12
5	Bt. Sale	D15
6	Mwanace	D10
7	Ali Kasunka	C6
8	Mbalasyao	C1
9	Atawile	C7

Fields

Fields

⑤

⑥   ④   ①

②

⑦   ③

⑧   ⑨

Bush

Bush

VILLAGE PLAN: ALI KASUNKA
(*Not to Scale*)
217

APPENDIX C

SKELETON GENEALOGY, HUT COUNT AND VILLAGE PLAN: MENI SECTION OF MAJAJA VILLAGE

Only hut owners are shown in the genealogy.

HUT COUNT

Hut No.	Owner	Gen. Ref.	Hut No.	Owner	Gen. Ref.
1	Meni	B4	19	Bt. Taimu	D6
2	Empty		20	Kitchen to hut 18	
3	Asinjisyeje	C8	21	Bt. Woci	D7
4	Girls' dormitory		22	Ngwaluka	nil
5	Sayisi	D11	23	Bt. Tayali	D5
6	Disused		24	Bt. Saidi	D9
7	Bt. Nyili	D1	25k	Bt. Saidi	D10
8	Bt. Mlungusi	D3	25	Bt. Gwenembe	C4
9	Bt. Duwa	E1	26	Ali Asini	D4
10	Bt. Wemba	D2	27	Boys' dormitory	
11	Aciwanjila	C1	28	Bt. Cinunga	C3
12	Bitiya	B1	29	Bt. Juma	nil
13	Esinati	C6	30	Asausyaga	B2
14	Bt. Mlenje	C5	31	Palinjeje	D8
15	Amina	B3	32	Bt. Majaja	B5
16	Bt. Cibwana	C7	33	Ambulaje	C12
17	Mosque		34	Elbi	C11
18	Cilewi	C2	35	Lusi	C10

The following huts are not included in the genealogy:

Hut 2—Empty.
Hut 4—Girls' dormitory.
Hut 6—Disused.
Hut 17—Mosque.

Hut 20—Kitchen to Hut 18.
Hut 22—Ngwaluka, a non-relative.
Hut 27—Boys' dormitory.
Hut 29—Bt. Juma, a relative of Ngwaluka.

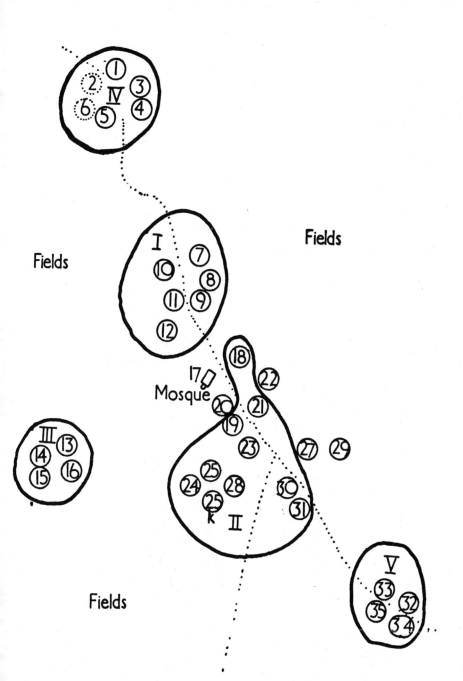

Fields

Fields

Fields

17 Mosque

VILLAGE PLAN : MAJAJA
(*Not to Scale*)

APPENDIX D

GENEALOGY AND HUT COUNT : CIKOJA VILLAGE

HUT COUNT

Hut No.	Wife's name	Gen. Ref.	Name of husband	Gen. Ref.
1	Amaenda	D14	Mbwana	C11
2	Ayesi	E8	Katoli	D33
3	(Boys' dormitory)			
4	Bt. Tepani	F37	Mapila	E52
5	Bt. Beula	E19	(outsider)	
6	Aniya	D15	(outsider)	
7	Bt. Amamu	E14	(outsider)	
8	Alusi	D16	Ali Mkwinda	C13
9	Lunjela	E13	(outsider)	
10	Ajumo	E25	Musa	D7
11	Bt. Mwamadi	G10	Nkatawila	D20
12	Bt. Bwana Isa	F16	(outsider)	
13	Bt. Amisa	E4	(outsider)	
14	Asubiya	E9	(outsider)	
15	Abena	E30	Rajabu	F20
16	Bt. Selemani	D19	(outsider)	
17	Nseweta	E60	Salimu ii	D3
18	Bt. Kacenga	D40	(outsider)	
19	(outsider)		Ali Tepani	E40
20	Alima	D22	(outsider)	
21	Abiya	D23	(divorced)	
22	Kalingule	E38	(outsider)	
23	Akumbiripe	E31	(outsider)	
24	Bt. Ciwina	E33	(outsider)	
25	Bt. Mwenye	C14	(outsider)	
26	Bt. Mwanjele	E55	(outsider)	
27	Alusi	E57	(outsider)	
28	Bt. Cininga	E59	(outsider)	
29	Asidaya	E56	(outsider)	
30	Tuweneje	E54	(outsider)	
31	Bt. Ulanga	D34	(outsider)	
32	Bt. Lilomba	E53	Jauma	F7
33	Bt. Cikwenga	F64	(outsider)	
34	(outsider)		Cilimba	F1
35	Bt. Madi	F10	(outsider)	
36	Bt. Aliya	F11	(outsider)	

HUT COUNT—*continued*

Hut No.	Wife's name	Gen. Ref.	Name of husband	Gen. Ref.
37	Bt. Ntalika	E3	(outsider)	
38	Bt. Kimu	G1	(outsider)	
39	Atawile	E50	(outsider)	
40	Bt. Maperera	D32	(outsider)	
41	(outsider)		Kausi	F3
42	Mege	F28	(outsider)	
43	Bt. Mbwana	F2	(outsider)	
44	Ayuyeje	F29	(outsider)	
45	Kasingati	F30	(outsider)	
46	Asimama	E6	(outsider)	
47	(outsider)		Cikoja VI	E7

Note : The genealogies for Appendices B, C and D have been inserted as folding plates at the end of the book.

Q

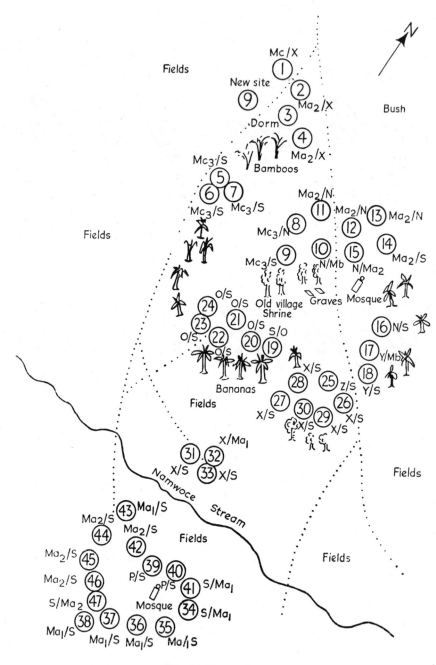

VILLAGE PLAN: CIKOJA
(*Not to Scale*)

KEY TO CIKOJA VILLAGE PLAN

Ma = Senior segment of dominant matrilineage, i.e. descendants of Ncilaga (C5).

Mb = Second segment of dominant matrilineage, i.e. descendants of Bt. Mkwinda (C6).

Mc = Third segment of dominant matrilineage, i.e. descendants of Lunjela (C8).

Ma_1 = Descendants of Atabiya (D1).

Ma_2 = Descendants of Amaliama (D2).

Mc_1 = Descendants of Amaenda (D14).

Mc_2 = Descendants of Aniya (D15).

Mc_3 = Descendants of Alusi (D16).

N, O, P, X, Y, Z = Patrilaterally-linked lineages.

S = Outsiders.

Mc_1/B = A female descendant of Amaenda married to a man from B patrilaterally-linked lineage.

APPENDIX E

FACTORS ASSOCIATED WITH THE PRESTIGE OF ADMINISTRATIVE VILLAGE HEADMEN

THE various social factors influencing the prestige of Administrative Village Headmen, as manifested in their right to wear scarlet headbands or to hold initiation ceremonies as described in Chapter IV, operate simultaneously. In order to assess the independent influence

TABLE XXX

DISTRIBUTION OF MARKS OF PRESTIGE AMONGST ADMINISTRATIVE VILLAGE HEADMEN POSSESSING DIFFERENT COMBINATIONS OF SOCIAL CHARACTERISTICS

| Invader | Kinship | Village size | Religion | Number of Village Headmen | | | | | | | | Total | Proportion with no marks of Prestige |
| | | | | With headband | | | | Without headband | | | | | |
				Both	Boys	Girls	No rights	Both	Boys only	Girls only	No rights		
1	1	1	1	7	1	—	—	8	1	3	11	31	0·3549
1	1	1	0	2	—	—	—	3	2	1	4	12	0·3300
1	1	0	1	2	—	—	—	1	1	5	22	31	0·7097
1	1	0	0	1	—	—	—	2	—	1	15	19	0·7895
1	0	1	1	2	—	—	—	2	—	1	14	19	0·7369
1	0	1	0	1	—	—	—	—	—	—	2	3	0·6667
1	0	0	1	—	—	—	1	—	1	—	14	16	0·8750
1	0	0	0	—	—	—	—	1	1	1	2	5	0·4000
0	1	1	1	—	—	—	—	4	1	5	8	18	0·4444
0	1	1	0	—	1	1	—	1	—	5	3	11	0·2727
0	1	0	1	1	—	—	—	—	1	6	24	32	0·7500
0	1	0	0	—	—	—	—	—	—	1	7	8	0·8750
0	0	1	1	2	—	—	—	6	4	5	41	58	0·7069
0	0	1	0	1	—	—	—	2	3	2	30	38	0·7895
0	0	0	1	—	—	—	1	—	1	6	65	73	0·8904
0	0	0	0	—	—	—	—	—	1	1	31	33	0·9394
Total				19	2	1	2	30	17	43	293	407[a]	

[a] Excludes 17 headmen for whom information was lacking on one of the characteristics.

Invader	1 =	Of Invader Stock
	0 =	Of Newcomer or Original Stock
Kinship	1 =	Direct Kinship with Chief
	0 =	No Direct Kinship with Chief
Village Size	1 =	More than 36 tax-payers
	0 =	Less than 36 tax-payers
Religion	1 =	Same Religion as Chief
	0 =	Different Religion from Chief.

of any one of these factors we need to hold constant the effects of the other three.

We may do this by examining the distribution of symbols of prestige among headmen possessing different combinations of social characteristics which we know influence the prestige of headmen. In Table XXX the social factors, i.e. the origin of the headmen, their kinship with the chief, the size of the villages under them, and their religious alignment, are reduced to dichotomies and the headmen with the sixteen different patterns of characteristics distributed according to the combination of marks of prestige they possess.

We may look upon this tabulation as 2^4 factorial arrangement in which the proportion of headmen without marks of prestige are set out for each combination of factors.[1] The effect on any one factor acting independently of the other three may be estimated by the difference between the proportion of village headmen without marks of prestige among those with a positive factor in combination with any arrangement of the other three factors, and the proportion without marks of prestige among headmen with a negative factor and the same combination of the other three factors. For example, we notice that the proportion of headmen amongst those who have Invader Status, some kinship connection with the chief, *larger* than median sized villages and the same religion of the chief is 0·3549. The proportion of such headmen amongst those who have Invader Status, some kinship connection with the chief, *smaller* than median sized villages and the same religion as the chief is 0·7097. The difference between these two proportions, i.e. −0·3528, may be looked upon as the independent effect of a headman having a village larger than median size on the possibility of his having no marks of prestige. Since with four factors there would be sixteen possible combinations, eight such differences may be calculated and averaged to obtain the mean effect of village size on the possession of marks of prestige.

The proportional effects, however, are not directly additive so that some suitable transformation of the proportions to an additive measure must be made. Half-logits have been used in this analysis. From these values the weighted mean effects of the factors may be estimated together with their standard errors and critical ratios.[2]

Using this method the half-logit effects of possessing the various social characteristics upon the proportion of headmen *without*

---

[1] We use the proportion *without* marks of prestige in order to avoid zero values. Zero values would make it impossible to use the method of analysis we adopt below.

[2] The method is fully described in Yates, F. *Sampling Methods for Censuses and Surveys*, London, Charles Griffin & Co. (1953), pp. 314–17.

marks of prestige, their standard errors and critical ratios are as follows:

	Half-logit effect	Standard error	Critical ratio
Being of invader stock	—0·159	0·137	1·16
Having kinship with the chief	—0·563	0·134	4·20
Having a larger than median sized village	—0·685	0·127	5·39
Having the same religion as the chief	—0·107	0·138	0·78

From this we see that the size of the village has the largest and most significant effect on the prestige of village headmen, kinship with the chief also has a large and significant effect. Being of Invader stock has a small and marginal effect, while having the same religion as the chief has no effect on the prestige of Administrative Village Headmen.

BIBLIOGRAPHY

A. WORKS OF DIRECT BEARING ON THE YAO OF NYASALAND

Annual Colonial Report, No. 472, British Central African Protectorate, 1904–5.
Census Report for Nyasaland, 1945, Government Printer (Zomba, 1946).
Correspondence re operations against Slave Traders in British Central Africa, London, H.M.S.O., C. 7925 and 8013 (1896).
Report of the Consul and Acting Commissioner Sharpe on the Trade and General Condition of the British Central African Protectorate for April 1896 to March 31st, 1897. Accounts and Papers. (Africa) No. 5 (1897), C. 8438.

ABDALLAH, YOHANNAH B., *Chiikala cha Wayao,* edited and translated by Sanderson, M., as *The History of the Yaos,* Government Printer (Zomba, 1919).

ABRAHAM, J. C., *Census Report for Nyasaland, 1931,* Government Printer (Zomba, 1931).

BUCHANAN, J., *The Shire Highlands,* Blackwoods (London, 1885).

BURTON, SIR R. F., *The Lands of Cazembe : Laçerda's Journey to Cazembe in 1798,* translated and annotated by J. Murray (London, 1873).

CARDEW, C. A., 'Nyasaland in 1894–5', *The Nyasaland Journal,* i, 1 (Jan. 1948), 51–5.

DUFF, H. L., *Nyasaland under the Foreign Office,* George Bell (London, 1903).

GARBUTT, H. E., 'Witchcraft in Nyasa (Manganja, Yao (Achawa)), communicated to the Writer', *J.R.A.I.,* li (1911), 301–4.
'Native Customs in Nyasa and the Yao', *Man,* xii (1912), 20.

HETHERWICK, A., *A Handbook of the Yao Language,* S.P.C.K. (London, 1902).
Note on Yao in *Nyasa News* (Nov. 1893), 64.
'Some Animistic Beliefs among the Yaos', *J.R.A.I.,* xxxii (1902), 89–95.
'Islam and Christianity in Nyasaland', *Moslem World,* xvii, 2 (April 1927).

HYNDE, R. S., 'Among the Machinga People', *The Scottish Geographical Magazine,* Edinburgh, viii (1891), 656–63.
'Marriage and relationship among the Yaos', *Nyasa News,* vii (1895), 217–218.

JOHNSON, W. P., 'Discovery of the Source of the Lujenda', *Proc. Roy. Geog. Soc.,* viii (Aug. 1882), 480–4.
'Seven Years of Travel in the region East of Lake Nyasa', *Proc. Roy. Geog. Soc.,* viii (Aug. 1884), 313–36.
'The Yaos : a defence and a Suggestion', *Nyasa News,* ii (1893), 55–8.
'More about the Yaos', *Nyasa News,* iii (1894), 77–80.
Nyasa, the Great Water, Oxford University Press (London, 1922).

JOHNSTON, H. H., *British Central Africa,* Methuen (London, 1897).

LAWS, R., *Reminiscences of Livingstonia,* Oliver & Boyd (Edinburgh, 1934).

LAWSON, A., 'An Outline of the Relationship System of the Nyanja and Yao Tribes in South Nyasaland', *African Studies,* viii, 4 (Dec. 1949), 180–90.

LIVINGSTONE, D. and C., *Narrative of an Expedition to the Zambesi and its Tributaries, and of the Discovery of Lakes Shirwa and Nyassa, 1858–64,* John Murray (London, 1865).

MACDONALD, DUFF, *Africana or the Heart of Heathen Africa* (2 vols.), Simpkin Marshall & Co. (London, 1882).

MAPLES, C., 'Mtonya', *Nyasa News,* i (Aug. 1893), 192–6.
'Unangu', *Nyasa News,* ii (Nov. 1893).

MITCHELL, J. C. (with GLUCKMAN, M., and BARNES, J.A.), 'The Village Headman in British Central Africa', *Africa,* xix, 2 (April 1949), 82–106.
'The Political Organization of the Yao of Southern Nyasaland', *African Studies,* viii, 3 (Sept. 1949), 141–59.
'An Estimate of Fertility in Some Yao Hamlets in Liwonde District of Southern Nyasaland', *Africa,* xix, 4 (Oct. 1949), 293–308.
'Preliminary Notes on Land Tenure and Agriculture among the Machinga Yao', *Human Problems,* x (1950), 1–13.
'The Yao of Southern Nyasaland', in Colson, E., and Gluckman, M. (eds.), *Seven Tribes of British Central Africa,* Oxford University Press for the Rhodes-Livingstone Institute (London, 1951), 292–353.
'An Outline of the Social Structure of Malemia Area', *The Nyasaland Journal,* iv, 2 (July 1951), 15–48.
'A Note on the African Conception of Causality', *The Nyasaland Journal,* v, 2 (July 1952), 51–8.
Marriage among the Machinga Yao (MS in the I.A.R. Library, Lusaka).

MOGGRIDGE, L. T., 'The Nyasaland Tribes, their Customs, and their Poison Ordeal', *J.R.A.I.,* xxxii (1902), 267–72.

MURRAY, S. S. (compiler), *A Handbook of Nyasaland,* Government Printer (Zomba, 1932).

M. T. K., 'The Yaos in the Shire Highlands', *Nyasa News,* iv (1894), 121–3.

O'NEILL, H. E., 'Journal from Mozambique to Lakes Shirwa and Amaramba', *Proc. Roy. Geog. Soc.* (1883–4).
The Mozambique and Nyasa Slave Trade (1885).

ROWLEY, H., *The Story of the Universities Mission to Central Africa from its Commencement under Bishop Mackenzie, to its withdrawal from the Zambesi,* Saunders Otley & Co. (London, 1886).
Twenty Years in Central Africa, Wells Gardner, Darton & Co. (London, 1889).

SANDERSON, M., *A Yao Grammar,* S.P.C.K. (London, 1922).
'A Note on the Ceremonial Purification of the Yao', *Man,* xxii (1922), 55.
'The Relationship system among the Yao', *J.R.A.I.,* l (1920), 369–76.

SCLATER, B. L., 'Routes and Districts in Southern Nyasaland', *Geographical Journal,* ii (Nov. 1893), 403–23.

STANNUS, H. S., 'The Wayao of Nyasaland', *Harvard African Studies* (1923), Varia Africana, III, 229–372.
'Notes on some Tribes of British Central Africa', *J.R.A.I.,* xl (1910), 285–335.

STANNUS, H. S., and DAVEY, J. B., 'Initiation Ceremony for Boys among the Yao of Nyasaland', *J.R.A.I.*, xlii (1913), 119–23.

THOMPSON, J., 'Notes on the Basin of the River Rovuma, East Africa', *Proc. Roy. Geog. Soc.*, ii (Feb. 1882), 65–79.

WALLER, H., *The Last Journals of David Livingstone in Central Africa from 1865 to his Death*, John Murray (London, 1874).

YOUNG, E. D., *Nyassa, a Journal of Adventure*, John Murray (London, 1877).

B. OTHER WORKS CITED

BARNES, J. A., 'The Fort Jameson Ngoni', in Colson, E., and Gluckman, M. (eds.), *Seven Tribes of British Central Africa*, Oxford University Press for the Rhodes-Livingstone Institute (London, 1951).
Politics in a Changing Society, Oxford University Press for the Rhodes-Livingstone Institute (Cape Town, 1954).

CUNNISON, I., *Kinship and Local Organization on the Luapula*, Communication from the Rhodes-Livingstone Institute, No. 5 (Livingstone, 1950).

DIXEY, F., 'The Distribution of the Population of Nyasaland', *Geographical Review*, xviii (April 1928), 274–90.

EVANS-PRITCHARD, E. E., *Witchcraft, Oracles and Magic among the Azande*, Clarendon Press (Oxford, 1937).
The Nuer, Clarendon Press (Oxford, 1940).
Some Aspects of Marriage and the Family among the Nuer, Rhodes-Livingstone Paper No. 11 (Livingstone, 1945).

FORTES, M., *The Dynamics of Clanship among the Tallensi*, Oxford University Press for the International African Institute (London, 1945).
The Web of Kinship among the Tallensi, Oxford University Press for the International African Institute (London, 1949).

GLUCKMAN, M., 'The Kingdom of the Zulu of South Africa', in Fortes, M., and Evans-Pritchard, E. E. (eds.), *African Political Systems*, Oxford University Press for the International African Institute (London, 1940).
The Economy of the Central Barotse Plain, Rhodes-Livingstone Paper No. 7 (Livingstone, 1941).
Essays on Lozi Land and Royal Property, Rhodes-Livingstone Paper No. 10 (Livingstone, 1943).
'Kinship and Marriage among the Lozi of Northern Rhodesia and the Zulu of Natal', in Radcliffe-Brown, A. R., and Forde, C. Daryll (eds.), *African Systems of Kinship and Marriage*, Oxford University Press for the International African Institute (London, 1950).
'The Lozi of Barotseland', in Colson, E., and Gluckman, M. (eds.), *Seven Tribes of British Central Africa*, Oxford University Press for the Rhodes-Livingstone Institute (London, 1951).
'Succession and Civil War among the Bemba—An Exercise in Anthropological Theory', *Human Problems in British Central Africa*, xvi (1954), 6–25.

HICHENS, W., 'Islam in Africa', in Arberry, A. J., and Landau, R., *Islam To-day* (London, 1943).

KUPER, H., *An African Aristocracy*, Oxford University Press for the International African Institute (London, 1947).

PIM, A., *An Economic History of Tropical Africa*, Oxford University Press (London, 1940).

RICHARDS, A. I., ' Mother-right among the Central Bantu ', in Evans-Pritchard, E. E., and others, *Essays Presented to C. G. Seligman*, Kegan Paul (London, 1933).
' The Political System of the Bemba Tribe—North-eastern Rhodesia ', in Fortes, M., and Evans-Pritchard, E. E. (eds.), *African Political Systems*, Oxford University Press for the International African Institute (London, 1940).
' Some Types of Family Structure among the Central Bantu ', in Radcliffe-Brown, A. R., and Forde, C. Daryll (eds.), *African Systems of Kinship and Marriage*, Oxford University Press for the International African Institute (London, 1950).

SMITH, E. W., and DALE, A., *The Ila-Speaking Peoples of Northern Rhodesia*, Macmillan (London, 1920).

WILSON, G., ' An Introduction to Nyakyusa Society ', *Bantu Studies*, x, 3 (1936), 253–91.

WILSON, M., *Good Company : A Study of Nyakyusa Age-villages*, Oxford University Press for the International African Institute (London, 1951).

INDEX

Abdallah, Yohannah B. : 24, 24n.

Aborigines : defined, 62 ; clanship with chief, 71f. ; ethnic affiliation, 65 ; kinship links with chief, 70 ; proportion Administrative headmen among, 89 ; proportion entitled to initiation rights, 97 ; religious affiliation of, 66

Achisi Yao : 24, 71

adelphic succession : 157

affinal relationships : 183f. ; kinship terms and cross-cousin marriage, 199

African Lakes Company : 19

Agricultural Officer : 7

Akamwini : see Husbands

Ali Kasoka : village headman, 87

Ali Kasunka : village, 140f., 179

Amangoche Yao : 25

Amasaninga Yao : 25

ancestor spirits : mystical powers of, 126, 138, 178 ; connected with curse, 138, 178

ancestor worship : 133-4 ; in pre-White times, 31 ; by modern chiefs, 52f. ; and initiation rights, 80 ; and rainfall, 53 ; expresses unity of village, 139 ; fallen away among village headmen, 52

Anglo-Portuguese Convention of 1891 : 28

Arabic greetings : 83

Arabs : 18, 22, 23, 29, 67 ; influence on names, 46n.

arson : and chieftaincy, 55

backbiting : 137

Barnes, J. A. : viii, 2n., 45n., 152n.

Bemba : 36, 63, 71

birth-pang confessions : 146, 166, 185

Black-White relationships : 27

bloodshed : and chieftaincy, 54

'blowing water' : 138, 165, 166

breast : synonym for lineage section, 134

British rule : appointment of consul in Nyasaland, 28 ; establishment of, 28, 39 ; treaties with chiefs, 28

British South Africa Company : 30

brother-brother : relationships, 154, 174

brother-sister : relationships, 145f., 151 ; incest, 146, 180n. ; kinship terminology, 147

Carrall Wilcocks, E. : 7

cash income : 21

Central African Archives : 7

Chamba, chief : 48 ; son of Kawinga I, 68

Chamba chiefdom : 16, 85 ; scarlet headbands in, 95

chicken ordeal : 123, 153, 156, 173

chief : and the village headman in pre-White times, 33 ; bureaucracy of, 44, 45, 123, 213 ; modern position of, 57, 83, 107 ; position in Administration, 57, 83, 107 ; position of sons of, 69 ; ritual performed by, 34, 52 ; subjects of in pre-White times, 34

chiefdom : as an organization of villages, 47 ; composition of, 58 ; disputes over boundaries of, 47 ; offences against, 54 ; social relationships at the boundaries of, 47

Chikala-Chaoni range : 8

Chikowi, chief : 49

Chikweo, chief : 14, 30, 48, 66 ; clan-name of, 74

Chikweo, chiefdom : 85, 86 ; scarlet headbands in, 95

Chiwalo, chief : vii, 4, 48, 50, 62, 186 ; as administrative village headman, 87 ; sister's daughter's son of Kawinga I, 68 ; struggle

groups of, 24 ; historical background of, 22f. ; invasion into Nyasaland, 25 ; origin of, 24 ; traditional home of, 14, 22, 61

Printed in Great Britain by Butler & Tanner Ltd., Frome and London